Not Always There

*A Powerful Memoir of Love,
Courage and Perseverance*

HELEN MARGARET BACHO
GODFREY GRAHAM ROBINSON

Not Always There
Copyright © 2023 by Helen Margaret Bacho & Godfrey Graham Robinson

Tellwell Talent
www.tellwell.ca

ISBN
978-0-2288-9353-0 (Hardcover)
978-0-2288-8756-0 (Paperback)
978-0-2288-9354-7 (eBook)

Dedicated to two people
To Jeff for Staying Alive
And to
My anchor L.D. who caught
me before I drifted away

Table of Contents

Prologue

DEATH

I died this morning. At 6:55. I was seventy-nine years old.

Helen, my wife of thirty-three years, had her arm around me. She sat very close holding my hand and encouraging me to let the angels take me away. I'm not anxious to leave my body. It will be the end of holding her hand, listening to her, feeling her warmth.

But there's no point in staying. I am skin and bone now. I haven't eaten or drank for eight days. The hum of the oxygen machine is constant. I don't have the strength to move. She told me it's okay to go. She said she will be okay. I don't want to prolong it.

It's been a good life. I want to tell you about it.

I hope I can keep my facts straight and tune you in to my journey with Helen for the past eleven years. From the day we first got the dementia diagnosis, it's been a rough and ready story, and I want to share it with you.

You might have the same diagnosis. You might be a doctor, a nurse, a carer or someone who wants to experience and understand what crept in and out of my brain on this slow downward slope.

There's lots of blanks, but oftentimes I'm aware of my surroundings, the faces, the love, patience, compassion. I'm aware of the other side, too, the lack thereof. Come into my world of confusion, frustration, despair, fear, indignity and aggression contrasted with love, laughter, happiness, music and contentment. We will definitely touch on more. Believe me.

Introduction

LIFE

This is our love story and our eleven-year journey coping with the ravages to my husband's brain. It is a record of our struggle with a new concept of living together and the toll it took on both of us.

Jeff made no notes. He couldn't write or even talk coherently about his steady decline and the shock of not knowing where and who he was anymore.

I endeavoured to convey what he would be thinking in the situations he encountered and how he coped. But, of course, I couldn't really know what he was thinking, so it's like "shadow writing." I'd known him so well over our thirty-three-year relationship. His thoughts and actions are expressed through my perception of them.

This book is close to the behaviour I saw. I'm telling his true story but giving him back his personality not as declining but how he was living in the decline, however obscure that may sound. He's going to tell you stories he experienced at home about being lost and confused, and the activities he could no longer cope with or perform with safety. This led to his involuntary admission to two hospitals, his time in a transitional residence and then his last four years in a permanent residence.

His story is written in italic script to differentiate from mine. It is a chronology of the eleven years we lived in the moment, and it is embellished with our connection and disconnection. In his approximately five years in care, I visited him five to six times a week from 10:00 a.m. to 3:30 p.m., taking two buses and a train (his residence placement was inconveniently located a long distance away). In those visits we always had a walk (when he was walking) in the mornings before lunch, ate lunch together, more walking, patio time and an afternoon nap. The routine varied somewhat depending on holidays and what life threw at me at times.

Chapter 1

WORKING TO LIVE

I married Helen, the woman I'd lived with since 1987, on a blustery day in 2009 at the famous Inukshuk statue along English Bay. We were so thrilled to finally be "tying the knot" and having a piece of paper that said Marriage Certificate!

It was a perfect day, apart from the weather (rain and snow), and we were all so happily gathered to celebrate our wedding. The reception was held at our lovely apartment. It wasn't a big group, nor was it planned much in advance, so some key friends were missing. But there were some surprises—my best mate from England and his wife made the flight!

I was sixty-eight when a neurologist diagnosed me with possible vascular dementia/possible Alzheimer's disease. Memory loss—the small, seemingly inconsequential forgetfulness— showed up around sixty-five. No one in my family had experienced dementia that I knew of. It's been mostly heart-related problems in my family.

I played rugby, always the sport I loved (and still do), from the time I was a child in England. In the late 1960s, I was living in Montreal and playing for the Brit Lions when I was selected to play for the Canadian national team. I was presented with my rugby "cap" in 2009.

It can be a brutal sport with lots of broken noses (eight), broken fingers (all of them at one time or another in my career), sprained ankles, dislocated shoulders, bruises everywhere and broken ribs. Concussions were a natural result of playing a sport without wearing any sort of protection for our heads. I remember having at least eleven concussions, a few requiring bed rest. But you know what? With all the injuries, bloody noses and fingers, we just played on! Fitness was always a high priority. We kept in top form for this hard-hitting sport.

In hindsight, I have to wonder whether the concussions contributed to my brain deterioration. Much was made in the '70s about contact sports and the onset of dementia. Be it boxing, football, soccer or rugby (I'm sure other sports as well), contact was always at the forefront, and this included hard hits to the head.

I had an unfailing love of rugby all my life. Do I think the concussions might have contributed to my memory loss? I do. I also participated in high-risk sports such as downhill skiing and scuba diving, so there could have been many factors.

My wife often reminded me about the time I was driven home, supported by my mates, with a concussion and broken ribs. What a mess I was, crawling on the floor as it hurt too much to stand and walk while recovering after such a brutal game. I was at home alone because Helen was visiting her parents in Ontario.

As I reached my sixties I still played with old friends, but other interests occupied my time. Then it became a game I watched on television or if I had tickets to watch live!

I went to grammar school in England, enjoyed literature, and prided myself on my vocabulary and the ease with which I picked up French; I was fluent after living in France on an exchange programme. German not so much but some Spanish. At the age of seventeen, I went to live with my aunt and uncle in Rhodesia (now Zimbabwe) and worked there as a tobacco farmer for a couple of years. I then embarked on a six-month journey on a Danish tanker to see the rest of the world.

I eventually emigrated to Canada, got married, moved back to England, and had three children. I worked in the food industry with my younger brother until the early 1980s when we moved to Vancouver. Circumstances changed. It was a big adjustment for the family, and our marriage was already in trouble, so we eventually divorced. My children were in their teens—a broken marriage and family. My daughter went with my ex; my two sons stayed with me for a time but then ventured out on their own seeking independence.

That brings us up to the late 1980s when I met my future wife, Helen, in the deli I was running. Within a year we were living together.

Helen was a court reporter for thirty-five years, six of which were with the Senate of Canada as a Hansard Reporter, long before we met. She was very good at computers and taught me to "read" the stenographic notes she took in real time. Eventually, I had my own computer and transcribed depositions and court work. We spent time travelling to Europe on various job assignments, and we worked as a team for years.

We lived in each other's pocket. She enjoyed many of my sports and became an avid follower of rugby and soccer, and we always enjoyed the Olympics. Scuba diving fascinated me, but it was a tough sport in the murky waters of England where I qualified as a certified diver.

On an Australian rugby tour, my wife jumped at the chance to take a five-day intensive diving course on Fitzroy Island. She was in her early fifties and passed with flying colours despite her claustrophobia. The diving course culminated in her first dives logged on the Great Barrier Reef. What an amazing feat for her as she was not a "natural" under water and needed lots of practice!

Life revolved around diving and our work. We worked hard so we could go on holiday and dive. When we did our final dives together, I had well over four thousand and she had 360. We made several trips to the Red Sea, the Caribbean, La Paz on the Sea of Cortez in the Baja Peninsula, and we often went for dives at home in Vancouver. We encountered all kinds of fish, fantastic coral, dolphins, and whales, and we were always guided by how much air we had left in our tanks before having to surface.

We met interesting people in so many walks of life and shared the camaraderie of exploring reefs with other divers and educating ourselves about the underwater environment. What a diving pair we made—Helen with her underwater camera and me searching for photo opportunities, always working as a team without discourse. Helen was my soulmate. We found each other, and it really was a romance made in heaven. We lived a life with hard work, rewarding trips, seeing the world, and diving!

Who would have thought dementia would rear its ugly head and change our lives forever? It left us helpless, hopeless, heartbroken and in denial. We worked through the anger, sheer frustration, impatience, and agonizing emotions together. Luckily, there was also humour.

We need to concentrate on the humorous episodes. I plan to tell you about some of them.

My wife is my journal. She remembers things I've forgotten so we now collaborate on writing my side of things even though we don't discuss it as such. She's my "shadow writer." She knows the details of the past years up close. I'm almost eighty now.

THE GORGEOUS CHICKEN MAN

In late December 1986, my flight descended into Vancouver International Airport in heavy fog—as was so often the weather on this coast at this time of year. I strained in my seat to catch a glimpse of a break in the fog while enduring all the noise, the whining of the plane, and the bright lights that only accentuated the fog and what I perceived as quite possibly the end of my life. The lowering of the plane's wheels made me jump like a rabbit. Obviously, I was not a good flyer!

That was the beginning of a new chapter—new job, home, city, friends. I had lots of trepidation leaving Ottawa and moving to a place so far away. I had travelled within the United States in my early twenties, so I didn't feel too uncomfortable about moving. Flights are at your fingertips so you're never really far away. I was looking for a break from all the snow and cold in Ontario and Quebec.

Two days after landing in Vancouver, my nieces from Ottawa arrived, as did the moving van, and we started sorting out my belongings in a condominium I had purchased months before.

Exploring the new neighbourhood, we noticed delicious looking chickens turning on a rotisserie in a deli close to my place. Standing at the window I spotted this good-looking guy with sandy hair and sparkling blue eyes.

"Now there's someone I'm going to check out soon!" I said to my nieces.

But we were on a mission that week. We spent the whole time getting me organized because they would soon return to Ottawa, so gorgeous chicken man was put on hold!

I had secured a court reporting position with a freelance deposition company before I left Ottawa. What a new and exciting life it was for me to be living in one of the most beautiful cities in Canada. I was surrounded by mountains, water, endless avenues of exploration, opportunities to meet people, and Vancouver would become my base to travel from.

As my nieces departed, I was easily lured into that deli by those golden rotisserie chickens slowly turning in the front window and the promise of a succulent feast for dinner. A bell jingled as I opened the door and stepped inside. The shop was warm, and the savoury smell of the roasting birds filled the air. My stomach rumbled. Jarred from my reverie, I looked up to see a boyish smile beneath two of the bluest eyes I'd ever seen. The man patted his stomach to answer the question on my face.

"Happens all the time when they're out," he said, jerking his thumb towards the chickens.

With the other hand, he absently brushed a lock of sandy hair from his face. Any embarrassment I might have felt at my noisy stomach melted at his peculiar mix of age and youth, the playful smile coupled with the crinkles at the corners of his eyes. I knew, with sudden certainty, that I'd be making a lot more visits to this deli.

He was a surprise. We flirted. We joked. We laughed a lot. But only in the deli for those first couple of months.

We were both busy with our agendas, but our paths would cross as we were dating others, frequenting the local pubs and dinner spots, and constantly running into each other. We were slowly getting to know each across the counter of his shop, and finally our mutual attraction realized a dinner date. I later found out his two mates were after him for months to ask me out and were even threatening to ask me out themselves if he didn't make a move. My closest new friend in Vancouver, Kendal, cautioned me about where I was going to buy my chickens if it didn't work out!

That's the beginning of a thirty-three-year relationship with a man who was diagnosed with dementia when he was only sixty-eight years old.

I am going to share our ongoing struggle, the highs and lows, the laughter and tears, the positives and negatives over these years. I've never written a book, but I need to reach out to you and talk about our wonderful life together despite the ravages of this disease. I hope I can give you some understanding of the plight we shared.

Perhaps you will discover some tips to keep yourself on track if you ever have to face an incurable mental health problem like his.

It was the year of EXPO 86 in Vancouver, a busy, exciting time to live there! Jeff was recently divorced. I was a widow for many years as my husband died suddenly at a young age. I didn't have children. At the time we met, Jeff's two sons were living with him, and his daughter was in another province with her mother, his ex-wife.

After our first date, we began an exciting romance and fell in love so quickly that we were both staggered. It seemed so easy to connect in a close, intriguing relationship that never floundered. Soon we moved in together. Time flew by at breakneck speed!

The deli changed hands with little profit to him, but we combined our talents and I taught Jeff how to use a computer. I was a court reporter so he needed to learn this new language of translating "notes" written in code at a speed of 225 words a minute into English. It took time to teach him to decipher ("read") my notes, but within a year we became a team—an efficient and competent working team.

He was a traveller with so much knowledge of the world, people and their customs. The cases I was engaged in so often had me delving into reference books. I was exposed to many life tragedies—murder, fraud, you name it! What an education I was so fortunate to have doing trials and depositions particularly in medical malpractice, architectural, criminal litigation, jury trials—a whole gambit of interesting but, of course, sometimes tedious and boring tax cases. He had such a knowledge of the world from his travels that I could envisage us as a really successful team.

We worked together for a few years in Vancouver and then decided to pursue other venues as Jeff had British and Canadian citizenship. He travelled to London and used Vancouver contacts at the Royal Courts of Justice. Jeff spent a few weeks having interviews in London with the possibility of working in Britain either in court or freelance depositions. We were approved for part-time work in the Royal Courts of Justice in London, and what a celebration that was!

We soon moved to London and secured accommodation within walking distance of the Royal Courts. It was a time of exploration and experience. I didn't have a working visa so Jeff was hired as he had British citizenship. We would be working as one of the teams which consisted of a court reporter to take shorthand notes in the trials. Jeff was the transcriber who translated the words to English by applying the shorthand machine code.

The language, customs, geographical locations and venues were fascinating to me, and I had the best guide as he had spent most of his life in England. We loved exploring the markets, museums and live theatre on weekends. It certainly was a new world for me! What a bright star he was, mentally and physically!

The next few years opened up opportunities to do deposition work in France, Germany and Switzerland. By 2001, we were back in Canada and were soon offered a two-week deposition job in Germany.

The day we flew from Vancouver to Germany was September 10, 2001. We landed in Germany in the early hours on September 11, and we didn't understand why there seemed to be panic everywhere. When we checked in at the hotel, we discovered the horror that was unfolding in the United States—the terrorist attack on the twin towers in New York City.

I think it's safe to say most of us can remember quite vividly where we were and what we were doing when we think back to a historic moment like the first man on the moon, the assassination of John F. Kennedy and so many other historic moments. The 9/11 terrorist attack is certainly one I will remember. The destruction of the twin towers affected our life and career path, and we ended up moving to Switzerland for a couple of years.

Two fantastic years of travel and work flew by, and we spent our money as quickly as we earned it. Neither of us thought too much about saving; we just booked the next dive trip and enjoyed our days together. Take it as it comes! We didn't own a house, car or much of anything of value apart from the odd painting or two. We both had a keen interest in auctions and all our possessions were bid on so we seldom bought retail.

However, trouble was on the horizon due to my hearing. Two of the most important qualifications of a court reporter was excellent hearing and writing on the stenographic machine with high speed. I started to notice my hearing was changing and became compromised so I could no longer work with confidence. It slowly reached a point where I was not able to keep up as I was hesitating about what I was hearing. The writing was on the wall that we couldn't sustain this lifestyle.

That's when we came back to Canada for good.

We worked on compilation of appeal books for a while but then decided to dabble in auctions and try selling items on eBay, a hot site at the time. We registered and proceeded to buy and sell as a team. Jeff was in charge of bidding on items at live auctions, packaging what we listed and sold, and regular trips to the post office. I wish I could say we made a lot of money—we didn't—but we could always pay the rent, put food on the table and plan for other opportunities that might come up.

We were fortunate to spend our summers on the beaches in Vancouver, cycling the sea wall, swimming in the bay, and having picnics. We were extremely happy!

Luckily, Jeff's decrease in cognitive ability progressed slowly. Little changes were happening to Jeff but not making a big impact on our lives at first. I had become used to filling in the blanks when words couldn't come to mind for Jeff. He would so often say, "Helen, finish this story for me." Friends and family were beginning to notice. We were faced with a struggle we yet had to comprehend—the beginning of the downward spiral of unimaginable pain and sadness while Jeff coped with his brain slowly being chipped away by dementia and dying.

He was physically the same man—strong and fit—but we were spinning in circles some days. There was more change, more danger. The safety of those around us and in our apartment building became a concern. Chaos at home followed, and we had to make choices about the future.

You might wonder why I'm writing about our eleven-year struggle with Alzheimer's disease. I wanted to show how the unexpected can happen to a partnership and within a family when such a diagnosis occurs. After a myriad of tests over six months, we were left in a state of fear and untold distress for the immediate future. This disease struck quickly and silently.

Happily married couples expect to live, love, work and retire together to share peace and pleasant days. With Alzheimer's, that no longer existed. We no longer had a path forward to happy cheerful days of realizing our goals realized; that was upended in a heartbeat. Our world became totally unglued.

How did we cope?

Can there be any plan to make the journey less troubled?

Are there any hints that could reduce the sheer loss of everything we counted on and hoped for as we headed into our future?

How could we survive the really difficult decisions we had to make to continue existing without losing our ability to function?

Where does one get the strength to carry on?

Where does the faith and hope come from to stop us from jumping off a cliff or a tall building?

There is the one who has the disease and then there's the one who watches over the one who has the disease. The fear and distress of the diagnosis threatens both, but the burden of help and stability ultimately falls heavily on the watcher. It's no longer an even 50/50 sharing—it only gets more and more acute for the watcher in ways that can initially be extremely difficult to comprehend or weigh to the fullest.

My husband and I shared an immensely close, tight bond of unconditional love and trust. It was put to the test with dementia.

Chapter 2

JEFF'S DECLINE

In March 2008, my husband's sister was quite ill—close to death—with heart problems, and we went to see her in hospital on a rotational basis scheduled by her family so she would always have someone there. We adhered to the plan—so I thought. But when Jeff went, he couldn't find her. Hospitals are a maze and many people have difficulty figuring out the layout and trying to find the right room, but even when he asked for directions, he still couldn't find her. He'd come back home and say, "I didn't see her. I kept looking at and following the directions, but I couldn't find her."

That was the first inkling that something might not be quite right. Jeff was sixty-eight years old.

In the fall of 2008, two of Jeff's long-time rugby mates met him for lunch at my suggestion. I hoped they could shed some light on the situation as I thought I was imagining things. They were struck by the changes, so I got Jeff to the doctor.

In January 2009 when we went to the hospital for his tests, we were calm and discussed his many rugby concussions with the neurologist. I was staggered at all the tests he needed done—something like ten over the next five months.

I noticed Jeff struggling to finish jokes, losing items, misplacing keys and glasses. He possessed a slight confusion that easily could be attributed to getting older. Jeff and I had talked about his memory problems surfacing so often, and we promised to always be together at home and do our best to get through the changes. It doesn't always happen that way though, does it? Where were we heading? How could we cope? We had no idea how quickly this might progress as we struggled with acceptance, safety and exhaustion.

I clearly recall mornings when Jeff was so muddled up. It always helped to get out, so we often walked to Costco, about a thirty-five-minute walk.

Some days he seemed calm and we would organize breakfast together. The only problem was trying to find a few things he put away. They eventually turned up, but he seemed to be all in a tizzy about things more often than not. He thought people were coming for dinner and we didn't have the food yet, and he started raising his voice to a shout, "We've got to cancel! We've got to cancel!" He was all mixed up with the timing. I convinced him that we would have a great time on that Saturday, which was the day they were coming, and he seemed to calm down.

Jeff got very agitated about small things and made issues about them, something he would never even have thought about doing in the past. He was just such a great guy and we had such fun out together, always joking and laughing. And there was nothing he liked more than cuddling on the sofa and relaxing!

I would start crying out of the blue as I guess I was frustrated. I couldn't see solutions, but then I would talk myself into being positive, like, *Don't get in a flap over little things.* I tried so hard to make him happy as he was becoming so unhappy a lot of the time. If I was showing any unhappiness Jeff became distressed and started crying, too, and asking, "What's wrong with me? Why can't I understand anything anymore? I can't read like I used to." I had to make sure I put on a "face" that everything was okay despite the chaos and confusion. We were waiting for the results and maybe the doctors could help.

My workload increased as I kept having to change things around, put things in different places, do a big search for hours for something that had always been right at hand in the same spot. We'd had an Inuit carving of a howling wolf sitting on our mantle for years. I sold the item on eBay and had been paid, but when I went to package the carving, it was not on the mantle. I asked Jeff about it and he acted like I must have lost it or sold it earlier. We searched the apartment for days in every nook and cranny without success, so I had to refund the buyer and send an apology that it was dropped and had been damaged. Two months later, I found the carving wrapped in tissue in the bottom of my bureau where I kept bits of clothing I seldom wore! He had hidden it probably because he didn't want me to sell it.

"Look, I found the wolf carving," I said, putting it back on the mantle. "Let's just keep it for us."

He smiled from ear to ear!

Jeff began doing some strange things—upside down, inside out, backwards, and that was just getting himself dressed. He was losing his ability to understand what order to dress or what to put on. I had to laugh to see him in my long housecoat for breakfast tied with a string he found somewhere, as it certainly didn't fit him. The sleeves went up to his elbow—it would look so obvious to anyone but him.

He sometimes knew that he had done things in the wrong order after he'd done it. One time he was peeling carrots and instead of putting the peelings into the garbage, he put them into the bowl of salad I had just finished making. It was only when we were about to eat the salad that I noticed all the peelings were mixed in.

He was so keen to help with breakfast and was hurt if I told him to sit and relax.

"Please let me help," he would say.

But it was easier to help him through his indecisions like how many place settings, how many pieces of cutlery, how many glasses and what kind to put out. He had developed a block about numbers.

When hosting dinner with friends, he insisted on setting the table for dinner. One person's setting got three forks and no knives, another setting just a soup spoon (and we weren't having soup). His mind seemed jumbled. To rectify it seemed to hurt his feelings and he wanted to know why I was changing everything he just did.

His conversations were getting complicated and hard to follow, and I think that can be said for those trying to chat with him as well. I got so frustrated sometimes I remember saying, "Just tell me straight what you want to say," as if that was the solution. I was as confused as he was it seemed.

He had two tests left to complete—a heart ultrasound and then the MRI, which would result, we hoped, in the diagnosis.

He tried hard to be good-natured most of the time and we carried on with our regular living, it seemed, but there were an increasing number of things that went on that made me stop short and wonder. He often said, "I'm blank today," or, "I can't think straight," so he knew something was not right.

We went grocery shopping one day, and he went to the liquor store next to the grocery shop to pick up a twelve pack of beer. He sat on a bench outside the grocery shop waiting for me. We walked home, but he left the beer under the bench. We went back right away—wishful thinking! Not there! A present for a happy camper! We got another twelve pack.

When we received a notice for a rent increase, he blew his top, something that was so unusual and unexpected.

"We're moving out of here! I'm going to tell them what I think about this increase!"

"We get an increase every year and so it's nothing new," I said.

"We've never had an increase, ever!" he shouted.

I quickly learned there were some things I shouldn't mention as he was definitely reacting with agitation and aggression—characteristics that were not previously in his personality but were arising more and more.

Jeff said he was being pushed to have these tests but there was nothing wrong with him. When our case worker came over to discuss options, Jeff got into a fight with him for no reason, stormed into another room and yelled for me. I excused myself and Jeff said, "Just get rid of that guy right now." He was in denial. He was angry, and he demanded that I tell him what he was doing wrong.

"How about if every time you do something differently from before I'll point it out," I asked.

He was all for that until I started following up. That's when he had to agree that he was doing things differently. He actually chuckled about it and started to say, "I've messed up again." He started to say that a lot.

He was going off to the post office without the parcels, without money and without his bus pass, just walking out the door and saying, "Bye!" I would jump up to check that he had everything and he wouldn't have anything. He became aware that he needed some help, and it was becoming obvious he couldn't do this on his own anymore.

Every moment could change quickly. His speech was even changing to a slight slur. He would put money "away." We would tear the apartment apart trying to find it before we went to the post office. Fortunately, I had a little stash in the office, so we used that, but he was so upset because he thought he had thrown the money out with the garbage. It turned up in the bottom of a candy dish in the back of a cupboard—somewhere we both hadn't looked.

I tried to convince him to put his bus pass and money on a clip thing we had by the door as soon as he got in the door, but it was difficult even for me to change our habits when we weren't fighting an unknown disease. There I was trying to make him do it and I didn't even follow my own instructions!

I had so many moments of despair over his condition as I knew he was not the same. We could no longer have the same conversations. I was not sure we were even having conversations anymore. He brought up the strangest things and was amused about something I couldn't comprehend or follow. He talked about trivial things he never would have mentioned before.

Where was it all going?

It wouldn't get better unless something was done about whatever "it" was. I got more frightened every day thinking it might be Alzheimer's. I feared he would just get worse, but I didn't want to think about that. This great strapping, energetic guy just going downhill broke my heart every day.

We had been biking a lot on some gloriously sunny days, and we happened upon a crafts fair. The crowds were thick, but we tried to stay off the beaten path. There were all kinds of food and souvenir kiosks set up, so we locked our bikes and walked around and ate some amazing dim sum! We were joined by a couple looking for a table. Jeff got in a chatting mood, but he was getting so mixed up; it was like he wasn't listening. The guy had said a couple of times with really pointed emphasis—I could hear irritation in his voice—that they didn't live by the water. The couple looked at him and at each other with strange looks. I turned to Jeff and said, "Let's go," and we rushed off. They just stared and said nothing.

Each day seemed to be challenging. Jeff kept screwing up. I asked him to put the stove on, and he put the kettle on instead with barely any water in it. We had a whistling kettle and I could hear it and I said, "Oh, you decided we'd have tea."

"No, I put the oven on," he said, but then he realized his mistake.

More confusion in the kitchen. He opened a beer and poured for three instead of two. Little incidents like passing by the stove and leaving the elements on high and just walking away. I walked into the kitchen and the stove was red hot. Fortunately, no pots on it!

He flooded the bathroom sink twice in three or four months. Because we lived in such an old building, the water moved quickly to leak into the apartment downstairs. The tenants were fine the first time, but the second time they had guests over and it was leaking on their dining room table as they were eating. We were becoming unpopular to say the least!

Jeff was becoming unpopular with me as well, as he started peeing against the wall near the toilet and not in the bowl. After a few times that happened and there was pee everywhere, I made a habit of walking in after him and pointing out what he was doing.

"No, I peed in the bowl. That's just water on the floor," he said.

I had to be so watchful, eyes everywhere.

He kept saying, "What's going on with me? What happens to people as they get older? Is this it?"

I hugged and held him as he got into moods of dejection and rejection.

"You don't love me anymore," he would say.

He was becoming more childlike every day and depending on me like I just couldn't believe. What was going to happen? Couldn't we get it fixed so all would be like it was before? It was like we had no control—we didn't actually—and no matter what we thought or said, it just happened. I shed lots of tears, and I had no one to rant and rave to. At times, I just wanted to jump into bed, cover up my head and wish life would go by quickly so I could go somewhere quiet and peaceful with no worries.

There was a show on TV with a scene that kept coming back to me. The family was so anxious to have a Christmas holiday somewhere sunny together and they were waiting at the airport for their flight to be called. In the meantime the granddad, who had Alzheimer's, took his grandson to see the planes taking off. Their flight was called, the family searching for them, but grandson and grandad were standing by a big window watching their flight take off saying, "Wow, look at that one!" The family all treated him like he was really special even though he had just screwed up all their Christmas plans. They knew he was as happy to go on holiday as they were but his cognitive level interfered and changed it all that day.

I could see that happening to us. I was so conflicted trying to stay happy and positive, but the opposite seemed to be happening. It was one worrisome incident after another. If you had a broken ankle, you could get it fixed, but there was little to be done with senility and dementia. I just didn't know how to handle things anymore. I tried not to confront him, but I was ignoring things that stared me in the eye.

Our days of roaming the auction halls were quickly coming to a close as Jeff could not comprehend the sequence with bidding. He couldn't write anymore. He now simply denied it and thought I didn't know.

So many things kept happening that created a muddle in our lives. I went out grocery shopping and left Jeff to retrieve the clothes from the dryer, which he did, but instead of sorting them into our separate piles on the bed he put them all away in his chest of drawers.

"Where's the clothes?" I asked.

"Haven't you noticed? I put them all away," he said.

I didn't say a thing but just started taking them out of his drawers and sorting them into my spaces.

"You are so ungrateful," he said as he stormed out of the bedroom.

I was shocked, as this was such an unusual way for him to react.

I read lots of articles on the internet about dementia and found Jeff fit every category in the mild level—the first stage. One of the questions the neurologist focussed on was Jeff's rugby career and how many concussions he'd had had. I read that twenty, thirty or more years later, concussions could be attributed to early development of Alzheimer's and much research was going into that area.

Jeff and I talked about dementia often and he would bring it up, so he seemed okay talking about it. He said he felt quite insecure over those past few months, and I assured him I would stand by him come what may. He described some of the rugby games after banging his head severely. He would vomit, get disoriented, have bad headaches it would take many days to get over. One time when he was playing Old Boys rugby (over 50s), he had to be driven home by two mates as he was so unsteady on his feet and needed help up the stairs. That might have been a concussion as he was sick to his stomach and had a very bad headache. So I even experienced it happening to him in the twenty-three years (up to that time) that we'd been together.

We awaited the MRI results which scanned his brain and would show if the tangles of cords were mixing and dying. One article I read showed one's brain in all the stages and how it affected the six or seven areas of the brain. With some people it was the front, others the side, and others the back, so each of those sections determined motor functions, cognition, memory and so forth.

He seemed content to rest a lot, sitting on the sofa with me, watching TV. He often did not want me to budge.

THE TEST RESULTS

We sat in the neurologist's office holding hands while the doctor told us Jeff had a type of dementia that could be vascular dementia or the early stages of Alzheimer's. He recommended seeing our GP and getting some of the new medications like Exelon, Aricept or others as a start. We walked out of his office holding hands and not saying much.

I often felt I was an ignorant anomaly. Because of my concern about Jeff and our own lives, I was so distracted that I was missing a tragic situation involving a lovely old lady in our building, Vivian, who was suffering with undisclosed problems. I knew nothing about dementia and did not think that was her problem. Even when her phone was disconnected and her Hydro bill not paid (she was a recluse), I didn't suspect anything. I paid her Hydro and set about helping her get the phone reconnected.

Vivian was a wonderful neighbour. She came to our wedding at Inukshuk on the beach and I hadn't seen her so happy in years! As she was a single eighty-four-year-old woman in close proximity, I used to bring her meals to share. After a few weeks I went to retrieve my dishes, but she was quite reluctant to let me past her threshold. When I finally coaxed her to let me in, the dishes were piled high! Weeks of unwashed dishes—including mine! She was fiercely independent and would not let me wash them and shooed me out. I then made a habit of phoning for delivery meals for her as her phone still wasn't working. Little did I realize that whether it worked or not she couldn't figure the phone out anymore. So ignorant was I, but I hadn't read any of the literature at that point. Like most people, I didn't know anything about dementia.

Can you believe I did not suspect what her disease was?

As the days, weeks and months passed, she got worse and I urgently requested her sister in Toronto to come help her. She could not function or talk about anything. I knew she was having a problem that needed checking but she wanted no part of that.

Within a couple of weeks of her sister arriving, she left her home of thirty-five years to go live in Toronto. She certainly balked at leaving. They asked me to convince her to go and she did go after much coaxing. It was in the middle of a hot summer day. She put on her fur coat, waved goodbye and that was the last I saw of her. In hindsight, it is difficult to believe I only suspected Alzheimer's. Perhaps I was in denial about her, and about Jeff.

I agreed to help with the disposal of her household goods in her large two-bedroom apartment, and I helped her niece sort through her clothing, mementos and so on. You probably know people who keep every bit of paper, clothing, souvenir of travels. Well, multiply that by twenty and you have her apartment. Nowadays they call that hoarding. She had brand new shoes in their original boxes piled to the rafters in her apartment, clothes with labels never worn, SO MANY *National Geographic* magazines, and a full set of *Encyclopedia Britannica*. It is hard to describe the clutter.

I kept in touch with Vivian through her sister, but a month later she fell, broke her hip and died in hospital shortly thereafter. Following this upsetting news, I enrolled in courses on dementia at the Vancouver General Hospital to educate myself on the subject.

We decided to try to stall Jeff's dementia with one of the suggested medications, but Exelon made Jeff sick to his stomach. By this time we had contacted the UBC Alzheimer's clinic, discussed his symptoms with the neurologist there and continued with another battery of tests.

The UBC clinic concluded that he had dementia, more than likely Alzheimer's. They prescribed Aricept, and we hoped it would stall the disease.

My husband had started an achingly slow decline. I noticed a similarity to episodes with Vivian, and I was, like so many of us, just not aware of the stages and symptoms of this disease. I harboured huge regrets of not being cognizant of what I was staring at with Vivian. Why she couldn't open jars anymore; why she would let her phone and Hydro lapse; her increased seclusion. But because I didn't know about dementia, I tended to think it was old age or senility. In hindsight, it seems obvious that her senility was dementia.

Three years before the diagnosis, we had our wedding celebration at the Inukshuk Statue on the beach in the West End of Vancouver. It was one of the happiest days of my life and we didn't stop smiling all day. Our lovely friend Vivian, who had shared so many meals with us, was present that day. We were still smiling. We hadn't lost track of our relationship and closeness. I missed the "old Jeff" all the time. I never stopped missing him—how he once was—and the way we travelled and explored, his British background and my Hungarian. Learning, always learning—laughter and contentment.

MEDS & TESTS FROM OUR GP

Our GP wanted to perform some verbal and drawing tests with Jeff before granting approval for some expensive drugs which might be partially covered by our medical plan. The whole idea, the doc said to me privately, was that if he failed the tests we would receive approval for payment.

The doctor started with the questions.

"What's the date?"

Jeff didn't know. He got all mixed up about where he was living—couldn't figure out whether he lived in Canada or British Columbia or Kelowna. It didn't get any easier for him from there. He had to repeat three words after a pause and he forgot all three. Our doctor asked Jeff to spell the word "world" backwards. He couldn't do it.

Jeff was then to read what was on a sheet of paper and follow the instructions. The instructions said, "Close your eyes."

"If I close my eyes then I can't see what's on the paper," Jeff said.

He just kept asking, "So what now?"

I was not allowed to coach him or give hints.

He was directed to take a piece of paper in his left hand, fold it in two and place it, folded, on the floor. Doc had to repeat the instructions three times. Jeff took the paper (not paying attention to which hand), tried to fold it with one hand, opened it up, threw it on the floor and stomped on it with his foot! We couldn't help but be hysterical with laughter as by this time he was laughing too.

"That's what I think of these tests!" Jeff said.

We all couldn't help but laugh at the antics he was going through despite the seriousness of the situation! A light moment for the day! Unfortunately, this also showed us he couldn't count anymore, could hardly read, and he couldn't draw a clock.

He failed, so we got the drugs 90 percent paid.

EARLY 2012

Over the next two years, my husband continued to decline. Little things became more obvious—hiding items, always losing his keys, unsure of where he was going, needing to plan days in advance of a get-together with friends. I started to compensate for these shortcomings by not providing details to him of any plans, hiding his keys so I could find them, and keeping an ever-watchful eye.

I had no family support in Vancouver, but Jeff had family living there. His sister sporadically gave support, but she had her own medical problems that seemed to far surpass what her brother was going through. I was mostly unaware of the plight and history of his sister's husband's parents who both suffered, and eventually died, from dementia.

Chapter 3

UNSETTLING LIFE AT HOME

VISITS TO MY SISTER IN HOSPITAL.
EARLY 2010

My sister had a serious operation. Her family made arrangements, like shifts, to rotate days to see her in the intensive care unit. My wife and I went on separate days so my sister would always have someone there for her if she awakened.

Something strange is happening though because I can never find her room. I know hospitals are confusing mazes but even after getting directions several times I forget what floor I'm on or where to go. I spend what seems like hours searching for her but finally give up and go back home.

My wife asked how my sister was and I told her, "I couldn't find her." I didn't want Helen to know how hard I looked as it worried me that I forgot the directions so easily.

Next time she gives me a note with clear directions and we go over them together. When I get to the hospital I can't find the note. It was in my pocket but not there anymore, so I was back to square one with the same old story.

I hate going to hospitals anyway, and so I told a little white lie. "My sister is the same," I said, even though I couldn't find her and didn't see her.

CRYING IN THE MORNING. JANUARY 2010

Why do I have to wake up crying all the time? She's right next to me in bed but the tears won't stop. She talks to me and holds me and says not to worry, but I am worried. I can't remember things. I have strange dreams and I wake up crying, not just a tear or two, but they just keep coming. She tries not to cry with me and makes our breakfast. I sit quietly waiting just staring out the window.

I am so tired after breakfast. Sometimes we sit at the table and I ask her what's happened to me. She says I have some memory problems. I've heard the word dementia and Alzheimer's bandied about but I don't think I have those.

I don't want to run back to bed but she says, "Let's go lie down for another few minutes," and it's very soothing and special to have her holding me.

Why would I cry when she's right here? She hasn't done anything, but every now and then she stamps her foot, and I saw her pounding the duvet one time when I came to see where she was. She was crying, but I got her through that and gave her big hugs.

HAPPENINGS IN THE NIGHT. FEBRUARY 2010

My hearing aids sat on my bedroom dresser at night so my hearing was vastly reduced. One night I was startled awake by Jeff saying, "Wake up, your bath is ready."

Yikes!

I said, "What's happening?"

He was standing there with a towel wrapped around his waist, wet hair, wet body, water dripping all over the place. I couldn't believe it.

I jumped out of bed to check the bathroom, and the tub was full of his used bathwater. Before I tucked him in earlier, I asked if he wanted a bath and he said no, so it must have been on his mind. In other bath-related mishaps, he often washed clothes—underwear and socks mostly—in the tub while he was having a bath. Then he would drape the wet items over the rod with water leaking all over the floor. Didn't give it a thought.

I declined getting in the tub. I was really nervous as I wondered how many people he had woken up with the water running at four o'clock in the morning. It always was so quiet at that time, and the walls were thin in this ancient building!

We were up so we decided to have an early breakfast.

"How much longer do you think I have?" he said.

He had a lot on his mind and began crying. No wonder he couldn't sleep! He was thinking about his future. I put on the brave face and told him he had at least ten years. I knew it was difficult to predict with a disease like this. What did I know?

Jeff often set the table for three or more, and he had major confusion filling the salt and pepper shakers. It was hard to imagine all the goings on. It was one thing after the other.

Jeff's attention span was now miniscule. He would start a project, like cleaning silverware, not finish it and leave everything in disarray. He decided to clean the kitchen drawers one day, so he pulled them all out and then put them in the wrong order so nothing fit. He just walked away from it all. He was so impatient opening the bottom bin in the fridge for the veggies that he broke it. Fortunately, there was an old spare fridge downstairs in the laundry room with a new bin so I swapped it for our broken one.

These "mistakes" just kept adding up, and I wondered what was coming next. It was still manageable despite the chaos, but little did I know just how bad it would get very soon. Some days I dreamt of going on a holiday, sitting on a beach and not thinking about anything. It had been five years since we had been on a holiday, but I didn't see it happening any time soon.

POST OFFICE RUNS. SPRING 2010

We work as a team. Helen gets the parcels and envelopes together and puts them in my black mesh basket. We made a plan that anything to mail will go on a table in the hall in a designated black mesh basket. She doesn't tell me when she puts them in there, but she will give hints like, "Have you looked in your basket?"

When I do look, the mail is waiting for me. My job is to put extra sticky tape on the larger envelopes, place the return address on the front in the corner and put on the airmail stickers. Could it be any simpler?

Yet I screwed it up more often than not.

I put the addresses on upside down or on the back of the envelope or on top of the addressee. The airmail stickers don't look like they used to as I see there's sometimes three or four when there needs only one. I tried my best.

When I go into her office and ask, "What's happening? Why are they messed up?"

She says not to worry, that she will fix them. She makes me a cup of tea and then I have a nap.

When I wake up, the envelopes are all done and we head to the post office together. I carry the parcels in my backpack and I have the money in my pocket. The two posties are patient and wait for me to empty the backpack. I spread the money on the counter and let them take the right amount. I put the rest back. We laugh and are happy and cheerful.

We then head to Costco for a smoked meat sandwich and French fries. We pick up just a couple of things, mainly our favourite BBQ chicken, and head back on the bus.

MORNING WALK ON THE BEACH

Another beautiful day!

She's made a picnic with deli items and we're ready to go for a day in the park.

We're walking on the beach, but first she is going to get us a Tim Horton's doughnut and a coffee as a breakfast treat. She asks me to wait on a big log on the beach, and I promise not to move.

"Please don't move."

She's gone up the street to get our treat.

I'm tired of waiting. Why is she taking so long? Where has she gone?

Did she tell me to meet her in the park? I can't remember the plan, but she's nowhere in sight so I better get moving so I can find her. I think she went ahead of me. Or did she? Maybe she went back to our apartment. Yes, I think that's what she said.

So I hurry back past the Inukshuk statue and go home and up the three flights of stairs, but she's not there. I'm tired. I decide to stretch out on the sofa.

I wake up hungry. She's not here. I stand at the window and see her across the street. I head down the stairs. I think we got our signals crossed.

We eat our picnic on a bench outside the apartment.

We come in, warm the coffee from Tim Hortons and eat the doughnuts.

EVER WATCHFUL

It was getting more and more difficult to make a plan and keep Jeff in my sight. It was hard to imagine how the person I left sitting on a log with lots of space around would suddenly get up and leave. I came back from a Tim Hortons with coffee and treats, and he was gone. I was stunned and had such a feeling of confusion that he was gone. But where? It never occurred to me that he would walk back home, so I walked in the other direction—to Stanley Park—to find him. After an hour or so, I decided to go back home and there he was waiting for me.

"Where were you?" he said.

FEEDING HORSES IN THE FIELD

My sister has found three horses to feed carrots to in this field, a stallion and two mares. He's so majestic, almost all white.

Helen always backs away as she is fearful of horses, but I've got the carrots sticking out of my pockets and that alone lures them to come to the wooden fence.

He often looks me in the eye and I feel compatibility with him. He lets me touch his beautiful face.

Eventually I give up all my carrots. The stallion always does his best to stop the mares from getting anything.

I could stay with them longer but we're only visiting.

I try to get my sister to take me there when we have outings together. I can lie in bed thinking about their power, but, like me, their freedom is curbed; they are fenced in. There seems to be a fence around my thoughts so much of the time as well. One minute I'm talking away and the next my thoughts are blank.

FEEDING HORSES IN THE FIELD

Jeff's sister took Jeff on outings to a fenced-in area where horses were exercised. Petting and feeding carrots to horses was such a soothing experience for Jeff. That ended after a few months as the horse owners, who didn't know exactly what was being fed to their horses, starting discouraging feeding out of an abundance of caution.

WORKOUTS WITH COACH WAYNE

I'm just so lucky to have a friend who picks me up to go for a workout at the gym in his condo. We are old rugby mates from playing together for many years. He's in charge and leads me to keep myself fit. We do these exercises every couple of weeks, if not more often, and I must be getting lazy as I'm not as enthusiastic. Sometimes I would just like to have a nap, but we get through with my coach. We then have a sauna.

We go off for a lunch together. He always pays. I have money but he insists on paying. One time we went to the casino and he gave me $20. I thanked him and put in my pocket. I'm not a gambler, but it's okay to watch others.

It's great to get back home and have a snuggle and a rest on the sofa. Helen unpacks my workout bag, and it seems I picked up Wayne's towel and can't find mine.

We are getting ready to call it a night, and I start undressing. "Look at you!" Helen says. "Those aren't your underwear!"

She starts to laugh as she realizes I took Wayne's underwear by mistake. Believe me, there is no mistaking for my wife. Wayne's are full waist jock underwear, soft cotton with an opening in the front, and mine are tight with no openings. Perhaps Wayne took mine so he could try a different fit and observe his wife's reaction!

LOST ON GRANVILLE AND BROADWAY. 2012

Time to buy some birdseed and chat with my birder friends from Quebec, in French! They are so knowledgeable about birds, and we buy a big bag every couple of months. It fits in my backpack.

My wife usually comes, but today she's busy making dinners for the freezer.

I've got the correct amount of money and I get on the bus out front. Then I wonder which bus I take, but it comes to me to go across the Granville Bridge and get off at the big intersection.

I get off and start walking towards the birdseed store, but I'm getting tired and haven't seen it yet. I'm standing at an intersection and everything looks the same. I don't know where I am. A nervous feeling comes over me as I know I'm lost. What to do? I walk some more and finally ask people if they've seen the birdseed place. One person tells me it's far away. Maybe I've been walking in the wrong direction.

I am back at the corner of Granville and Broadway after asking for help many times. My knees are bothering me. I get on a bus going back across the bridge. The bus driver tells me where to get off after I told him I live on Beach. I finally see some familiar stores and landmarks.

I walk the rest of the way home. I've been gone a long time and she's very worried. When I see her I burst into tears and tell her I got lost and had no idea where to go.

What is happening to me?

We have a cup of tea. We hold each other.

"We'll go together tomorrow to get the seed," she says.

"Then I will show you where I went wrong," I say.

Can it get worse? I'm really worried as I never get lost. I'm the one who uses the compass underwater and leads the group of divers in the right direction. I have, or at least I had, a keen sense of direction.

LOST ON OUR BICYCLES. SUMMER 2012

We're all pumped up for a sea wall cycle but decide to check our bikes out at the corner bike shop. All is well, bikes looking good.

Really nice guy helping us. I get muddled, but Helen speaks to him and gets everything in order.

She's ahead of me and we're enjoying all the boats tied up in the marina.

Quick as a flash she's gone—she's nowhere in sight. I look all over but can't find her. I don't know what to do. I keep searching. Then I decide to go back to the bike shop. Maybe she went there.

I ask that nice guy if he's seen her.

"No," he says.

"I will just wait," I say.

It seems a long time has gone by, and I am standing outside watching everyone in case I spot her.

This car pulls up and these two big guys get out. The nice guy talks to them and then they come over. I ask them if they are rugby players. We have a great chat about sports. I tell them I'm waiting for my wife. They say that's okay and ask if I know my address. I never forget my address, so I reel it off. They say we should go see if my wife is there. We can have this nice guy guard my bike.*

We are not far away from home, and we get there quickly. I stand in front of our door with these two guys who could easily be on my rugby team. I buzz Helen. She answers and I say, "I met two great guys but they want to meet you."

She buzzes us in. She looks relieved that we're here. She invites them in and chats with one while I talk rugby with the other. They are so friendly! They write something down and then they leave.

Helen and I hug and stay close to each other. We talk about what could have happened, but by this time I'm starving. We have a quick bite and a cup of tea. We then walk with her bike to get my bike.

The nice guy in the bike shop says, "Hey, you found each other!"

Then we do a spin around the sea wall. I'm always in the lead and she's always behind me now.

*Helen's note: The guy from the bicycle shop called the police as he was worried about Jeff. I had mentioned to him that Jeff was forgetful due to dementia.

BUS CONFUSION

I'm waiting like always for her downstairs while she grabs last-minute items for mailing at the post office.

The bus is coming but she's not here yet. He's a driver I know and stops and I get on. We start chatting. The bus pulls away. I turn to say something to Helen but she's not there. I get these panic feelings. Where is she?

I ask the driver, "Where is my wife?"

He says, "I haven't seen her."

I just know I have to get off this bus. I have my satchel of mail but I don't know where to go. Somebody please help me figure it out.

I get off the bus and start in a direction I think is where I came from.

I see familiar shops but the panic of not knowing where to go fills me. I keep walking towards the water as I know we live close to the water.

A big bus pulls up and there she is! I yell and jump with joy! We hold onto each other.

We go somewhere different to mail our letters. I am worried and frightened but she says, "Everything is okay, we'll have a treat for lunch."

We walk to Stanley Park and everything settles down. She picked up some food on the way. We sit on a park bench and she puts her arm around my shoulders and I fall asleep. I'm safe now.

LOST IN STANLEY PARK. 2012

I used to really love doing yard sales, but they really tire me out these days when I have to stand and talk to people. Gabbing doesn't come as easy.

She decides to have a sale with another tenant but I want to walk along the sea wall. She says I might get lost. I can't imagine getting lost as we do this route all the time. I decide to go. She cautions me to be careful.

It's beautiful out and I get to the Lost Lagoon and sit on a bench and watch the ducks and swans. Then I decide to go see the artists in the park as I have a South African friend there and it's a great way to connect with him. I walk and walk but I can't find them, and that's strange as they usually are right where I'm looking.

I'm getting really hungry. I'm not sure if I'm going the right way. Not as much looks familiar except lots of trees. I'm just walking along and this police car pulls up. There are two officers who ask me if I'm okay. They really look familiar and I ask if we've met before but I don't remember the uniforms. I ask about rugby, if they play, and we chat for a bit. They tell me I shouldn't walk in the middle of the road. I wasn't aware I was in the middle of the road.

They ask me for my address and I tell them—I never forget my address—and one of them checks his computer. Nowadays everyone is always looking at cell phones or computers.

They ask me if I'd like a ride back to my place. I hesitate as I don't want to be a pest but my knees hurt, and I think it's a far walk. I'm starving so I say okay and I join them. We take a scenic route and they are so agreeable and easy to chat with.

I see my wife among all the sale items in the front yard. My wife's face drops when she sees this cop car pull up at her yard sale and I get out!

"Oh, my god," she says. "What's happened?"

I'm smiling and say, "I've met two cops and we've been chatting rugby and they offered me a lift as I'm so hungry and I told them you would have my lunch ready!"

We go upstairs and there's my egg sandwich. She makes a cup of tea. The one cop joins us upstairs and we chat away.

I can hardly wait to eat and have a nap! I am just so happy to be home with Helen. There are some good people around.

THE PRIVATE CLUB. FEBRUARY 2013

Helen is taking me to meet a British couple who run a private members club for people diagnosed with early onset Alzheimer's.

They are such a nice couple—she's short and tiny and he towers over her!

I'm told I don't quite fit the diagnosis to be under sixty-five but they are willing to stretch it a bit as I'm sixty-eight and have had this illness for years—probably before sixty-five.

They will have me join on a trial basis starting in two weeks. On a Wednesday I will meet them at 10:00 and spend the whole day until 4:00. Because I'm a walker it really helped win them in my favour as they spend the afternoon walking to various venues.

Helen and I will go by bus together in the morning and then she will meet me at the club at 4:00.

Here's what goes on at the club:

It's a one-of-a-kind club with approximately twelve members who meet Tuesday, Wednesday or Thursday. My day is Wednesday. We start off with coffee and baked goods. Then we read newspapers and discuss articles among the group. After that it could be gym, a movie, music.

Lunch is at a specially organized restaurant for us. It's delicious and we can choose our food.

Following that is a walk as a group with the British couple and a team leader. Weather permitting it can last from one to two and a half hours. Gelato is always the afternoon treat.

I'm feeling my way and very tired by 4:00.

After a month of scheduled Wednesday visits, we decide to use HandyDart, which saves my wife from taking me there and picking me up.

All was going really well but I often don't like the team sports, and I would like to leave and be with Helen and have a nap.

SPRING & SUMMER ROUTINE - SETTLING IN

We were managing. Life was changing at a rapid rate. The club was a godsend as Jeff seemed keen, with encouragement I might add, in going on Wednesdays to be with the group of like-minded people. But he always said upon his return that he was tired and his knees hurt from walking.

Unfortunately, the routine didn't settle him but made him think he was missing something because I was not there as well. There always was a hint of anxiety and suspicion when he questioned what I was up to while he was at the club.

We spent a busy summer at our usual haunts in Stanley Park, on our bikes, having picnics, sitting on the beach, going in the water, catching sunshine, talking a lot. But it was obvious how much Jeff was changing. He lacked comprehension and experienced so much confusion about the smallest things and the adjustments we were making. Although he generally didn't complain, he definitely was not as chatty or energetic. We were coping on a different level.

We joined weekly groups like Minds in Motion, which was a programme for exercise and discussion with family members lasting about half an hour. The goal was to help us cope and be inspired with more diverse activities, but Jeff couldn't seem to join in. He wouldn't engage with people and got restless after about ten minutes.

I was going to a monthly group meeting for carers, but despite instructions to him to rest and stay home, he would turn up at the meeting standing outside the glassed-in windows looking at me. Someone said once, "Isn't that your husband there?" It sure was. There he was knocking at the door trying to join in. I'm sure his isolation and inadequacy in communicating was obvious to him, and he was fraught with frustration without me there to talk to and comfort him.

Living in our apartment began to raise some security questions among the other tenants. The news about Jeff's decline travelled quickly, and we learned about the stigma dementia carries. It made people nervous and cautious. Options and choices were an ongoing discussion with doctors and people in similar situations. No one wanted to live apart. It was a subject I thought I would never even have to talk about much less make serious choices about, and now it was a reality.

Jeff was not aggressive, but he was unpredictable at times. His ability to help with household chores, grocery shopping and so on was at a totally different level than previously.

His confusion was obvious and his fear was palpable. I was like a mother with a young child, and I had to watch his every move. But I couldn't just put him in a stroller. My energy sagged as the days passed, and the emotional strain of losing what was once Jeff was devastating. He was a Jeff who couldn't write or read books, couldn't handle money to buy food or go outside on his own. I was continually frightened and fearful of the future as I noticed his decline, forgetfulness, and lack of ability to comprehend situations or our relationship.

I tried very hard to explain "things" to him but it was not registering anymore.

NEW MOUNTAIN BIKES. AUGUST 2013

We decided to get upright mountain bikes at Costco. We cycled home on them and were happy with our purchases. Oh, they worked so well, but they were heavy to cart up and down a floor to the basement laundry room where we kept them locked up.

A month later, we decided to go biking to the park after we finished the laundry. I was hauling the dry clothes upstairs while Jeff unlocked the bikes out back. He came upstairs and said everything was ready, so we got ready with our packs.

We went out back and the bikes had disappeared—just not there. We were panic-stricken and searched all over. Then I thought maybe he hadn't really brought them outside. He said he had and "leaned them right there" indicating our two building dumpsters. He didn't lock them. They were not there.

A tenant in the building leaned out his window and said he saw the bikes leaning against the dumpsters and then saw two guys ride off on them. He didn't know they were ours or why they were there. In a matter of ten minutes they were taken. They weren't locked, just leaning there.

To say Jeff was upset is an understatement. He started crying.

"What are we going to do?" he said over and over. "I can't do anything right anymore. I make so many mistakes."

"Let's just take our old bikes and go to a bike shop and get some air in the tires," I said, which is what we did.

What a bad experience. It reminded me just how his mind was not working like it used to. He would never leave the bikes without locking them to something. But that's the disease. There was no point in chastising him as he was devastated. I only made things worse if I pointed out what he should have done or what choice he should have made instead of the one he did.

THE PRIVATE CLUB. OCTOBER 2013

I don't want to go with HandyDart. I'm tired. I want to stay home with Helen.

But HandyDart arrives, and she tells me she has lots to do today and will be coming to pick me up today after our walk.

I don't want to do things with the group. I want to be with Helen and stay home.

She walks me downstairs and I get on the HandyDart bus.

Lunchtime comes and I don't want to join in. The leaders phone my wife but can't reach Helen. Then they call my sister and she comes to get me. We arrive back at my place but Helen isn't there.

I keep watching out the window for her. She eventually shows up. She tells us that she went to meet me at the club but found out I had left already. She didn't have her phone with her.

I am so happy to see her and we hug, and I say, "Please don't make me go back there."

My sister leaves with a worried look on her face. Helen and I go for a walk on the beach. We are together now. I'm happy this way. I don't want to be away from her.

THE RESPITE PROGRAMME

It was brought to my attention that a new respite programme was working out quite well for people with this disease. It gave both parties a break from each other with a one-or two-night stay. I was encouraged to give it a try and made arrangements for Jeff to go to the respite centre for a couple of nights, but they also asked that I didn't get in touch with him during that time so we could get used to being apart. More him than me.

RESPITE VISIT. OCTOBER 2013

Helen tells me that we need to try this place as a two-day overnight as her sister in Ottawa is quite ill and she needs to be with her. I don't quite understand.

I say I think I would be okay on my own in the apartment but she says we need to try this in case she needs to stay longer or go more often. She doesn't want to worry about me having mixed-up days.

So she makes some arrangements. My sister drives us to this place they call the respite centre. I'm staying Saturday and Sunday night and she will be back to get me on Monday morning before 11:00.

I get my backpack settled in this room and immediately someone invites me for tea and biscuits. Helen and I kiss goodbye.

I chat with people. I walk around. I'm restless. I watch a bit of TV. We have a nice dinner. I get ready for bed but I'm not sure about sleeping here.

I wake up in the middle of the night and don't know where I am. Someone steers me back to bed but I tell them I want to leave. Right now! They say I have to wait. I get back in bed and then jump out of bed and rush to the door to get outside and start banging on the door asking to be let out. I am naked and I don't want to be here. I keep pounding on the door that won't open. People come and try to talk to me. I keep saying, "Where is my wife? Help me please, where is my wife?" They give me some tea and a pill. I finally go to sleep.

I'm not happy being locked in here. I can't come and go as I please. They don't understand that I feel like I'm in jail. The next day passes and they invent all sorts of things for me to do but none of it interests me. I ask many people, "When can I leave?" Over and over again.

That night is a repeat of the previous night with me standing naked banging on the door asking to let me out of here. I feel so tired and alone and desperate. Where is Helen?

Monday morning can't come soon enough. It's just after breakfast and my bag has been packed for hours. I just stand around with my bag waiting for the doors to open and waiting for Helen.

At last my wife arrives and I rush to her and say, "Let's go, let's go." We leave quickly. We stand at the bus stop and I ask her why I was there and why was I locked in and not allowed to leave. I say this must be what it's like to be in jail. She says not to worry, we're going home. I am so happy when the bus comes to take us home.

THE PRIVATE CLUB. NOVEMBER 2013

Oh, why do I have to go on HandyDart this morning? I try to reason with my wife to let me stay at home with her and we can go for walks on the beach. All to no avail. HandyDart comes on time.

We get there and I am not feeling secure or safe. I need Helen. I want Helen here. My knees hurt. I'm tired. I don't want to be with these people. I don't want to talk. I don't want to have lunch with them. I don't want to go for another walk.

The leader tries to phone my wife on one of those silly phones they all have glued to their ears. I try to take her phone away and want to fling it in the garbage. I run out into the traffic as I want to get away.

The tall one rushes over and we talk. He convinces me to join them for lunch. He makes phone calls.

Suddenly my wife appears. I am so happy to see her and we hug and leave for the bus. She saved me from the big walk. I can hardly wait to put my feet up and have a nap.

My wife is not happy that I didn't want to stay. I tell her I really just want to stay home with her. I don't want to be with these people and walk and walk. We cuddle together and I have a bath. Then I rest in the bed.

COMPANIONS FOR JEFF

I made arrangements for companions to spend time with Jeff so I could get a bit of respite and time on my own or meet up with friends for a bite. They found a most congenial guy who loved to play cricket—something Jeff played—and they connected really well.

ERIC.SUMMER/FALL 2013

Where did they find a gem like him?

One day he appeared at our door and invited me to go for a walk on the beach with him. Helen had groceries to do and errands.

So Eric and I explored the sea wall, chatting about cricket. He is so well read and full of jokes.

I really enjoyed the walk. I ask about where Helen is but he says she had lots to do.

We walk slowly at my pace and sit frequently on the benches.

After our first visit together he comes often—sometimes twice a week—and I look forward to seeing him. We never run out of things to talk about. He can easily walk my feet off and I do have sore knees.

The stairs back home can be difficult after a long walk.

We go to a Safeway café and have a coffee and a dessert for me.

She gives me pocket money but he always pays.

Chapter 4

INVOLUNTARY ADMISSION TO HOSPITAL. JANUARY 6, 2014

On the sixth of January 2014, Jeff and I walked to a hospital and had Jeff admitted. He had been extremely agitated over the past three months, causing sleep deprivation for us both. Our case manager, friends and other support people constantly encouraged me to think about placing him in a home because it was easier to do it this way than having an ambulance take him.

I didn't know what I expected, but it wasn't what I anticipated happening. Had I known what it was like, I never would have admitted him. But hindsight was always a glaring truth. I needed help. I had no energy left. I was in a daze and crying a lot. I just couldn't handle the stress of watching Jeff every moment of my waking hours.

To my knowledge my husband had never raised a hand to anyone. He was a gentle man with a free spirit. We spent so much time together going on picnics and getaway weekends. I was sitting at home lamenting my decision and started reminiscing about what a team we used to be and how adept Jeff was at handling presentations to schools about diving and saving the seas.

A contact at UBC wrote to us about a German couple looking for accommodation in Vancouver and wondered if we would be interested in renting our apartment to them for six months. We jumped at the chance and decided to move to La Paz, Mexico. Everything came together except for an injury Jeff incurred playing rugby two weeks before we were to depart—three broken ribs. We continued with our plans. In addition to his discomfort, it also meant he couldn't dive for a few months due to lung expansion as he descended, but he still could snorkel and swim.

In May 1995, we found a house to rent in a secure, gated property with a beautiful backyard and garden that was close to the downtown area. We took Spanish lessons twice a week and cycled around the city (the house came with two ten-speed bikes). We invited friends to visit and stay in the spare rooms and many of them came—a couple from Australia, a few dive buddies from Vancouver, and Jeff's oldest son.

We organized exhibitions of our blown-up photos in a couple of hotel lobbies. I shot pictures of the sea life right in the Sea of Cortez, which attracted many students from the University of La Paz. They invited us to have an exhibition of our photos at their university with Jeff giving a talk about saving the seas. It was well-received by the large group and they had us cut a ribbon. It was a simply marvellous time in our lives.

Jeff was so quick to learn Spanish and even helped educate some young students. He also met with them once a week at a pool and encouraged them to pursue diving.

It was so hard to imagine that here we were with Jeff being so incapacitated with a dementia-related disease for which there was no cure. The comparison was staggering.

I didn't sleep the night he was admitted. I went to see him the next day, and I was totally shocked. He was tied down to the bed in restraints, and he begged me to help him get to the bathroom to pee. It was like no one trusted him. I told the staff I'd go with him and that he wasn't a violent man. We walked together to the toilet and he went about his business. I couldn't believe staff were so nervous that he was now in restraints.

What had happened overnight? What had I done by admitting him here?

All of this was so shocking. I was unprepared. I stayed with him. I was sure he was on some medication by this time, as he was slurring his words and walking in a tentative swaying manner—criss-crossing his feet. I waited with him while he ate his dinner.

I left for home to have my dinner. When I came back around 7:00, I just burst into tears when I saw that he had a guard by his bed and he was shackled to the bed with restraints. I was told that he was determined to leave and they could not keep him in bed "unless restrained." It was the most disturbing thing I've ever seen. I consulted with a doctor and it was only then I realized that once I agreed to his admission, I had little to say in the matter. I just couldn't stop crying.

What have I done? What was I thinking?

I wanted him back home with me, but it was too late. He had been admitted. He was given medications I was not consulted about and had no say in.

Days passed. He was always restrained. He was agitated. He was aggressive. He tried to attack the guard. I'm sure he couldn't stand the sight of me as it was me who brought him into this situation. I couldn't stand the sight of me when I looked in the mirror. How could I have done this? Jeff was yelling, trying to get out of bed, lashing out at anyone, just so upset. Who could blame him? What could I do?

Each night after visiting hours, I walked home and cried myself to sleep—if I slept. This was not the plan, but what was the plan anyway? They would not release him to my care until they decided it was safe, so we were stuck. I couldn't have him back home, but I was so worried and distressed that all I could think about was getting him back.

I had many discussions with the doctors and staff. Within a week, plans were being put in place to move him to a different hospital which was more conducive to treating patients with dementia and thereby following a specified course of treatment. He was transferred after ten days. They wouldn't allow me in the transfer vehicle, so I had to find my way to this new destination. I got there after he arrived.

This was the beginning of a push and pull to have some say in his care, his medications, his life. I couldn't kid myself and think I could be there all the time, so the doctors did what they felt they needed to. I was his persistent advocate and I wanted to be involved in his treatment and medications, so I made no bones about telling them that. Jeff was a stranger now in so many ways—certainly not the man I married—but it was still my responsibility to ensure he was treated with humanity and respect and that he wasn't simply drugged for the rest of his life.

The despair I felt to have been cut off from him posed the most trying, helpless, hopeless and guilt-laden days of my life.

FIRST HOSPITAL STAY. JANUARY 2014

I'm trying to figure out how it is that I'm in this hospital tied down to the bed.

There is a guy in a uniform sitting in a chair next to me but he doesn't talk at all. At first he did say that they are trying to clear up some kind of infection I have.

Helen comes to visit me twice a day and I eat my meals with her. She gets me out of bed to walk but I find my walking is very shaky and erratic. Even my speech is different—kind of slurred. When she leaves they make sure I don't get out of bed in case, I guess, I might run away. For sure I would. I don't want to be here. I feel like I'm in jail like that other place I went to where I was pounding on the door to get out at night but only worse.

My wife tells me I'll be coming home soon when we clear up whatever infection I have, and that I have to be patient. I am so happy to see her and want to leave with her.

It's not easy. I am locked in this bed for "safety" I hear them say.

The food is not too bad though, and they give me lots of treats.

I've moved to the seventh floor but that doesn't change anything—I'm still locked in here. There is talk among staff that I will be moving soon to another place.

It's a confusing, mixed-up place and time. I want to be on the beach and walking outside in the fresh air.

Why are we being separated? I want to be with Helen.

Chapter 5

PSYCHIATRIC HOSPITAL. JANUARY 2014

I wake up on a gurney bed, strapped in, and loaded into a vehicle. I can hear them talking. We're going to another hospital to help me get rid of a bladder infection.

They tell my wife there is no room in the transfer van for her so she has to find a bus to get out to this hospital.

We arrive somewhere. I've got a room with a curtain instead of a door to the toilet.

It's antiseptic, full of people wandering the halls trying all the doors, none of which seem to open except to a few people. I will be good so it will open for me.

I'm not happy as everyone wants to be in the toilet room with me. Don't like people with me in the bathroom, and so I try to push them away. All I want is to pee in peace and privacy. So I continue to push them away.

Next thing I know two men in navy uniforms have my arms while two nurses have my feet and I'm being carried to my bed. I'm immediately strapped in with a belt across my chest and restraints on my arms and legs.

They won't listen to me. I just want privacy while I pee. You can't talk any sense to them.

That's how Helen finds me when she gets here. She is very upset and shouts at people to undo the restraints and bed belt. She is crying and we cry together. How did it come to this? What's happening? I hear the whispers.

"It's a psychiatric hospital."

One guy wandering the hall tells me it's a "loony bin."

I remember when my son tried to live with his mother, my ex-wife. He had bipolar and she couldn't handle the situation as it was rumoured he was unpredictable so she arranged for a psychiatric assessment. They had to take my son in a straitjacket as his strength and determination not to be restrained was super strong. It seems like déjà vu. Like father like son.

TWO WEEKS LATER

None of the doors open.

I remember a movie with Jack Nicholson, I think it was, something about flying over the cuckoo's nest.

People come and go and some yell and scream and when that happens the dreaded Chair arrives. It's this big chair with belts for your arms and feet. It takes some doing to strap a strong squirming person in that Chair. In the name of safety to yourself and the staff, reasons are invented to spend time in the Chair— not enough staff, people not wanting to talk with you, constant breaks staff need and everything has to be written down with a pen.

You'd think in this so-called computer age, the staff could punch a few keys but no, it's all longhand, and if they put you in the Chair they can do what they want to do. Ignore you whether you are quiet or not. If you cause too much of a fuss, you are put in your room all alone to sleep as they put stuff in your food. I won't take the medications so why am I slurring and sometimes barely can walk?

I hate the Chair. I think some of the people waiting on me don't like me and want to see me strapped in to show their power. Once they decide I'm having a spell in the Chair, that's it, I'm stuck. I can squirm, shout, moan, curse and it's to no avail. It can result in being put in a room facing the wall, all alone with the door shut.

You learn to stay quiet and just maybe someone who loves you will come to visit you.

I hear a loud demand to unbuckle the Chair. Helen has arrived. It gets unbuckled as now they don't have to watch me because my wife is there to do that so they can have an extra long break or do what needs to be done in a hospital like this with so many people.

I really don't like it here.

There's a guy across the hall from my room standing in his underwear yelling at me, "Where's my pants?" How would I know?

SETTLING IN TO THE CUCKOO'S NEST

My memory seems to have more blanks than normal and there is a need to forget the place with all the power-hungry guards and staff.

They lump all dementia patients into a category. "If they are not restrained in the the Chair, well then let's give them more drugs so we can have our breaks, do our job and go on to the next day."

Helen loves me a lot though and she doesn't want me restrained nor full of drugs. She's trying to get them to understand that we have feelings and need to be treated with dignity. I hear her say this word "dignity" often. I really want to leave with her. I don't want to stay here. I don't want two women standing by my side in the bathroom watching while I pee or poop.

I try all the doors. Everyone tries all the doors. None of them open to us—only to doctors and nurses. We sit close to the entrance door hoping we can dart through.

THE LITTLE BISTRO

I listen to them and I know this is a loony bin and all the guests have problems and can't leave. It's another jail. We're locked in. I can only hope someone who loves me will try to move me somewhere else.

I ask my wife over and over when can I go home and she says she's working on it. She shows me a calendar she made and crosses off the days I've been here. One day she says it will be soon.

I can't believe it! At last I'm allowed to go outside through the locked doors with my wife for a short break in the fresh air. She has found a little bistro that makes cappuccino coffee and we head for it. It's very cold outside and I'm bundled up and we walk hand in hand to the café.

It is freedom for a short while but I get cold so I'm okay going back in to the warmth as I can have a nap and rest my aching knees.

We often go to the bistro now that we've found it. She has to have her phone with their number in case we slip on the ice and fall. It's tempting to run away, but how far would we get?

DAY PASS WITH WAYNE

She tells me we are going for fish and chips with Wayne, my rugby pal, and to see the beach. He arrives and we are so happy to see each other. We walk to his car—I am unsteady today.

I feel very groggy and tired and yet I woke up so enthusiastic. There must have been something in my drink. Why would they put the rape drug in my drink when I'm going out with my wife and a rugby mate? I actually have trouble walking.**

I can't follow the conversation. I sit in the front passenger seat; Helen sits in the back. The drive flies by and we go to the beach at Jericho. Wayne and my wife hold either arm as I can barely walk, but we sit on a log and I watch the water. I feel so out of it and helpless not being able to amble on my own. I'm actually afraid I'll fall down asleep right there.

We get to the restaurant and they help me get seated. I'm still so unsteady and groggy. I manage some food and a sip of beer. I am very quiet as I can't talk without slurring.

We get back.

My wife and Wayne are very upset, and I know they leave as I can't communicate with them. I am just so tired.

(**Note by H: Ativan was put in his drink in case he needed calming. It spoiled the day for the three of us.)

ANOTHER DAY PASS WITH WAYNE

I'm so happy as Wayne has showed up to take me for lunch with my wife.

She tells Wayne it was brought up to the doctors that I was safe with them and I didn't need anything to calm me.

We headed off to this great restaurant which is close to the railroad tracks—trains go by all the time. I get a really good seat so I can watch them.

We order beer and Reuben sandwiches with French fries. We have such a good time. I feel so happy and we are laughing a lot. Wayne is telling me some updated rugby news.

On our way back we stop for an ice cream cone!

What a surprise though as we run into my eldest son who just happens to be in the area. We buy him a cone too as he kept grabbing mine. My son had come to visit me once but got in a big fight with staff as he gave me a Swiss army knife. He wasn't allowed back in.

It was a really good day to drive around and have lunch but I'm also anxious to have a nap as I'm very tired.

We kiss and hug goodbye. I'm tucked in and my eyes are closing.

ATTEMPT TO RETURN HOME. FEBRUARY 2014

There is talk of moving Jeff to another hospital/residence.

After a couple of months at this psychiatric hospital, things were not working out that well. We discussed having Jeff discharged to my care with the help of a nurse who lived in the same building and would be in constant touch with us.

I think I was in denial that Jeff was that problematic, out of control or even hard to control. I was exhausted taking care of him, but I remained that way even though he was in hospital as I kept thinking there had to be a middle ground where he could get settled in and I would somehow be more at ease.

In any event, there was talk of a "transitional residence"— in between a psychiatric hospital and a permanent residence for dementia patients. All the residents would be dementia patients and/or patients who needed to be in a psychiatric hospital with twenty-four-hour care.

First, we tried having him discharged to my care with all kinds of provisos and different medication to help him adjust to his condition. My nurse friend and I had trouble just driving him home as he wanted to get out of the car in traffic. We would stop for a traffic light and Jeff would try the handle. I had to muster all my strength to hold him back even though he had his seat belt on.

Eventually we settled down, but he was a different man and not malleable at all. He wanted to go outside and was extremely restless. I think he was suffering from "sundown" episodes—it was the time of day when his energy changed for the worse. He seemed to get highly agitated, exhausted, restless, not in control and more confused than ever. It was so obvious—despite my wanting my husband home—this was probably not going to work as the progression of the disease made it too difficult to judge his actions and make the right decisions.

We tried a few nights, but I had to take him back to the hospital. I was terribly upset that it wasn't working. We had a meeting and were working on transferring him to a "transitional hospital," which happened three weeks after he returned.

In the meantime, his son did come to visit, but, unfortunately, brought his father the wrong kind of gift—a Swiss army knife—which was immediately confiscated. It happened during an evening visit when I wasn't there—only heard about it—and his son got into an argument with staff, exchanged words and was banned from coming back.

My husband did have some visitors, but I think they were shocked at his disarray and confusion. On one of these visits, Jeff was running down the hall dressed in an open gown, clutching papers and unable to talk clearly or to understand them. He kept laughing at a joke only he got and was just so mixed up. I believe the medication he was receiving had a lot to do with this strange behaviour. I noticed my friends' tears at seeing him in this condition, especially knowing how active, fit and alert he was playing rugby with this French mate who was visiting with his partner. They mentioned how sad it was that he was like this after spending such wonderful years at dinner parties together.

ATTEMPT TO RETURN HOME

She kept telling me we would be leaving soon. That's what I want—to go back home. At last it's happening but I don't know when.

One morning we get packed up and my wife and our nurse friend CA arrive to take me home. Riding in a car. Oh, happy day! Every time we stop I want to get out quickly.

And there we are back at our apartment. I just can't believe I'm back where I want to be. I have a nap and then a snack. I ask her where everyone is. I want to go out and walk, so we go outside.

I'm not sure about things. I feel mixed up. We walk along the beach but I'm tired from going up and down the three flights of stairs. We sit on benches and I say hello to lots of people. Some answer and some don't and look like they don't know me, but I recognize most of the people as so many of them look alike.

We get back in the apartment and have tea and I want to leave. She convinces me to have a bath and a nap.

We do that and she prepares dinner. We watch TV. I'm waiting for things to happen but nothing does.

I get tucked into bed and she settles into reading, but I am restless and get agitated and walk around naked and don't know where I am. I keep coming into the living room, and I don't know what's happening. Where are all my friends? Where's everyone?

She gives me a pill and we snuggle back in bed. I wake up and she's asleep, I look out in the hallway—I want to go some place but I can't figure out where. All of a sudden she is standing beside me in the hallway and asks, "What's wrong?" I start to cry. I hold her and say, "I'm lost." I don't know what to make of anything anymore. She cries with me and we go back to bed. We try to sleep.

Chapter 6

MOVE TO WISTERIA. FEBRUARY 2014

Wisteria Hospital was a "transitional placement," but it was, nonetheless, a hospital. It was different from normal hospitals because all the patients had some type of dementia and were waiting for permanent placement to a residence.

The advocates of the patients were given a choice of location they would prefer for their loved one, but the choice was not always adhered to if an opening came up somewhere else. They still remained on the waiting list for their preferred location when and if it came up.

When choosing a transitional hospital, a patient was assessed by type of care needed—most being lockdown, which was twenty-four-hour care. The choice of residence was narrowed down by hall dimensions, room size and whether the patient required a private room or not. If someone was in a wheelchair, they required a residence with the appropriate means of hoisting the patient into bed or for the toilet if they couldn't stand or walk. A number of residences for Alzheimer's patients were not available for our needs as some didn't have ceiling hoists for wheelchair transfer to bed.

The list was quite short for my husband, and chances of an opening didn't look promising in the near future. It was only natural that I would choose a place not too far from my home to save all the travel time, especially since I didn't drive or have a car and had multiple buses to take. My first choice would have been in Yaletown because it was close by, and there was no question that my husband would definitely have a private room due to the stage of his dementia.

A placement could come up at a week's notice or less; if the patient's team were ready for someone's placement, then only a phone call comes to the one advocating and agreement needs to be secured quickly. If an opening came up and the team agreed it was the perfect transfer to residence for that patient, then the advocate had little say. If the move was not agreed to by the advocate, then the cost of staying at this "transitional placement" would be double or more per day. In essence, it was better to agree, as the patient was still on the waiting list for the original placement.

So those were the rules and regulations.

Wisteria was in a great setting with a huge mature outdoor garden that was well-groomed by the gardeners, a BBQ pit and fantastic trees. In the spring the garden was alive with birds, blooms, buds and flowers!

There were five floors, the fourth and fifth being twenty-four-hour care lockdown. Two floors were not lockdown but had restrictions. At any given time there could be twenty patients on each of the fourth and fifth floors—usually an equal division of males and females. It was a culturally mixed hospital, and many staff spoke more than one language.

There were many corridors connecting to a staff station where the head nurses sat. There were a couple of open balconies with chairs, but residents were only allowed there when accompanied by family or friends. The food was simple home cooking, and patients ate in a large dining room close to the nurse's station. Along the hallways were paper dispensers and small water fountains. There were lounge chairs and a large television, and it was quite a spacious place. The doors to enter and exit were locked and required a special key, as did the elevator.

The patient rooms had a separate sink and toilet, a single bed with bureaus and a chair or two. There was a common patient bath/shower room. Items could be added, if acceptable, by staff caring for the patients. A private television could be set up at minimal cost. You could decorate the walls to a limited degree—a message board, photos and so on.

Safety was a top priority. Some patients walked, others were in wheelchairs and still others were on gurneys and often stayed in their rooms depending on their level of wellness. The door to each person's room had a key, and rooms were generally locked. There was a tendency for patients to wander into the wrong room, so locking was advised to keep Jeff's personal possessions safe. A constant visitor, like myself, would get a key.

Visiting hours were from 8:30 a.m. to 8:00 p.m. A visitor was encouraged to purchase a meal if there were extra portions available so they could have breakfast, lunch or dinner with their patient. A meal had a set price, minimal, and was paid to the server. We could sit privately to eat or join a group at a long table.

The premises at Westeria were well taken care of, neat and tidy, and offered lots of recreational activities, exercises, crafts. There was excellent care from capable and friendly staff.

The move from the psychiatric hospital was coming up quickly for Jeff, and I was busy preparing myself to organize his room and clothes and meet with the staff. Jeff's doctor felt Jeff would fit into this new environment well as he was always engaging and charming and enjoyed meeting new people. At that moment he was one of the lucky ones (if we can call it that) as he was not yet incontinent, could eat without being fed, and mostly recognized family and friends. He was fairly fit and could walk without assistance, but he had inherited his arthritic knees from his mum. Despite his obvious pain at times when walking, he was proud and independent.

It was anyone's guess how the transition would go, but I was hopeful for a more settled time and less worry for both of us.

A NEW EXPERIENCE

A big bus came and took me to a new place. There was no room in the bus for Helen. She said not to worry that she would meet me at this new place. She said I would like it there.

She was standing there at the entrance waiting for me and we walked into this really large place with gardens and lots of open space.

I had a new room. We moved my stuff in there. Then we were having a cup of tea and biscuits.

We wandered around the halls and looked at everything. I sat on the bed while she organized the chest of drawers with my clothes and shoes. There was no closet though.

The bathroom was large so I tried out the toilet. She put up a photo of me on the side of the door with my name on it. I was standing on a beach in the West End many years ago. I looked at it and read my name and said it out loud.

We had lunch together which was a delicious soup and an assortment of sandwiches. We then went out into this beautiful garden with lots of trees and tulips blooming, and there were benches and chairs. We walked all around.

I was tired so we went in. I had a nap and she crawled in and cuddled beside me.

She was gone when I woke up but I found her talking to some nurses and I sat with people and talked.

We decided to have dinner together and the food was really good. It was a new place to sleep. It didn't look like she would stay.

I tried all the doors but they didn't open.

EARLY MARCH 2014

Helen told me that my daughter (she is also a Helen), who I hadn't seen for seven years, will be coming up from San Diego to visit me soon for a few days. She is my daughter from my ex-wife.

My wife and I go for walks in the garden. We are restricted to the grounds but there's lots to see and she brings treats for me and always lots of fruit. We often go out in the morning before lunch and stay outside for an hour or more.

She often stayed and had lunch with me and we sometimes had dinner together. She came often.

I'm getting to know lots of people. I even met up with someone I knew—it was the guy across the hall who could never find his pants from the crazy, mixed up place with lots of yelling, the Chair, and those strange people.

Don is his name and he reads newspapers all the time. So I often join him at breakfast and we read newspapers together and talk a lot about all sorts of stuff. He's energetic, walks quickly, so we walk around together in the halls often and eat snacks together. We often eat dinner at the same table. It's great we found each other again.

My wife tells me my daughter is coming tomorrow. She tells me I will be seeing my daughter on my own. My wife will be back in a few days.

It's confusing here and I wake up not knowing where I am. But I know where the toilet is.

WISTERIA. EARLY MARCH 2014

Jeff's daughter from a previous marriage came to visit him as he was slowly settling in to Wisteria. She lived in San Diego and was accompanied by Jeff's sister.

I was not a party to these visits so I can't comment on how Jeff reacted or anything else, but he hadn't seen his daughter for seven years. I hoped he recognized her (as long-term memory is so often intact) and that they had good visits.

The doctors and nurses told me that Jeff was not adjusting that well to this new environment and seemed very confused and agitated. One doctor in particular suggested that I "stand back" with my visits to let him adjust to this new venue and give the staff a chance to get to know him and vice versa. I was coming every day to be with him. I wasn't happy to "stand back" but decided if that would help Jeff, then I would give it a try.

That was the advice on a Wednesday, so I didn't visit on Thursday. I phoned a few times and they said everything was fine. I didn't visit Friday either. When I phoned Saturday morning, a nurse told me he was in a restraint chair without clothes on and that he couldn't be moved because there was a child running around and they were worried about the effect it would have on the child. Or words to that effect. I was stunned. Jeff was in a restraint chair? *What was going on?* I asked what he had done, and she declined to say. She said he was fine and that I didn't need to come visit.

I was aware there was a chair with a buckle which was used for safety for patients who sometimes walked around unsteadily. But it seemed there was a different chair with a locked strap, which was where they put Jeff. No one called to let me know he was agitated to that extreme. If they had, I would have taken a cab to get there as soon as possible on the Friday when it happened. I stayed home Saturday, but I felt confused by conflicting messages which I interpreted as him being fine but yet he was in a restraint chair.

I decided to visit on the Sunday as I was concerned that he might be having a lot of confusion with having his daughter back in his life for a visit. It was a good thing I went and they didn't know I was coming. As I walked in, a male nurse rushed to me, seemingly alarmed, and said Jeff was in what he called the "quiet room." He took me there. As I approached the room, the door was ajar with a table so anyone could see Jeff and his state, although his back was to the door.

I called to him. He was by himself, tied down in a restraint chair and dressed only in a diaper. His eyes were vague, vacant, and he could barely talk. He seemed heavily medicated. He was trying to tear the buckle off. He saw me and started crying, so I held him and comforted him. I was trying not to cry myself, and I wanted to find out what happened.

Another male nurse suddenly appeared and wanted me to come down the hall and chat about it, but I wanted Jeff out of there—like right then. Not a second more was he to remain in this restraint chair. He needed to be taken into his room and put in his bed. I was very insistent.

Was I in an uproar? You bet! I tried to control myself from yelling but asked them to please let me take him to his room. Once there I insisted he be put to bed. He seemed to be in a stupor and out of it; he just lay there shaking for a couple of hours.

I was terribly distressed. I confronted one of the doctors who was on the team—the one who told me to "stand back."

"This is how you are letting him adjust to the new staff, is it?" I asked, beside myself with anger and grief.

I eventually got the story from someone on the team. Apparently, he had messed the bed that morning with a bowel movement which triggered a reaction by him. He had always been private about his toilet habits, and being handled by nurses did not sit well with him. Apparently, he lashed out. He simply wanted to crawl on the floor and didn't want to go back to bed, so they injected him with

Ativan to sedate him and got him into that restraint chair and put him in that room all by himself.

I stayed by his side for hours. At one point I managed to get him to eat a wee bit of food.

He woke up a number of times during the afternoon. Because he was not incontinent, he said he had to go pee and wanted to go right away. I pressed the nurse button, but he unsteadily but quickly got out of bed. I could tell it was urgent to pee, and he staggered around and was so confused that he almost peed in a wastebasket. I steered him to the toilet.

He was stark naked and started peeing. And then, horrors, he had a bowel movement standing up just as two nurses walked in. It was mind-boggling and shocking to see; it was a so out of the norm and just a horrendous mess. It looked like he wasn't even aware of what was happening. The staff who arrived were fantastic, and we got him back to bed, changed and cleaned, but he was still so groggy. He settled down, went to sleep and I left for home an hour or so later.

I was so weary and couldn't believe what had just transpired.

When I returned home, I immediately composed an email to everyone on the team and copied my lawyer, our GP and various others. I threatened to add the UBC neurologists who had been involved in his care over the years. I was so shaken up I could hardly write clearly. I was so angry and disappointed in his "team" and the doctors.

I received emails back from members of the team to set up a meeting with them soon to discuss what happened and what solutions might overcome this misunderstanding. What were the options?

I pointed out many times in a number of interviews when I first arrived at Wisteria with Jeff that he very seldom took medication, even with his rugby injuries. When he came home with broken ribs, a broken nose or a dislocated shoulder, medication like Ativan was definitely not the answer. I repeated many times how sensitive he was to drugs and how he preferred to just deal with the pain, so I couldn't understand why he was so medicated all of a sudden.

The meeting came about quickly. I laid out my case, my objections and some ideas that might help with his care. I did not criticize the staff. The nurses seemed caring and helpful, but none of them were aware how agitated and aggressive he would get if strangers were around him when he used the toilet (despite the fact I had pointed this out numerous times). I did get an apology from the doctors about the restraints, and they said they would never use them, nor Ativan, on Jeff again.

Could I trust them?

I read this paragraph of my email to those at the meeting:

> My husband is not a wild stallion waiting to be broken, but that's what it looks like. He's what he is and who he is. He has Alzheimer's and has agitation and aggression which is part of the disease, but surely all patients don't get put in restraints when they can't be handled for the so-called "safety issue"— that's what keeps being said to me "the

safety issue." What about guiding him in another direction, calming him, giving him something to do? That doesn't seem to be what's happening at Wisteria. I went into great detail about the restraints practice at the psychiatric hospital, and everyone who heard my description seemed shocked, but this is exactly the same scenario happening here. Three weeks before Jeff was moved, I had phoned Wisteria asking about restraints, and someone told me they never use restraints. They said it had happened—and I quote—"Only once in twenty years on a difficult patient," so I was very encouraged and trusting.

There were six people at this meeting, and I knew they heard clearly and understood what I had to say. I felt I had accomplished something as I didn't see the chair being used like it was previously. It was not only Jeff who suffered this so called "safety" solution. There was always the question of safety, and other methods were being chased down to see if something else might work without buckling someone in—a one-on-one with a nurse, sports on TV, folding laundry, different activities.

When Jeff got tired, he started undressing anywhere he was. It was a sure sign that he needed to nap, and if they were not too busy surely they could take him to his room and he could go to sleep. If they ignored him, he would just take all his clothes off anywhere and lie on the floor, even in the dining room. Whenever he was agitated, there was a reason: fear, too hot, too cold, hungry, tired, knee pain.

There was no doubt I was emotionally upset with the turn our lives had taken. We were not able to be together under the same roof except for day visits. It was a helpless, hopeless, sad, grieving time for me. I never thought it would be so difficult to face the days without him every morning and night. It was an empty life without him, a huge adjustment for me. I had little interest in the future for myself, and I prioritized seeing and being with him. I wanted to spend most of my time visiting him and helping him through his good and bad days.

As soon as I took him outside to the garden, his whole persona changed—smiles, clapping, laughing, trying to talk. He was relaxed and examined flowers, bushes. We tossed a football around. I read to him as he sat on the bench. He looked at magazines. We enjoyed every moment in the sunshine, and there were lots of songbirds in the garden. We always had tea and treats.

A couple of days after the bathroom incident, he was walking like he had Parkinson's. He had trouble eating. His eyes were vacant and often unfocussed. Knowing him as I did, I recognized that he was suffering from the worst humiliation due to the bathroom accident. I tried to ease his mind and said, "We all have accidents, so try not to worry about it." He looked at me with huge tears in his eyes and obvious sadness at this intrusion into his life.

I had discussions with his team—the lead general practitioner, his psychiatrist and other professionals—so we could work out what his needs were. I rue the day I brought him to hospital as an involuntary patient. I was hoping he would be in a happy, safe environment with lots of helping hands, but that day of admission constantly haunted me. It took time and counselling to steer me in the right direction. I needed to stop beating myself up and ensure I was working with the team to make Jeff's life manageable while easing my mind. I could say it was a matter of survival on both our parts for him to be taken care of and not to remain at home together.

The team had agreed to let him crawl on the floor if that was what he needed to do (my suggestion), and there was a room he could do that without disturbing everyone. But that episode seemed to have been a one-off as I had not seen him do it again nor did the staff—so they told me—after that one time.

He had settled down. We had permission to go outside any time I visited. We always walked around this beautiful garden, mostly holding hands and enjoying the fresh air. I brought him special treats like the odd McDonald's or fish and chips, which he asked for many times and ate with such gusto!

Meanwhile, I started taking some workshops to educate myself on the stages of Alzheimer's and other types of dementia, and they helped me comprehend what I would have to face in our struggle together.

The old Jeff would never hurt anyone, but the new Jeff, agitated because of his brain disease, might. I think it was hard on him to experience these high emotions of fear, frustration and agitation. If he could not be calmed in other ways, then drugs were a viable option. I guess that was what the doctors on his team were trying to accomplish, but it was stated clearly that these medications would be discussed with me beforehand. When a new drug was brought up, I did some research. One drug that bothered me was called Risperidone, which was mainly prescribed for schizophrenia and not dementia, so I expressed my views about it. His psychiatrist assured me he was given the smallest dose possible.

It was a difficult adjustment for both of us, but he seemed to be making friends at a rapid rate, and I could tell he was much happier as the days progressed. It was amusing one day to see four people sitting at a table together. One was Chinese, another one spoke French. Jeff and Don were listening to the Chinese guy and agreeing with him, but he was chatting away in Chinese. I had to laugh!

SETTLING IN AT WISTERIA. SPRING 2014

It was a strange room as it didn't have any closets. Where did they expect you to hang your jacket, your scarf and your hat?

I thought if I tried pulling at this wall, there could be a closet behind it. I was wrong. All I got was all this pink asbestos stuff coming out. I took most of the wall down and what a mess I made. They weren't too happy to see what I'd done. I said I was looking for a closet. So they covered all the exposed pink stuff with plastic and taped it down.

A few days later, I was taking all my clothes out of the drawers and the more I opened and pulled the drawers, the more it was angling to fall over. And then it did right on me but I escaped with only a bump or two. Huge crash and nurses helping me up.

There is not much to do in this room.

I seemed to be getting in all kinds of trouble as the taps just did not work so I worked on them and broke them off. The plumber came and repaired them.

Then I did it again, trying to get the water running, and this time the water was gushing out and I didn't know what to do so

I went and sat on the bed in the corner against the wall as the water was flowing towards my bed. I knew I was in big trouble when the water started seeping under the door and down the hall but I was frozen on the bed just staring at the water flowing by.

They had the smallest sinks, not enough space to wash my runners so I washed them in the toilet bowl water but they didn't like that much as then I had dripping runners on the heating ducts which I had already taken apart as they make a lot of noise.

They took my chest of drawers away.

So I was left with only a locked cupboard because I would take all my stuff out, put it in my satchel and be ready to leave but they only took everything out and put it back in the cupboard. I heard them calling me a "busy bee."

But there were paper dispensers in the hallways so I was never out of paper. I grabbed a few sheets every time I went by, often emptying the whole dispenser. I hope they didn't find out it was me.

On rainy days we sat on the balconies as they had an overhang and it was fresh out there. Helen and I would have tea and sweets, often my favourite doughnuts from Tim Hortons!

SO MANY ADJUSTMENTS TO WISTERIA. SPRING 2014

The other day when I arrived at 9:30, Jeff was sitting on his bed, shoes locked in the cupboard and he was crying. I held him and tried to comfort him. He couldn't tell me anything. I cheered him up as I had gifts, and I distracted him with a rugby magazine and some pictures on my iPad. We had breakfast together.

Seemed like the disease was progressing. He was hardly talking and seemed very confused at times. He was not happy. That was obvious to everyone.

After breakfast he was peeing in the corner of his room—aiming for the garbage can. He seemed to be having trouble figuring out how to pee and defecate, whether he should be standing or sitting.

We went for a walk in the garden. Cheered him up immensely. At last some big smiles. He kept asking me, "When can I go home?" A constant question. It must have been on his mind all the time—going home.

He was going to be seventy-four in April, and I planned to bring him fish and chips plus a big cake for everyone to share. We talked about our past adventures together. He could talk a bit but not whole sentences, only a string of words. He would start the sentence and I tried to finish it, hoping that was the thought he had.

The gardens were so lovely and we both enjoyed them. He always had a nap in his room with me when I visited, and I was just small enough that I could squeeze against the wall. We cuddled and slept easily. But I was very worried about him. He had tough days—distracted and worried looking—so I often stayed to have dinner with him. I was especially sad these days as I wanted him not to be forlorn and was so hoping things would work out well for him in this new place. But he seemed very troubled.

Speaking of trouble, he rearranged his room and it got complicated. The plumber fixed the taps, then the plaster man put the wall back up and repaired the heating duct a couple of times. The maintenance guys liked him as he talked to them. They told me he was very strong to break the taps and tear down the wall—they wondered if he was a carpenter or plumber before coming to Wisteria.

THE ABANDONED RCMP BUILDING SITE. SUMMER 2014

I see her walk through the door and I'm sitting having lunch! I am just so happy to see her and I announce to everyone, "She's here!" They all glance at her coming to my table. I get up and hold her in my arms. We have big hugs, and we have a coffee together and I finish my lunch.

As always, we go to my room and get my coat and hat and, hand in hand, take the elevator downstairs and head outside into the fresh air.

She gives me her backpack to carry and she always has treats or fruit, a bit of chocolate.

My favourite walk is to the abandoned RCMP building which is now used to train students. That's where we're heading today. It's just across the street—a short walk.

We walk all around the grounds, watch chickadees bringing food to their young, watch the building across the way going up. And best of all, we look at the snow-capped mountains in the distance!

We find places to sit as my knees always ache. She always holds my hand when we walk as I can be unsteady on my feet. Some days we are out there for well over an hour, especially if the weather is sunny and warm!

Sometimes we bring a plastic covered mat to sit on the grass; sometimes I nod off a bit. We stretch out and talk about the past. I've come to accept where I am, which means I'm in a place where people keep an eye on me and there is always danger I could get sick and be in big trouble. I often ask her when I will be going home. She holds me and tries to convince me that it will be in the not-too-distant future. She looks very sad when we talk about that and says she misses me very much and wishes we could be together all the time.

On one of our visits to the building, we spotted a coyote and followed him. The coyote had three youngsters that were like teenagers. We sat on the grass watching them watch us. It was a wonderful encounter. Helen took a picture of the coyote.

THE BEACH. JUNE/JULY 2014

Jeff had been doing well in the summer of 2014. He seemed content and was making lots of friends. He was definitely popular with the ladies and the staff. We went outside every visit I made, which was usually five days a week.

Jeff was not incontinent and was still wearing his own underwear. He rarely had an accident as he seemed on time going about his business.

He kept asking to see the beach, so I had a plan in mind to present to his team. After several meetings they approved trial day outings for him with me on warm and sunny days. The plan was to walk to a bus, go to the Canada Line and then get a Beach bus to our old apartment where I still lived—a familiar area for him. It would have been too costly to take taxis, and I didn't drive or have a car.

One provision was to get him back for dinner at Wisteria. I had been warned that it could be upsetting when he returned from the Beach Avenue apartment to

Wisteria, and it might change the dynamics of his settling in. I was willing to give it a try this summer even once a week for a change of atmosphere and pace. I was not sure whether I was following the right course, but he seemed so eager to see the water and beach again.

THE NEW PLAN

She's arrived and I know we're going somewhere!

I've had breakfast and she says we are going out to a special place for lunch today.

What a great feeling walking out the door and heading to the bus stop. I'm carrying her small backpack and we're holding hands as always. I keep smiling at her.

Wow, it's busy out here with lots of cars zipping by. I can see the bus stop and a bench and can hardly wait to sit down—these knees of mine are acting up again.

We get our bus, then the SkyTrain, and then the familiar little bus to our apartment. All those steps and I'm tired already.

We make it! I see our apartment in front of me. I slowly go up the three flights of stairs and I collapse in a heap on the sofa. She makes a cup of tea and we have a biscuit. I'm looking around but I can't stay awake so I know I'm just going to nod off. I know she has lunch to make so I relax.

Lunch is ready. We go out to the beach—my favourite area. We have roll-ups to lie on and a large towel but I can't sit still. I need to walk, so she says "Okay, let's do that." I go down to the water's edge with her. There are lots of people. It's busy. We stay for a while enjoying the sunshine.

Then we head back to the apartment and I decide to have a bath. It calls for another nap and we enjoy our time together.

Time to get back for dinner. We're back and it's so good to be where I know where things are and see the familiar faces. Everyone saying, "Hi, Jeff." She leaves me to have my meal with Don and says, "See you later." A hug and a kiss. My evening unfolds looking out the window, watching television and chatting with my friends.

RASH OF VISITS

Several of our friends had come to visit that summer. It was not easy for them to see Jeff as he was compared to the twenty years most of us had been friends. I understood their reticence to visit as it likely reminded them of their own vulnerability to aging and how life could change. It looked painful for them. It was painful for me. I was not sure what Jeff thought—I could only guess—but at times he looked troubled and confused around them.

Unfortunately, the day his dive buddy and wife came to visit for the first time was the day Jeff had been discussing suicide with Jay, one of the activities directors. The encounter was brought to my attention as soon as I walked in the door, and a half hour later his friends arrived so it certainly must have had some impact on their visit; he was in such a troubled mood. It would be hard to recover from that visit and come again, but I encouraged them to visit any time.

Jay told me Jeff wanted a meeting with her so he could tell her some things. He asked her about dementia, whether he had Alzheimer's, and what was going to happen to him. He said what a nice clean place Wisteria was and that he felt fit and strong. He thought he had Alzheimer's as he heard people talking about it. He also noticed that his brain was not working all the time. Jay said this was an incredible moment for her and like no other. That he wanted to talk about suicide made her cry, and she said he was crying too.

Short visits were good. He always reached out to touch L's (the chocolate lady) hand when she came to visit, so there seemed to be the long-term memory with her (although I don't think he remembered her name). She always brought him chocolate and, as she, too, is English, gifts that he would recognize from the past.

The day trips had been happening twice a week for a few weeks, on Tuesday and Thursday when the traffic might be lighter. Jeff seemed happy to be "on the move," and we didn't take the stairs in the Canada Line but the elevator.

He tried to talk to people on the train and they just looked at him, some with distrust on their faces. It wasn't surprising as he was suffering from brain damage. Although I knew he was not an aggressive person, someone who didn't know him might look at his size—six feet—and as he did not look weak, they had a certain look of, *Is this guy* all right? in their eyes. The trains were quite open and people often stared at him. His Beach bus drivers remembered him. He just wanted to stand there at the front of the bus talking to them, but we encouraged him to sit down. He got quite talkative at times.

Staff at Wisteria told me he seemed agitated after some of the day outings. The doctors I had spoken to about the outings suggested that it might be an overload for his brain, requiring much more energy to catch up, which was why he slept a lot during and after these trips. He may have been getting confused by confronting long-term memories of where he once lived. Maybe his brain was questioning why he wasn't living there anymore. Could be a maze of questions possibly floating around and further confusing him. I decided to try just a few more.

I thought he would be so happy to just sit on the beach like we always did. But that's not how it turned out. He was pacing, wanting to get away, tired, and the trips on the bus and train were beginning to exhaust him and, frankly, me as well. I was doubling my travel time on those days. I was on alert all the time in case he fell. Stumbling on the stairs in our old apartment was a problem for him, and the familiarity of the old apartment seemed to confuse him.

MORE WISTERIA DAY PASSES?

We are off for another trip on the buses. I think I could easily just sleep today as my knees hurt from all the walking. I see the bus stop and can hardly wait to sit down.

We get to the apartment and I can barely go up the stairs. I have to sit on the steps and wait.

I have a nap and am so happy to lay on the sofa. Lunch is going to be inside at the window and then we will go across the street and stretch out on our folded beach pads.

We have a great lunch! The dessert is the best part—Eccles cake!

When we are walking towards a nice spot, I look back at the apartment but then I see our bus going by and think we are going to miss it.

I shout, "Come on, we'll miss the bus!" but she says, "No, we'll take it later."

I don't agree and I start to run down the sidewalk towards the bus. She's running after me. I wave at the driver. The bus stops and waits. We get on, and then I need to get off. I'm so mixed up.

The driver stops. I say to him, "We made a mistake."

We get off. We are walking back towards the water. She says, "It's okay," and I say, "Get lost, fuck off, just go away." I'm really all mixed up. Who is she? She looks worried and so she should be.

What are we doing here? Where am I? What is this place?

She says, "I'm Helen, your wife. Let's go back to the apartment."

We really struggle up the stairs but we make it.

She suggests a bath. I love that, and we do that. Then I have a nap with her close to me. I think I yelled at her but that couldn't be. I love her. I can feel myself drifting off but she's near me and that's what counts.

She tells me it's time to go back for dinner to the other place. But I want McDonald's. Things don't go that well in there. I need to wash my hands, so I go to the ice dispenser and cubes come out and there's no soap but I get my hands wet—it's a bit confusing and people are staring at us. Ice was falling on the floor from the dispenser. She's dropping things. We finish eating and catch the bus. It's a long trip back with the three buses and I can hardly walk anymore. My knees are killing me.

We get back in one piece. My friends all greet me. The nurses ask me how my day went. I'm anxious to sit at a table with Don, read his newspaper, and not walk. I give her a hug and kisses and she is on her way.

WELL, WE TRIED

After a few more staff meetings we decided to abandon the day passes. There was just too much confusion, walking and transferring to different modes of transport via elevators. That last trip exhausted me beyond anything I'd felt for a long time. I went to get him: three modes of transport; we went to Beach: three modes of transport; we went back to Wisteria: three modes of transport; I came back to Beach: three modes of transport! It was twelve changes of buses and trains. We had done it before, but that last time with the stress and his unhappiness and confusion did me in! I was an emotional wreck when I finally stumbled back up the stairs alone to the Beach apartment. I just cried for hours.

I don't know what I was thinking. I didn't think I was in denial, but I had high hopes that the beach would make him really happy and content. But the beach wasn't as important as I thought. He was not the same Jeff. He was a new person with changed and damaged brain cells.

I still had high hopes for a placement in the Yaletown residence. If that happened, we could walk to the sea wall. I had made a few visits to that residence. The rooms seemed small, but there were five or six floors. The common areas were lovely with a huge fish tank, a greenhouse and some birds. I looked at other residences that were close to where I lived, but Yaletown stood out as the ideal place for Jeff.

I returned to visiting with Jeff five days a week but trying to cut it down to four as I got really worn out. He was now using a cane to help him walk as his knees were arthritic and swollen.

I was watching the sun at 3:30 one day, and I was so tired. I couldn't drum up the energy to get Jeff out and stay there for another couple of hours. I don't know, five hours of constant attention to someone wears a person down.

As soon as I got home, I wished I could take him out to be with me again. I guess none of this would ever sit well with me—what I could and couldn't do—but I imagine it was a problem everyone in a similar situation faced. I had no idea what tomorrow would bring and how I would cope with the unexpected and unpredictable changes.

I sometimes had such profound grief come over me out of the blue. I was sitting with the TV on, just not even there, far away with memories and a wrenching heart. It just never stopped no matter what. Once we were swept into that dementia journey, the train just kept rolling along in a nebulous state of such sorrow and sadness. It was unlike anything I've ever encountered. I was so lost and didn't know where to turn, who to talk to or where to find solace.

The people without dementia are just as lost as the people who have it.

BEAUTIFUL AUTUMN DAYS

My sister and brother-in-law have come to visit me several times. I remember them. They look familiar. We chatted about our memories, or at least tried to. They had tea and biscuits with me. We sat in the sun or walked in the garden.

I also had a couple of visits from my youngest son, both times just after dinner. He brought a girl with him, and she and I got on really well—she's very pretty and friendly. My son played number 8 position in rugby but too many injuries to keep up with it. I haven't seen my other son here.

Don and I are often rearranging the furniture which is not popular among the staff. We like to push and pull tables and set them against the walls and that seems to be a no-no.

There's exercise classes, music, crafts and birthday parties. We do a lot of those activities. But we do so enjoy rearranging the furniture! We have a purpose and we accomplish something.

People come in to entertain but I find it very loud and it tires me out, so I ask Helen if we can go to my room and she always agrees. I need to lie down and not hear all that noise.

I go out in the garden every time Helen comes to visit; she often lets me decide if I want to go to the RCMP building area across the street or the garden off the music room. We always cover a lot of ground. We also wander some backstreets where there is a vacant school and a nice park.

I have now been given a cane for walking outside only as the floors are too slippery inside to use it. It makes it easier to walk. After the walk, we put the cane in the nurse's station. It has my name on it.

I've made lots of friends especially Jay, who directs us all. She's small like my wife and they get along so well. Jay and I have lots of chats—she's easy to talk to and I tell her all kinds of stuff that I wouldn't tell anyone else like not wanting to live anymore and would it be easy to commit suicide. She wasn't happy to hear these thoughts and I cried.

LATE SUMMER/FALL 2014

Jeff started using the cane for the walks outside, which meant not leaning on me quite so much. He seemed more independent, which was certainly a positive.

Back at my home front, I had a major move from our Beach Avenue apartment with the three flights of stairs. My new destination was a bachelor apartment in the West End that was much cheaper.

Moving day was August 14. Somehow I had to squeeze the contents of a large two-bedroom apartment of almost 1500 square feet into this tiny space of 425 square feet! Hard to figure that one out, but I did take my time planning the move and had an auction house pack three-quarters of our possessions, and I sold a lot of items privately.

I continued to see Jeff four times a week. His sister was visiting more often as she knew I had a lot on my plate with the moving arrangements. It was an emotionally exhausting time organizing everything, but I met the challenge and moved. I left our beautiful apartment. My bachelor apartment was close to Lost Lagoon in Stanley Park. It was a hotel that had been converted to 125 bachelor apartments. Peter Newman, the Canadian writer, once lived in this same building in the 1940s when he was attending university in Vancouver. It was a quaint, charming bachelor apartment ideal for one person!

On October 26, his sister and her husband showed up at Jeff's while I was there. They had a puppy with them called Newt. It was adorable to see Jeff holding Newt. We all went for a walk in the garden. It was a really pleasant afternoon. Jeff was walking with his sister, holding her hand and using his cane in his other hand.

Jeff had his routine, and I fit my time into four to five visits there every week. We always walked, had a meal together and napped. The months flew by.

Our "conversations" were loosely-phrased words spoken aloud. Jeff's few words would give me a clue to what might be on his mind. I would ask questions or talk about whatever the word he blurted out would be. If it was London, I described our days there and talked for ages about our memories together. At times I could tell I wasn't steering the conversation in the right direction as he would often just nod off.

Our first place in London was in the downtown hub just off Fleet Street. We found a small furnished one-bedroom apartment on Chancery Lane with a fantastic landlord. Kitchens in these apartments were so small that only one person could be in there at the same time. The washers and dryers cost three pounds each time, so we did all our laundry in our tub.

Our main contact for work came to London with his family to see the London Bridge and we invited them for tea. They had four children, and I think they were shocked at our tiny place. They had put us up in their very large home the first time we went to London for work, and the garden had an aviary and a huge vegetable garden. This tiny one-bedroom apartment with a kitchen only one person could be in at a time may have been a learning experience for the kids to see how fortunate they were!

Jeff and I stood in line to get tickets to see plays like *The Phantom of the Opera*—live theatre was such a wonderful experience that we stood in line for last-minute tickets often!

We went to fantastic outdoor markets on the weekends. We didn't have a phone or a television—hard to imagine today living without—but we cooked and did a lot of reading and sightseeing. He was born in London during the Second World War and had such a great interest in museums throughout his youth, so I was being exposed to his extensive knowledge about art and live theatre all the time. Such wonderful memories.

We celebrated our wedding anniversary in Wisteria in early December. I brought smoked salmon on bagels and a drop of bubbly. It was our first Christmas and New Year's living apart, but we ate together, opened our gifts, bundled up and walked in the garden.

There was such a mixture of nationalities within the patient population at this transitional hospital. Some got a placement quickly due to their level of care being less than what Jeff would need. Jeff and Don were high level care and very "busy," so it was not easy to place them in a residence.

At this stage, Jeff could not dress himself, shave, wash, shower or bathe on his own, and he required a lot of attention. Too much attention was something new he had to handle with a nice looking older British gentleman who took it upon himself to become his best buddy. Staff told me that this resident was making Jeff tea and trying to spend all his time with him. When I visited, they would tell this resident that I was married to Jeff and would introduce me to him saying, "She's Jeff's wife." They hoped he would get the message and not get attached to Jeff.

One day I was informed that this man was caught going into Jeff's room at 10:30 p.m. and sitting on his bed. Someone heard some shouting, and the rumour what that he was making inappropriate advances on Jeff. I was told that this resident was moved to another floor as his advances weren't reciprocated. It caused an uncomfortable situation for Jeff, me and, frankly, everyone.

We were almost into a new year, and it was difficult to believe time was going by so quickly. The disease was slowly progressing but fluctuating a lot. It was remarkable that he and Don remained close friends, and it served both of them (and the staff) well. They could communicate together, walk around and read newspapers. It was wonderful to see them laughing and joking together. Don hurt his foot, and Jeff pushed Don in a wheelchair while he was mending. They ate their meals together, sat on the balcony together and ate snacks. I never could understand what they talked about, but they managed a good friendship.

Don's wife came several days a week, and we often compared the problems we faced. Occasionally, she coincided her departure with mine and gave me a ride home if we happened to be there the same day.

JEFF'S FALL. MARCH 2015

March 6 was a beautiful day, and Jeff and I took a walk outside. Little did I know, it would be the last time Jeff would ever walk. We had a cup of tea, a cuddle in bed, and I left about three o'clock.

I received a phone call at 6:00 p.m. that Jeff was transported to hospital for X-rays as he was in a lot of pain, could not stand up and could not say what happened. Apparently, a nurse came into his room at dinner to get him as he hadn't shown up. He was lying in his bed moaning and pointing to his hip/leg. He was in real distress.

I rushed to the hospital to meet with the doctors having been advised by Wisteria staff that X-rays showed a cracked femur. Jeff was distraught and in a lot of pain, but they gave him some pain meds. We were just holding each other tightly as I leaned into his bed. I asked him what happened and he said, "I don't know. I can't remember anything. The pain is awful. Please stay with me." I didn't leave his side.

A doctor came late that evening to chat with me and said we needed to talk about an operation. There were only two options: He could stay as he was, but he would just lie in bed, get worse and probably die after six months. The other option was an operation but, depending on how he recovered, he might have to use a wheelchair afterwards. The doctor said that patients with dementia don't always recover well from a general anaesthetic, so I needed to understand that. But he pointed out a real positive on Jeff's side was how fit and strong he seemed to be. We decided on the operation.

The operation went as planned on March 9. Apart from being confused and being unable to eat on his own, he recovered well. I spent the next eleven days feeding him his meals in the hospital and staying by his side. A general anaesthetic, which was what he had, could have any number of consequences since he had dementia. His cognitive abilities could worsen or stay the same, and he could be confined to a wheelchair at least initially. The doctor seemed to think he would probably walk again after a period of rehabilitation. He had one visitor, his rugby mate Wayne, but I believe Jeff was somewhat muddled at first who it was.

There was no question he would need to use a wheelchair right after his release from hospital, so arrangements were made to borrow one from the Red Cross. That chair was too flimsy for a big guy like Jeff and the consensus from his team was that he would need a chair for quite a while, so we purchased a large Broda wheelchair; it worked so well for him. It was barely used (hence a great price of $1,000), so it was a good opportunity to secure it while I could.

He was soon discharged from hospital and started a programme of physiotherapy with a foot-peddling machine and standing exercises which we fit in on days I was there. He would stand and hold the railing and do up to ten repeats if he could. He couldn't move his feet in a walking motion or step forward. He could only stand.

In April, he continued using the foot-peddling machine to strengthen his legs and thighs. He was using it for half an hour every visit, and a physiotherapist was watching him use it while he was checking up on him. I had warnings that he might decline quickly after this fall, but he seemed to bounce back. Don even pushed him in his wheelchair!

He didn't seem to be able to walk yet, but he could stand as he was helped in and out of bed. I worked with a physiotherapist and we tried getting him to stand several times a day in hopes of his mobility returning.

In the meantime, we would go out in the garden every visit. He was bundled up, eating fruit, getting used to his wheelchair. He would push himself up off his feet with his arms on the arm rests. He did that a lot as he was not happy in the chair, really disliked having a belt buckled for his safety. So far, he hadn't figured out how to open it, but it was just a matter of time as it didn't need a key and there was a certain way to open it. I always made sure he was not looking as I unbuckled it!

SPRING 2015 - THE OPERATION

I broke a bone in my upper leg and had to go to the hospital. It was so painful. I don't know how it happened. I don't remember falling out of bed. I know I was in bed when they came in and asked me what's wrong. I just knew there was lots of pain in my hip and leg.

The next thing I remember was waking up in a hospital bed with Helen by my side. I've got a big scar and I hurt a lot when I move too quickly. A nurse and Helen help me go to the toilet. I can't walk on my own but there was a wheelchair and we do the transfers.

I'm hungry but I can't seem to handle the cutlery so she helps me with the spoon and the yogurt. We get it done together. I try to talk but it's not easy for some reason. I ask her where I am and she tells me and talks about the operation I had. Wayne comes to visit.

I want to go home but I have to stay for a while. Helen reads to me and she tells me stories and we talk about the past or at least she does as she's doing all the talking!

I get better. I finally get moved by van back to my room where the garden is. Helen comes later.

I have this big wheelchair that is so comfortable. I've met a physiotherapist and he wants to help me get fit again and walk so we start with peddling exercises on this foot peddler. Then we do standing exercises several times a week and every time Helen is here. They are preparing me for when I get to stand in this tall strange walker, and then I will try to move forward. They keep telling me it's coming.

The day comes to try the walker. I can stand but I can't move. I don't know how to walk anymore. I don't know what to do. They try moving my feet but I just stand frozen. They can't budge me. Two aides hold me and Helen tries to move one foot forward and it won't go forward. We try this many times without success.

We go in the garden in my wheelchair. I'm so happy to get outside. I clap and eat apples and pears.

Helen brings me McDonald's burgers and fish and chips. The flowers are blooming and it's beautiful here. I'm happy to be with her.

I want to walk and I can't. I keep pushing myself up off my feet straining the buckle. If it wasn't there I'd probably fall on the floor.

SPRING & SUMMER - REHABILITATION

This spring was all about healing, getting strong and staying fit. Because Jeff was now in a wheelchair and could no longer run around, tear down walls, empty paper dispensers, move furniture, break taps (four times), or get into trouble with Don, it would be easier to place him in a permanent residence.

Jeff was learning how to use the wheelchair effectively. The foot rests were detachable, which enabled him to move himself with his feet and pulling himself along the railings in the halls. It was quite a positive move forward for him. He still couldn't get out of the chair on his own and walk but could stand and do supervised peddling to keep getting stronger. Jeff saw his Wisteria physiotherapist regularly.

In the meantime, his psychiatrist contacted me about grief counselling because she recognized how unhappy, confused, out of sorts—whatever—I was becoming. It was a new situation for me, and she offered to give me guidance once every two weeks to talk about my fears as Jeff declined in this disease. It helped tremendously. She knew Jeff and was still part of his team. She understood what he was facing in this journey—what we were both up against.

Fortunately, Jeff and I continued to have a tight bond that seldom varied. I was always greeted with hugs and kisses. He was always happy to see me and vice versa. But having breaks from each other was also good for us.

He continued to have his group, his friends. He knew them and, therefore, he knew what to expect.

For his seventy-fifth birthday at the end of April, I planned a small celebration in the private back garden for some of our old friends to gather and celebrate this milestone occasion.

On my home front, a one-bedroom apartment had been offered to me for first of June, and it was an offer I couldn't refuse. Much as I liked the bachelor apartment and really had no intention to move again, when the chance came up to live in an apartment with a balcony that was close to Yaletown, part of the West End and had a bicycle path outside my door to the sea wall, I absolutely could not pass it up!

Jeff's sister had stopped her visits since October when they came with their new puppy. She emailed me that she was seriously ill and could not continue visiting her brother at this time. Jeff's three children from his previous marriage had not visited, phoned him or me or sent any emails or cards. His sister's children also had not visited or called. Why would that be? I invited them all to Jeff's birthday party but did not hear back from any of them either way. The nursing station had Jeff's family's contacts, but none of them reached out to meet up with him or me.

MY SEVENTY-FIFTH BIRTHDAY PARTY.
APRIL 2015

I was helping Jay with the decorations to be put up in the garden as someone was having a birthday party. I held the items in my lap while she stood on the ladder putting up balloons and all sorts of weird stuff.

Then I noticed the banner we worked on yesterday that said "HAPPY BIRTHDAY" with my name on it.

"Yes, it's your birthday tomorrow," she said.

I don't think about it much as what will happen?

Helen came in to have lunch with me. She was really bustling around but we sat together. I got changed and wrapped up in warm clothes as we were going outside—my favourite thing to do.

This time, though, one of the attendants came with us, and when we got to the garden there were many people there, clapping and smiling at me.

I recognized several people. They each took a turn to come down to my wheelchair level and have a chat with me. Mostly the chat was about rugby, always a safe subject with these rugby players around. I recognized these mates from twenty-five or more years ago. They showed up to chat with me and partake of cupcakes and champagne! Just a bit but it was so nice on my lips!

There was Wayne and Dave, my long-time rugby mates, and Mike, my dive buddy, and others but I'm not that good with the names. The tall one and the short, feisty one from the private club. Some good-looking women but I can't remember their names.

The weather was not good, windy and cold, but I was thought of all the time. A heated blanket appeared out of nowhere and I was wrapped up in it. We soon went inside and sat by the window and I recalled old memories with my dive buddy. We had some photo albums and that triggered more stories!

To say I am tired is an understatement. All the activity, goodies, new and old faces—some just hovering on the edge of my memory and then a quick flash and I see one of them way back running on the rugby pitch with me scoring a try!

The cards all say I'm seventy-five—could that be true? I never thought I'd live past fifty! I have enough chocolate goodies for months! My "chocolate lady" was here and I just knew she had some chocolate for me.

A last hug and kiss from the ladies, and I'm wheeled away to my warm bed with many hugs and kisses and "See you soon" from my poppet, the girl who is always in my dreams.

JEFF'S SEVENTY-FIFTH BIRTHDAY

It was a blustery, cold day with intermittent rain, but there was a great turnout for Jeff's milestone seventy-fifth birthday celebration!

Jay was so delighted to tell me that Jeff helped her the day before as she put up banners. They got along really well. She said he sat in his chair watching and kept telling her to be careful and not fall off the ladder. She gave him all sorts of things to do, and she said he was just so happy and smiled so much.

He was so happy on the day of his birthday! He knew it was his birthday. He told me they all sang "Happy Birthday" to him at breakfast and clapped.

When Wayne walked in, he said in a loud voice, "Wayne!" and they shook hands. He was engaging with everyone. It was chilly out, but a terrific nurse came with a heated blanket for Jeff. If you smile a lot and treat everyone with cheerfulness you certainly become a popular patient. Everyone had a turn chatting with him.

Several rugby pals from the past were part of the group. They had also been at a stadium to congratulate him four years earlier when he received his rugby cap for Canada.

Soon after we met, Jeff told me he had played international rugby for Canada in the 1960s. He had lived in Montreal at the time and was quite involved with the team. He even played games against the famous All Blacks and other well-known rugby clubs.

When he lived in Rhodesia, he played with the local rugby club. When we went on the cycling trip to England and France, we went to his old rugby club in Cheltenham and some of his jerseys were hanging on the walls. He joined many clubs and played on a regular basis. I would often go scuba diving on a Saturday with like-minded friends and he would play rugby for the SnowCaps or other teams.

One of his sons had tried for several years without success to have him presented with his rugby cap, but it hadn't gone unnoticed as it finally did happen in Vancouver at one of the rugby matches. His sister, her husband and many old rugby friends attended the cap ceremony.

It was lovely to see the couple from the private club come to wish him a happy birthday. It was hard to know if he remembered everyone, but he was smiling all the time, happy to eat some cake, and he even took a sip of bubbly. He received cards from everyone and chocolate and other treats!

We didn't stay outside too long due to the weather, but we moved the party into a common room and continued visiting with him and each other for another hour or so. Jeff's dive buddy, Mike, whom I believe Jeff recognized, sat with him at a table and looked at a photo album I brought that contained photos from our diving trips.

Jeff was definitely getting tired by the end.

The only disappointment was all his family in Vancouver were invited but there was no response from any of them. He didn't even receive a greeting card from them. A real shame when it was a milestone birthday and his family lived right in the vicinity.

LIVING IN A WHEELCHAIR. SUMMER 2015

So many things changed when Jeff became confined to a wheelchair. He could no longer just walk into his bathroom and go as he could not stand on his own. He continued to wear regular underwear, but accidents were happening as staff couldn't be by his side every minute. He would fall asleep in his chair by the window and wake up wet, needing to be changed. Staff didn't come running when he said, "I have to go to the toilet." Because he didn't have one-on-one support, he might sit there for a while, which often led to an accident.

It was another new stage—the category of incontinence of bladder and bowel. He was having accidents in bed. Staff often reported that when they came to his room in the morning, he was awake, upset and there was poop everywhere. He made even more of a mess due to his frustration.

He was no longer the free agent he was when he entered Wisteria. It was a difficult adjustment for him, but it was also difficult to watch unfolding. The femur break and not being able to walk seemed to have affected his control. He was having trouble walking before with his bad arthritic knees, but now sitting in a wheelchair made him less mobile. But who was to know whether the catalyst was a decline in his cognition that led to ignoring these functions or the hospitalization with the anaesthetic.

There were rumours that his permanent placement could come up that summer as there was a time limit for staying in a transitional hospital. Using a wheelchair could result in him qualifying for residences other than Yaletown House, and we had to go along with our second or third choice of residence. I got the impression they were preparing me for the disappointment of not going to our first choice.

BIKE MISHAP

The days were so warm since May that I started riding my ten-speed bicycle to and from the hospital. Horrors of all horrors, at the end of June I collided with a pedestrian. It was a Saturday morning and there was heavy traffic on the road, so I was slowly biking on a wide sidewalk close to the Canada Line. Suddenly, this guy jumped out of his parked car and ran into me—like crashed into me— sending both of us flying to the ground. I went down with the bike!

It was such a shock as it was so unexpected and I was so unprepared! I had my helmet on and I still don't know how I landed—most likely on my side from being pushed over. The right side bike pedal gouged my leg below the knee so there was blood pouring. I had a bloody elbow and bruises on the back of my other leg. There I was lying on the sidewalk in a tangle with my bike. A little crowd gathered with concerned people getting me a bottle of water and bandages. Someone wanted to call an ambulance, but I just wanted help getting untangled from the bike. I was just shaking like a leaf.

The pedestrian was crying—he was older than me— and so upset that I was hurt. Fortunately he was okay. We waited until I settled down and then two people helped me stand—nothing broken, hallelujah! A chair suddenly appeared, someone was holding my bike, and bandages were applied over the cuts. It wasn't as bad as it looked at first! How lucky for me to escape serious injury! I was okay, just shaken up, and I had my helmet on. We were right in front of a pizza joint.

I tried to relax and knew I would be okay. I then decided to go ahead to the Canada Line train with my bike as it was just half a block away. A concerned, kind lady insisted on walking with me and my bike to the Canada Line, and I got my train. When I got to Jeff, I went to see the head nurse and she steered me to a chair and patched me up. Jeff could see the blood on my legs and was visibly upset.

"What happened? What's wrong?" he yelled.

We sat together as the nurse patched me up, and Jeff offered suggestions for where to put the bandages. We laughed when Jeff then found a cut on his leg and asked the nurse for a bandage. So sweet, naïve and innocent— probably what a child would do!

I got a painkiller in me, and we had an afternoon nap. I decided to take the Canada Line to Yaletown, and I stopped to thank the people in the two restaurants who came to my rescue. The pizza place sent me home with a pizza strapped on the back pannier. I was impressed!

Chapter 7

PERMANENT RESIDENCE

On June 28, 2015, I received a phone call that Jeff was approved for placement in a permanent residence. Unfortunately, it was not Yaletown but the farthest residence from my home of any of the possible places he could have moved to. I just burst into tears on the phone. I could not believe it. How could they make that kind of decision?

It would take two bus changes plus the Canada Line train. One of the buses was at Cambie and Langara College and then went to 48th Avenue—forty stops. Like forever! Surely they could be persuaded to reconsider? The trip would never take under an hour, and that meant a daily visit involving two hours just for travel time.

No one could blame me for being upset, discouraged, crying. I couldn't sleep. The system for placing patients had betrayed us. There was no explanation other than it was a place that had become available and had accepted Jeff. There was no negotiating on the place or date. I felt forced to say yes to this move to the boondocks. I had never felt so cornered and without any say about what would happen to Jeff.

My psychiatrist phoned me and said, "It is truly one of the nicest and best facilities in Vancouver. For Jeff's needs," she said, "it is number one." She told me she even fought to give me an extra day instead of "immediate." I could have refused, but then his room and board would be charged at a full daily rate, which was out of sight. He would be moved in a few days whether I liked it or not!

A good friend, Doria, said she would come over the next day, which was a Sunday, and take me to this residence so I could see where it was and how it looked. Another friend came with us, and I sat in the back seat and cried most of the way, especially as we got farther and farther from home.

We arrived at a low-lying building with no gardens and just cement and a parking lot out the front. We were given a tour, and it looked like a well-established, homey, comfortable spacious residence. But there was no proximity to the water or a garden. My friend was realistic and surprised me in her reaction to Jeff's move and my being so sad about it. She continually reminded me that it was Jeff's care that was important. She pointed out if they had chosen that place maybe it would be the best place for him, that I should take baby steps and look at the whole picture. She was right; it should have been all about Jeff, not me. If I died before him—dropped dead right that moment, heaven forbid—he would be somewhere that was safe for him.

In any event, it was their decision, and moving day would be in a few days—yes, a few days, even with my psychiatrist pleading for extra time. The move was to happen on a Tuesday, and she said that "it took all our negotiating power to move the day from Tuesday to Thursday."

As I continued to ponder this move, I knew Jeff's progression could possibly open the door to new friends and perhaps engage them in "his" conversations. What he would be affected by was any negative reaction by me to this move. I knew he loved me and was always aware of my reaction to situations I thought were unjust and injurious. I needed to put on a brave face and see how it went because there was still the possibility of an opening at Yaletown in the near future.

On a happier note, Jeff had been adapting well to the wheelchair, and he used his feet to paddle around and ably held onto the railings. He was free to move. It was obvious he had pain in his knees when he tried to stand, and he seemed exhausted after the physio he had begun twice a week with his new physiotherapist and me. Oliver was a charming, friendly addition to his twice-weekly exercises.

I think he had accepted that he couldn't walk, but then he would forget, of course, and want to just get up and go, so he struggled against the belt blocking that move. It was truly sad to watch him—a man who always had such confidence and pride in his physical ability to engage in sports, walking and dancing and always, but always, encouraging his friends to stay fit.

We both really enjoyed dancing and took every opportunity. We prepared for a two-step evening at a ballroom in Vancouver. He taught me the two-step but, alas, was so much shorter than him so it was difficult because I fell far behind and stumbled away. But we made the attempt, had an entertaining evening, him in his tuxedo and me in a gown. I probably needed higher stilettos to dance with someone so tall.

On our get-togethers visiting my family in Ottawa, dancing was high on the agenda. It was easy to imagine him dancing in a circle with four of my nieces, and they were so shocked that he could move like that. Little did they know that when he was a teenager at school in England, he won prizes for his dancing abilities. He had natural rhythm!

He wasn't at all shy chastising friends or saying something outright negative to them if they looked overweight and spurned exercise. He would look at some of the staff, and if anyone was overweight, he would whisper to me, "Oh, she is fat! She's got to lose some pounds" or "She needs to do more exercise." Being fit and not overeating had been ingrained in his health regime and he stayed at a constant weight and remained healthy, though I knew he was losing muscle tone being in the wheelchair.

MONTBRETIA RESIDENCE. JULY 2015

Something is going on!

She's here early and we're having breakfast together.

I see a porter pushing a luggage cart that is piled really high and it's parked by the elevator.

People come over to her and hug and kiss her and whisper things. Her eyes keep brimming up with tears but she looks at me and smiles that lovely smile!

I think I'm part of what's going on.

The tall biker is pushing my chair.

A few people look my way with tears but some come and give me a big hug. A couple say, "I'll miss you."

So I'm going somewhere but she's coming with me, thank god! We squeeze into the elevator and I see a big white van which says Transfer Vehicle. I'm greeted warmly and settled into a spot with lots of buckles and straps. She holds my hand tightly and says, "We're off to a new hotel."

Tall biker is with us. I haven't been in a vehicle for a while and it's mesmerizing seeing all the shops and streets flying by. It goes by quickly, too quickly, as I like seeing the sights. She tells tall biker, "It's such a far distance." They talk about whether she could bike here like she could at the other place. She counts the stops and says it's forty, so that's quite a distance.

We arrive at this new hotel, so much to see but all in good time. Lunch is coming and my chair is next to a long table which I share with another woman who has a walker. I try to say hello and she barks at us. Very grumpy lady!

Not sure what to make of everything and I think some of the same people are here. I recognize a short round one and she knew my name, so it must be her. So some of them came with me. That makes me happy.

My room has cupboards and it's cozy. I hear her say that often, "It's cozy." That's the word to describe it.

EARLY WEEKS AT MONTBRETIA RESIDENCE. JULY

Jeff settled in nicely. I found my way, met with the staff and got to know our new surroundings. There was a small kitchen off the dining area which was used for making coffee and tea and which had a microwave oven. We were on the second floor. There were four separate units in this residence—two lockdown and two for residents who could move about on their own and didn't have the same special needs as those in lockdown.

There was one balcony and a fish tank in this unit. We could sit on the balcony and look out, but unfortunately, it was a parking lot for the view; it was still fresh air outside. We could take the elevator down one floor to the main lobby and there was a long, narrow balcony we could use which had an overhang so it was a good place to be rain or shine if we couldn't go for walks during poor weather!

We were introduced to a fantastic activities director who played the piano and flute. Y was a tiny, talented, friendly dynamo with boundless energy. Jeff liked her right off. Residents had to be accompanied by family, friends or a paid companion. If there was entertainment on the main floor—singing or dancing or jazz—a resident could go with a care group to watch.

My life "on my own" away from Jeff had changed markedly. I moved from the bachelor apartment to a one-bedroom apartment in June 2015. I had been encouraged to go on an Alaskan Cruise for a week that summer—a cruise I won in a draw. Two other people I knew were already registered. I had a girlfriend on standby waiting for my decision so she could share the cabin with me as each winner was allowed a guest.

I was hesitant to follow through with the prize, so I discussed it with my psychiatrist. I hadn't had a break for a long time, so it was an opportunity at a time when Jeff was settling into his residence and getting to know staff and vice versa. My whole life for the past five or six years had Jeff as my top priority. I had never been to Alaska, so I decided to go.

The cruise took place the last week in July 2015. It was fantastic visually, and I enjoyed it. I did my best to keep worries about Jeff at bay and enjoyed the saunas, massages, spas and an outdoor as well as indoor swimming pool. I felt refreshed disembarking, but I could also hardly wait to see what Jeff was up to.

LATE JULY 2015

There's lots going on here!

I seem to be so busy doing exercise with this speedy, tiny, short girl. She gathers us up and we listen to live music downstairs. We toss a soft soccer ball around. She tried to get me to colour pages but I can't do that—can't do puzzles either. But what I can do is move around the halls, pulling myself along the rails, and meet people I haven't met before. There's some really friendly people. The nurses all take care of me.

In particular there is a lovely lady who speaks French, as I do as well, and we have become friends. She also has a wheelchair and we sit by the window together. She likes to rub my back. She's very friendly. I wonder what my wife will say when she sees us together.

I keep waiting and watching for Helen to arrive.

Rosie wants to come into my room but the staff are not happy about that. She has sneaked in a few times and the nurses caught her and have now locked my door so that doesn't keep happening. But we just meet up in the halls and sometimes at the meals.

I'm so happy as my wife Helen has arrived with apples and oranges. Also chocolate. I'm busy with my lunch but I stop so we can have hugs and kisses. She watches me eat and has a cup of tea.

I'm very sleepy so we go to my room, and she is putting up pictures and I'm watching her climb on a chair, warning her to be careful.

I wake up and we go outside for a spin around. I keep getting mixed up about the railing in the elevator to go downstairs and she's having a hard time prying my fingers away so we can exit.

We go around the building outside but there is not too much to see. They tell us we can go into this garden from the outside on the main floor. We see a few birds and watch the gardeners cleaning up plants.

SETTLING IN

They have me on a new routine of sitting on the toilet at 11:00 every day. Two days with no success. I try to do my "Tom Tit" but it only does it when it wants to.

I had a bath today. They gave me the cloth and I got to scrub and someone washed my hair. It was all so warm and I feel so nice.

Oh, look! She's arrived with her cooler pouch. She's giving me hugs and holding me in her arms. She's small so we can do that!

Rosie, one of my new friends, is motoring down the hallway with a bad look on her face and so agitated. We watch as a nurse rushes over but not quickly enough as Rosie takes a swipe at my wife's head. I don't understand why they can't be friends. Rosie is wheeled away but comes back twice more and says loud things in French to my wife. She hisses, almost spits, at her with what looks like such dislike. Is it me Rosie wants? She has been told I have a wife but she watches closely and finds her moments to be out of their view and gets next to me. My wife tells me I'm popular with the ladies.

I have a favourite friend who is very tall and so friendly. I read his name tag, and I think it said Snooton.* We chat a lot. He always wears different coloured outfits mainly beige.

She has carrots and cukes and we sit together while she peels them. Lunch comes and I'm still full from breakfast but the soup looks worth trying with that chocolate cookie.

I have a bit of carrot and cucumber. I can only eat half my lunch and I feel very tired and am nodding off. We wait for lunch to be over and we slowly go to my room for a nap. She's about to help me get in bed but I say, "Wait."

Oh, no, I can feel it wanting to explode.

"Please, please help me," I say to her.

She runs to the door and signals to Snooton and we can smell it but we're hopeful I can get on the toilet. She keeps saying, "Wait, wait, wait."

I'm in the basket hoist and can see the toilet, oh, yes, Snooton moves fast and I just touch the bowl and it's starting Big Time. She and Snoot are clapping and I'm smiling. She keeps saying "Push, Push!" She hugs me. Snooton chuckles at the absurdity of her hugging me while I poop. Both of them rub my stomach and tell me it's best to get it out.

*Helen's note: His name tag read "Newton," but Jeff gave him a new name!

THE UNPREDICTABLE INDIGNITY OF DEMENTIA

So much was working so smoothly except for changes with Jeff's toilet regime. He was being given suppositories and it was causing cramps as well as unexpected and almost uncontrollable needs to get on the toilet immediately. We were working on sorting this out with the rotating doctor.

I was sitting there reading and pondering about this new level of indignity. I never expected it would reach this level, but I soon found out incontinence was the norm with dementia. When it began, it would never get better; in fact, it could only get worse.

MID-AUGUST 2015

At last she's here, just in time for lunch. We're sharing a soup, she has one today too!

I'm feeling rumblings and I need to say something but the words won't form. I'm shaking my chair and trying to get out so I don't mess myself.

She unlocks the wheels and I go towards my room, maybe I'll be in time for the toilet.

No, it's too late—I give in and just moan and say, "Oh, no."

She knows. She tries to get their attention but they are busy spoon-feeding others. They say "soon," but after ten minutes she is agitated and asks if she can clean me up as it's spreading. Soon the back of the wheelchair and then the rug will be drenched with poo.

They are now alert as she is getting impatient and she says she wants to change me.

It's to the shower and bath as it's over the top in the level of clean-up. There is no point in resisting.

She's waiting and they put me in the basket hoist and then I'm in bed, very tired, but my eyes are closing. She's holding my hand and I know she will stay with me.

REMINISCING

As Jeff lay sleeping, I gazed at all the dive photos in the albums and remembered how close we came to tragedy on more than a few occasions. In July of 1992, we went on holiday to Cancun and took the ferry to the Island of Women—Isla Mujeres. We had dived there before. We decided to dive this challenging site later in the afternoon, but we would have the divemaster/owner with us on the dive.

Several currents come together at a certain spot, which seemed to attract thousands of fish. I had named this site The Dive of 10,000 Fish! We couldn't anchor the boat, so we quickly followed a line down or held onto your dive buddy. The current can reach eight knots—no exaggeration. I needed twenty-five pounds of weight around my waist because this was a drift dive. Jeff, me, our divemaster, and a Danish diver plunged in. All of us except the Danish diver were kitted in full wetsuits. I was breathless when I neared the bottom (at about forty feet) as thousands of fish parted for me. They all were about a foot away and I could hear them grunting! No matter which way I turned I saw walls ten deep of fish that looked like tuna.

The descent was no problem. There were a few craters we could slip down into to regroup where there was no current. We would swim out of the crater all together and just fly in the strongest current I'd ever dived in!

This marvellous dive started around 5:45 in the afternoon, and we ascended when we were close to 500 left in our tanks. It was a dive where I could hold my arms out like on the bow of the *Titanic*, except I was moving at an alarming rate. I had this panicky feeling the other three would get away from me, but we all moved with the same distance apart that we started with.

When we surfaced, the boat was nowhere in sight. Jeff blew a whistle but there was no response, no boat. It was starting to look like a movie where the boat forgets to pick up the divers. We were in the middle of the Gulf of Mexico and couldn't see anything close by. We floated, waited and waited. After about an hour we started swimming towards a mountain way in the distance. Jeff said we should keep our tanks on and weight belts and our jackets inflated, which we all did. It seemed like hours had gone by, but the water was calm and we were close together trying not to think about sharks and what was lurking under the water watching our progress to shore.

Darkness and quiet.

"Will we make it?" I asked Jeff.

The whistle died. There was no use shouting as there was no one around to hear us. But the mountain was getting closer. We could see lights flashing around the mountain so perhaps the divemaster's wife had a search party looking for us. But these were just dots of light on the horizon—it was still very far away. We figured we were out in the water for at least four hours by that time.

A few waves formed as we neared the shore. We were close enough to see all the rocks and the crashes of the waves on those rocks. That's where we were going to land. Jeff and the Danish diver paired off, and the divemaster and I were together. We saw an approach entry with a large rock on either side and that our plan was to land there together.

As we were about twenty feet from shore, we heard a huge wave creeping up on us. It crashed right into us and shoved us towards the rocks. I saw Jeff grab the Danish diver, lift him in the air and propel him onto the shoreline away from the rocks. The divemaster told me to put my mask and regulator in my mouth and hang on to him as another huge rogue wave was approaching. The shock of the crash and how the rip tried to pull us back out was distressing, but our weight belts kept us from floating away. Another wave that looked about ten feet high crashed over the divemaster and me. It dislodged my mask, and I could feel him holding on to me. We were tangled together and made it to a slightly higher set of rocks. I saw one of his fins go as his leg flew up and it was bare—no booties!

We rushed to the shore, and Jeff found an opening to come to our side of the rocks.

"Are you okay?" he shouted.

He took my weight belt off. I was quite shaken up. We were standing at the bottom of this mountain, and waves continued to crash in so we scrambled towards what looked like a path. We shouted when we saw some headlights shining into the water and we knew we were spotted. People rushed down to help us climb this steep mountain. We were bruised, hurting but safe and alive. We lost a lot of gear, but we needed to get out of there. My chest was aching on one side like I'd been punched in the back. It was now about 10:00 at night.

We were actually close to where the divemaster lived. The boatman had disappeared—we weren't told anything. It was such a relief that the divemaster's family—wife and three young children—were together again. We had hot showers in our wetsuits, ate and got back to our hotel. When we peeled off our wetsuits, the bruises were already blooming on both of us, but I was worse off than Jeff from slamming into the rocks. It was a most frightening experience to say the least. The next day we recovered some of our diving gear from the area indicated in this photo.

THE DOG DAYS OF SUMMER

I startle awake and she is reading by my side. I reach out to her and she crawls in beside me and we cuddle. It feels so good to hold her close like we used to do, and I can feel myself dropping off.

The rattle of the door wakes us up. Staff forgot to lock it although the "Do Not Disturb" sign is there. We see Rosie opening the door and staring at us. She looks so sad. I hold my wife tighter. They quickly wheel Rosie away.

We get ready for an outside wheel around and little treats she always brings, but this time I'm holding a little container with cut up cukes and orange peppers with fresh lime. I just can't resist—I eat the lot! I only smile when she sees the empty container and we haven't even reached our garden destination. Surely she knows I crave the "memory" food with piquant dressings. They don't even have mustard or ketchup here. She says she will bring me some to sharpen the taste buds!

END OF AUGUST 2015

I see her arriving!

Oh, oh, she's going to catch me and Rosie chatting. Rosie likes to caress my shoulders and is always right at my level even though her wheelchair is smaller. She really likes to be with me and it's nice to have friends here. She speaks French. I speak French too. I often see a very tall man come to visit her.

They are wheeling her away but the love of my life is standing there with a big smile. I like to call her my "Poppet."

I say, "Thank god you're here."

She gets close. We hug and kiss.

I've had lunch but she has a container with her. What a treat—shrimp and pasta! I can't help but reach for a shrimp. She always lets me have what I want in her special containers. She always made yummy shrimp dishes! She's promised me a Big Mac and fish and chips, so maybe that's coming soon.

At last we're going for fresh air and freedom out the front door. I sigh with relief and smile and tell her she's beautiful and that I love her. I say this often. I have so much to tell her but it starts coming out and then it's gone and she tries to anticipate what was on my mind and suggests thoughts I might have wanted to convey.

It's beautiful outside and I just rock in my chair and stay quiet. She produces a Pink Lady apple, whole, and I'm really chomping away and tell her it's good when she asks me.

Back upstairs she hands me an ice cream cone and it's wonderful and cool. When I finish my treat I don't see her but she did mention something about going to the dentist. She'll be back. She always tells me she will be back and will love me always.

The others here are chatting with me and we're looking at my photo album together that Poppet brought for me. It's of old friends, relatives and the underwater world when we enjoyed our scuba days together. The adorable seals who offered us rocks or shells carried in their mouths and dropped to us. Memories of mom sea lion basking on a rock partially submerged lowering her head to watch us play with the newborns. They seemed to trust us and almost knew we just wanted to love them and take these pictures. All the beautiful fans swaying in the current.

I try to tell my new friends about our experiences underwater. They listen and ask questions about some pictures. Some trigger an image of that time; others don't say anything to my memory except they are pretty. But I always remembered the slipper lobster!

CLAUSTROPHOBIA AND THE SLIPPER LOBSTER CAVE

Putting together that album of some of our underwater photos reminded me how I worked so hard to ignore caves and darkened areas underwater; I have a slight case of claustrophobia. Jeff and I talked about that often, which resulted in my getting a better camera and concentrating more on taking photos rather than the darkness or closed-in spaces.

I found out just how rewarding going into a cave could be on one of our dives.

Jeff disappeared into a cave ahead of me but turned back, grabbed my hand and pulled me in with him. He shone his dive light on this amazing slipper lobster, a crustacean I had never seen before. Unlike spiny regular lobsters, they are more heavily armoured. They are sometimes described as looking like a flattened armadillo. They also don't have the long antennae found in spiny American lobsters. I was frightened because it was pitch dark when he turned his light off. As he moved farther into the cave, I became even more apprehensive, but he pointed forward so I could see light at the other end of this narrow tunnel—our exit, so to speak. I trusted his confidence and amazingly skillful body language that helped me relax in tight areas. It helped me appreciate the caves rather than fear them. He had so much experience and was often asked to help lead larger groups.

LAZY DAYS TOGETHER

I'm watching and listening for the elevator. I think she'll come.
Yes, she's here! She's arrived with apples and an orange.
I'm busy with my lunch but interrupt it to give her a hug and kisses.
We really tried to do the toilet but so far just no go.
Dropping off, my lids are heavy.
I feel good. She's standing here by my side. We snuggle and caress our backs.

Next thing she's not there beside me but we are enjoying an apple. The basket has come and gone as the apple has my undivided attention.

We did a quiz today. She asked me who I loved and right away "Mike," my dive buddy, popped out. She said what about Wayne? I said I love him sometimes.

She asked about my sister and brother-in law but I know they've died. I tell her they are dead. I never see them. She asks about other people but I just don't know who they are so I remain silent.

It's so nice lying in bed having my ice cream cone and looking at my girl.

She has a sore tooth so has to go soon to her dentist but she always says she'll be back.

ENJOYING MONTBRETIA. AUTUMN 2015

We had settled into a routine with me visiting Jeff four to five days a week despite the long distance to cover to and fro. I was always hopeful Yaletown House would have an opening. I actually met with one of the managers there to discuss the possibility. She explained that one of the reasons an opening had not come up was because it was a five-story building with only two lockdown floors. If someone passed or moved from lockdown and a room became available, it seemed that the residents who were presently there who may have declining health had first choice of moving to one of those available rooms. It made a lot of sense instead of totally uprooting someone from a transitional hospital or another residence. Basically, it was a waiting game for Jeff and me.

There were some positives and negatives about Jeff being so far away at Montbretia. A big plus was that I got a lot of exercise going up and down SkyTrain stairs, getting off and on buses, waiting for buses, and walking to and from his residence.

Being far apart gave us both respite from each other as well. He could engage in activities with others and he had some independence. When I arrived, we were tight together doing walks, sitting in his room, having naps. At times, I think he must have felt he was put in the position of having to entertain me. That was okay had I left after an hour, but because of the distance I stayed for a minimum of three hours, usually five, and always planned my time around lunch so I could assist him with eating.

He was getting four or five days a week of foot peddling, which certainly helped with standing exercises, which we did every visit as well.

The staff had their routine with Jeff, and we tried to work around the days I was there. I took Jeff outside at every opportunity even just to wheel him a couple of blocks to the marketplace. No doubt pushing him in his heavy wheelchair gave me even more exercise.

This autumn was a busy time with him as he required help dressing into his outerwear, heavy coat and warm pants. It was remarkable to see the transformation when we went outside—a look of such happiness and lots of smiles, especially when I produced a fresh pear or apple.

Jeff no longer communicated much—it was sporadic and at times a word or two—but he seemed to comprehend what I was saying if I spoke slowly and used lots of gestures.

AUTUMN 2015

I'm so tired today. Suddenly she's here. Lunch comes but I can feel my bum starting to rumble and I tell her, "I have to go right now."

She takes me to my room and tries to get them to come change me, but they are busy feeding people who need help. Time is going by and she gets more and more upset and she gets their attention and we make it in time to the toilet.

It's good to be on the toilet and not mess the wheelchair as that often means a shower. They are all very happy with me and that I was able to go on the toilet.

I finish my lunch. I know she was crying but now all is okay. I have an ice cream but keep nodding off in my chair. She tells me we are going to lie down and I start clapping and helping to take my clothes off.

When I wake up the first thing that catches my eye is the note left for me on my bulletin board. Helen is reading and comes over and I point to the note. She looks happy.

"What does it say?" she asks.

I read it out loud—I surprised myself that I could read it—and she says that's her name. I smile and say yes. I am happy I can still read.

The note is always there in the mornings when I wake up and I read it every day. It says, "Hi Jeff, I love you." She sends hugs and kisses and it says, "See you soon!"

Looks like I'm losing teeth. I lost three upper teeth on the right side. Not sure how it happened but they aren't there anymore, just stumps. I've noticed blood on my pillow.

A joy to see my wife all the time. She had a Starbucks coffee and we shared an orange.

Sometimes I find it hard to tell what is food and what is paper.

Hot dogs for lunch today but she brought yogurt which we mixed with melon. After lunch a great spin around in the beautiful sunshine. Oh, a fresh pear, just perfectly ripe.

Our usual nap together, then an ice cream!

MID-NOVEMBER

I'm wearing a Remembrance Day poppy and so is Helen.

I see people are leaving and new people are arriving.

I haven't seen the lady who barks at the lunch table for a while and another guy I thought I knew.

We've got new people here so they've gone somewhere.

Rosie was after the new guy that just arrived but she still is after me.

She wheeled up to my wife and hit my wife on the arm the other day and yelled at her again. She has been doing that a lot and staff quickly move her away from us. It looks like Rosie doesn't want her to be with me, but she gets wheeled away by staff.

The activities director has a small rubber rugby ball that we toss around the group.

There is this wall siding along the door to my room and I was busy trying to get behind it and it all came off. I got black pitch all over my hands and legs as I had my shorts on, and it took so long to get it cleaned off—staff were not happy—and there is still some residue.

Helen comes often. I always feel good when she's next to me and wish I could go with her and be with her for always. I don't think I have a sickness but I can't go in a car with her now because of the wheelchair.

The guy came to fix the wall I tore apart and he said to me, "I want to meet your wife to tell her how strong you are." We were laughing together. I thought I was repairing something but looks like all I did was make a mess so it's hands off now to these sidings.

MONTBRETIA. DECEMBER 2015

Our wedding anniversary was coming up on December 4. I invited two of Jeff's close friends, Wayne and Mike, to join us for a lunch of shrimp, salad and a beer or two. I got Jeff dressed in a rugby jersey and he looked just great.

When they arrived, they greeted each other and I think he knew them. Jeff was smiling and seemed happy. We sat around a table but then he changed. He would not look at any of us and was bowing his head as he was eating. He didn't say anything and they could see he was confused and getting agitated. Before he even finished eating, he started rocking his chair, which is a sure sign he wants to leave. We were just outside his room, so I took him there. He rushed to take his clothes off, I helped him into bed, and he immediately fell asleep.

I was concerned, so I kept the door open. We continued with our lunch and concluded that hanging out with these two good friends was too much for him to absorb. We could see his distress. Perhaps he had forgotten them. Or maybe it really boggled his mind to see them standing and walking while he was in his chair.

Some visits worked; others didn't. This disease was unpredictable, and the reaction to visits and situations varied with everyone. I saw it constantly. One day a resident would be so uplifted, but the next time they had a visitor they were so confused and unsure.

Jeff bounced back from that visit and was amazingly alert the next few days. He was talkative and so happy.

"Your hair looks scruffy," he said. "You're a beastie but I love you."

Actual sentences!

As we sat by the window one day, he suddenly shouted "Champagne!" out of the blue. Where did it all come from? From a high to a low—changes were so unexpected.

We had a lot of time outside. He was in his element!

As the holidays approached, I found myself breaking into tears easily. We would be apart again. I kept trying to figure out how I could have him with me, but he needed twenty-four-hour care. That meant a battery of nurses, a house with ceiling hoists, wheelchair accessibility—it was just so expensive.

One of the best Christmases we spent together was in London. We were still in that tiny apartment with the miniscule kitchen, but it didn't stop me from roasting a chicken and preparing a feast for us. As the chicken was cooking we walked to St. Paul's Cathedral—only six blocks away—and listened to a service and sermon. It was just so beautiful and peaceful. We just couldn't believe we were so fortunate to be living this London dream on a Christmas Day.

When we were cuddling, he must have seen the wistful expression on my face.

"Can I come with you?" he said.

I just burst into tears. His voice kept haunting me with those words and the tears wouldn't stop. I knew it was this overwhelming grief and he was a lot to handle, but I kept thinking there must be something more I could do. I noticed the changes in his cognitive abilities, but I didn't want to see them. It was so difficult to carry on a lot of the time. I tried to convince myself I was okay, but I wasn't.

So I channeled my fear into hope for Jeff to walk again. It was just great that he was standing, peddling and having physiotherapy twice a week, but we had to figure out a way he could actually walk again. I was shown some photos of a new walker on the market called the Ultimate Walker, and we looked into renting it to see if that would help him. It was a positive idea, but I didn't want to get my hopes up; it had been so long since he had walked, and it might be an entirely inappropriate walker for him.

DECEMBER 2015

It's wonderful to tell the time again!

Helen brought me a special gift! Since our anniversary I now have this great big wooden clock on my wall. She also put up a series of huge blow-ups of favourite underwater photos which trigger events and places from the past. I love looking at them.

She tells me stories about the pictures, especially the ones about the elephant seal.

She also put up some great photos of me and my mum. She's the one I took after. She was a runner when she was a young girl and suffered like I do with sore knees.

Dad was a bookie, among other enterprises, and he loved the greyhounds. He died young in his early seventies.

My sister looks like Dad and she has had serious heart ailments for years. I think my sister and her husband must be dead as I never see them or hear from them. Could it also be said of my three children? I never hear from them either.

Helen tells me Christmas is soon and we'll have turkey together!

I have lots of problems with constipation and yesterday they had to do an enema. A special doctor came to see me and rubbed my stomach and I heard him say they will try to change the medication mix for my bowels.

How wonderful it would be to walk again. She put me on the bike foot peddler and I did ten minutes but only one stand as I'm very tired. She said I should have a little nap and then we'll go outside to wheel around!

CHRISTMAS 2015

It's Christmas Day! Everybody is wishing me a Merry Christmas!

Helen told me she's coming to share lunch and dinner with me.

She's arrived decked out in a colourful brooch and she brought a scarf for me!

They put one of those things up my bum and no sooner did we move my chair to the sun than I had to have a BM but I can't tell her or anyone in advance that it's about to happen. It now just happens. The staff are celebrating and I have interrupted them at a bad time. But they are so nice to me always.

Lunch was really good.

Now we're going to go downstairs and outside in the sun. We do a stand first as she wants to check something and, oh no, not another BM. I hear they gave me suppositories.

At last we are heading downstairs and outside to catch some sun and fresh air.

She brought apple pie and blackberries with ice cream for afternoon tea—my favourite treat for dessert!
I watched her decorate the table in the corner by the window. She tells me we are going to have the most delicious dinner with little bottles of bubbly! She has even brought some home stuffing she made like her mom used to make.

Chapter 8

JANUARY 2016

A new year started! Jeff and I had kept him peddling to strengthen his legs and hips, and we did standing exercises every visit. He was always anxious to stand up, and it was up to him how long he stayed standing. The wheelchair was always pushed close to the railings, so if he stumbled it was right there to catch him.

We were leading up to Jeff trying the Ultimate Walker, which looked like a big, square, aluminum box with a seat. It was quite roomy. This walker had tiny wheels but also slid along the floor as you walked and propelled yourself forward. It had a loose adjustable strap that went between the legs, and there was a bar opening that snapped closed for safety. It was fairly lightweight and there was a seat as well. Unlike any walker I had ever seen! I looked forward to seeing Jeff walking in it, and I believed it could happen soon! So we were making a plan for bringing it in and giving it a trial. If we succeeded, others would be able to try it as well.

Because Jeff hadn't walked since before he broke his femur the previous February, it was going to be a relearning process. Many people with dementia were not capable of walking after an operation and usually didn't recover and start again. Everyone's journey was fraught with their own issues, fitness, medication, and what stage they were relative to their decline.

No one really knew whether someone had Alzheimer's, Lewy body dementia or other forms of dementia until a brain autopsy was performed, so it was a family decision to push for physiotherapy for their loved ones. I often had this discussion with Jeff's physiotherapist, and it seemed to be up to the family how much effort they wanted to put in.

After hip or leg surgery, some patients can't walk again; others can. If someone was declining rapidly, we would want them to be comfortable and not force them to walk. But Jeff wanted to walk. He was determined to stand and peddle and follow the regime of fitness he had all his life. It was not stopping him now, so we were going to give it a shot. Walk or no walk.

Would he just stand there like before, frozen, or would he move?

Our care plan was for me to assist the physiotherapist, Oliver, twice a week. If it works well, we could have the walker available to us on the weekends, but I would have to take Jeff on my own. These were good, positive plans for the new year!

The flu season was in full swing, but Jeff's place seemed to contain the outbreak. We wore masks and were cautious when we visited. Only family were allowed for a while. Jeff had a slight fever one day in January and didn't look at all well. I spent the weekend with him and helped him eat and nap. He recovered but needed a lot of rest.

Trouble with staff started one weekend. One of the residents, a querulous woman who couldn't speak English mistakenly walked into Jeff's room while we were sitting outside of his room having tea. I chased after her and as I got close to her—she was near his bed—she slapped me hard across the face, almost knocking me over. I didn't see it coming and never engaged with this woman so it was quite shocking. Two staff came running as she was shouting. These two staff immediately said to me, "What did you do? You should have known not to go near her." Why would I have known not to go near her? No one ever mentioned anything about it. She always sat by herself, didn't speak to anyone, so I hadn't a clue about her level of fitness and cognitive function.

Staff handled it badly and caused a scene in front of Jeff. We exchanged words, and both Jeff and I were quite upset. The station head nurse got involved, but the strange thing was that no one asked how I was. I was fine. One of the two nurses even said in an unfriendly and loud voice, "Just go home." She had daggers for eyes. I was so upset. No way was I going home! I was there to be with Jeff.

Everyone can have their differences, and I suppose we couldn't expect everything to run smoothly all the time, but I thought it wise to write the manager. She said she was always there for me to discuss any problems I had with staff or with Jeff. After another incident the next afternoon with the same three staff, I asked for a meeting with her. Staff were trying to do their reports instead of cleaning up his room, which was such a mess. The smell was unreal; even the pillowcase and duvet were covered in scraps of poop. The manager told them to forget about the reports and clean up the mess—like right now. Chastising them in front of us and a few others who were around didn't help our relationship.

Things came out in the open about a number of issues—it was too complicated to write about at length, nor do I want to go through it all again. She explained how they follow each resident's "care plan" and that when family and visitors are around it could interrupt or interfere with that plan. It made a lot of sense. We went over the care plan, and I was only too willing to learn how to make it work for all of us. I also concluded that since most residents have few or no visitors that some of the staff resented my presence every other day. I "saw" things I shouldn't have and they know it. I had broken up fights and alerted them to residents wandering into rooms that weren't theirs.

I would be meeting with Jeff's physiotherapist soon, so I hoped the issues would be resolved. One of the "trio" had to apologize to me for her unprofessional behaviour in front of Jeff. That likely didn't sit well with her, but the truth was she lost her temper and lashed out at me with unkind words. I didn't want to start worrying about what went on when I wasn't around. Did I really want to know? Obviously, it was so important for me to have confidence in the staff and trust that Jeff was being well cared for.

There was no doubt that my constant presence affected them in positive and negative ways. On the positive side, I entertained Jeff, took him outside, fed him lunch, helped the physiotherapist and made sure Jeff had his exercise. On the negative side, I supposedly interrupted their routine. I was very aware they didn't like to be seen in a bad light, which happened often. Food would often get cold sitting in front of a resident who needed assistance to eat and no one heated it up. Many people from "the outside" will notice when residents reek of poop, but it seemed to take a long time to change them.

MID-FEBRUARY

Helen tells me I am going to try walking with an Ultimate Walker. She's promised I would walk and it's going to happen if I can make it happen. It's up to me now.

It's been a long time since I walked unaided. I'm anxious to try.

It's a big white contraption with a seat but does not have big wheels. You just rest your arms on each side and start walking and it slides along the floor. I am amazed at how it will work as it's so unlike any other walker I've seen.

Helen arrived with a Starbucks to share but she's busy getting me into shorts as these pants won't hold together in the back and that won't do for walking.

Helen and Oliver, my physio guy, go through the procedure of transferring me from my wheelchair. Then they close the gate and I'M WALKING!

What freedom! What a great feeling! I am so happy! I don't want to sit down in the seat. I just love walking again. But after three trips up and down the hallway, I'm tired and we know it's time to get back in the wheelchair.

Helen is taking pictures. I'm so happy. Helen is so happy! People are clapping! Everyone is watching! I can't stop smiling.

I hope it doesn't cost anything to buy it. Helen told me it might be free.

Lunch is noodles and chicken with a custard dessert. Then we get my shoes on and we're going outside because it's so sunny and warm. I think I'm helping by holding the doors open but Helen keeps trying to pry my fingers off the elevator door so it seems all in vain.

It's back to my room for a nap and cuddles until afternoon tea and sandwiches!

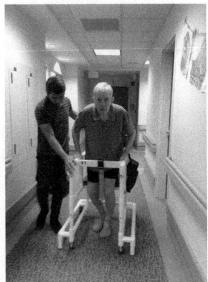

WALKING

I was so hoping this Ultimate Walker would work out for Jeff. There were so many questions about safety all the time. The biggest concern was transferring him from his wheelchair to the UW. We needed two people for that and staff seemed short. In the meantime, Oliver was going to help me every Tuesday and Thursday.

What a fantastic turnaround that Jeff could walk again! We had to give it a go and hoped he could do it.

He certainly didn't disappoint himself, Oliver and me! We were all just over the moon at his enthusiasm and determination to walk again!

Oliver and Jeff seemed to like each other and they always joked and laughed together. If we wanted Jeff to get up from taking a break, all we had to say was, "Let's go to your room!" Jeff would be up like a shot and almost trot to his bed and the comfort he felt. Oliver and I tried hard to increase the revolutions, but sometimes his knees made it so hard to keep going.

On Saturdays and Sundays, I got the UW out of the storage room. Jeff and I would do the transfer in his room, but staff were not allowed to assist. Jeff behaved most of the time. He listened to me and didn't try any tricks like propelling himself from the bed.

UPLIFTING SPRING

Poppet tells me my birthday is coming up soon.

I don't say anything as I'm not sure how to say things much anymore. I can get what she's saying and "hear" lots but it goes in my head and then unexpectedly it will pop forward and startle me.

Walking in my new cage is wonderful. They call it the Ultimate Walker. I rub my hands together in anticipation when I see Helen roll it my way for the transfer. It's not as hard now as I've been doing it every week, but there is still pain in my knees and that's to be expected.

Helen rubs my knees with a cream called antiphlogistine after our walks. I sit still as I like the heat, the attention and the smell.

After walking I just want to close my eyes and sleep for hours but she's here and always inventing new things to do. I told her today, "You're a pest. How about some quiet time, lady? You try walking with knees that hurt and pants that won't stay up!" I think I said all that to her. Or did I only think it?

Walking is strange—sometimes I can only tippy-toe walk; sometimes I criss-cross my feet and they don't want to go where they should; sometimes I want to just sit there and cross my knees. When they say I have to get going, I do, and as soon as I stand, it's magic to walk. Don't let anyone tell you differently. Pain or not!

MY BIRTHDAY. APRIL 2016

Oh, the sun is shining into my room. The nurses come in and shout, "Happy Birthday Jeff!" I'm smiling and they ask me all kinds of questions about how I feel today. They ask me if I would like to put on anything special but I leave that up to them.

They take extra care with my hair. I'm hoping when Helen comes I can look in the mirror with her. We are celebrating my birthday—no doubt about that as all the staff have now joined in with the dynamo exercise leader to sing during our break before lunch.

Helen arrives for lunch with lots of treats, butter tarts, chocolate!

We have cake, listen to live music and there's lots of noise but Helen will let me escape to the room whenever we want to. At one point a lead singer comes over to me and all the residents join in with his Happy Birthday song! Oh, I'm off to the room and peace and quiet!

I ask Helen, "Who are all these people?"

She tells me we're in a hotel where lots of people come and go. She tells me I'm seventy-six years old today. I find that hard to believe.

She also says I'm the second youngest out of twenty people! That I can believe, as there are some pretty old people here—I hear ages of ninety-two to ninety-eight!

After the noise and the band packs up, we go outside and sit in the sun as it's still shining.

SUMMER 2016

Jeff and I went for long wheelchair spins, and we often stopped at Starbucks to get him a cold coffee with whipped cream. As we strolled in that direction, I would tell him where we were going and his eyes would light up at the mention of a frothy drink! That was his favourite treat from there and guaranteed to make him happy. He would lean back sipping it through the straw!

He wasn't that good in the Red Cross wheelchair loan but tried to keep his feet on the foot rests. He had certainly changed; little things were happening that weren't there before. I was so startled when he threw a cup of tea on the floor. Another time, he started eating a paper napkin. He was subtly declining through the stages.

He used to say my name often, but hardly at all by that time. At times I thought he had forgotten who I was, but I could have been imagining it. I had my name printed on a card which I then wore around my neck when I arrived. He would examine it like he hadn't seen it before and would say my name out loud. Staff told me they had noticed that he would reach for their identification card, which was hung around their neck, and Jeff would say their name out loud.

His long-term memory showed up at the oddest times. A casual shift nurse named Hilda was looking after him one day. He turned her ID card over and read her name: "Hilda." I saw a sparkle in his eyes and he said, "My mum." Hilda really was his Mum's name! That was the nature of the disease. Watching his brain slowly die was agonizing, but then these wonderful, joyful surprises would suddenly pop out and balance it all.

Tears kept coming to my eyes while I watched him sleep, but then no one said this journey would be easy for either of us. I had my super memories of our wonderful years together, and I so often wondered what was flashing through his mind. Looking at the photo albums together sometimes made me cry, and I wanted to hide them all so I wouldn't be reminded of the changes. It was a huge tug on my heart, which oftentimes felt like a physical pain.

Shortly after we met in 1990, an opportunity to go on a month-long tour of New Zealand and Australia with the Twilighter Rugby Club presented itself. We would be billeted by hosts of those two countries. It was my first exposure to "immersion" rugby—games were played every couple of days in different venues. Unfortunately, Jeff, who was the number 2 (hooker), was injured during the second game so he was sidelined. It didn't stop us from attending all the games and cheering the Canadian team on to victories.

It was such a long distance trip that we made arrangements to stay an extra two weeks in Brisbane and meet up with a mate Jeff hadn't seen since he was in his twenties. They had travelled together after his two-year stint in Rhodesia. That first encounter for Frank and Jeff was extraordinary to watch (photo from 29 years ago)! His wife, Janet, and I hit it off and we made plans to spend time together. We rented a condo on Brisbane Beach in Surfers Paradise and went on an exploratory tour with our friends; it was an amazing couple of weeks. We looked at these photos many times, and I told Jeff so many stories of that trip.

Jeff and I then went diving in Fiji for ten days. We chartered a forty-foot ketch for five days in the Mamanuca

Islands. The captain had solar panels on his boat railings, so it was tough for me to get kitted up in the water—much to the hilarity of Jeff and the captain! There was some unforgettable diving and a BBQ on board every night of—what else?—lamb! Jeff was a leader by nature and made new divers like me very much at ease. He had such patience and gave me the confidence to trust myself and learn by following his lead.

I had amazing memories to fall back on, and I never stopped telling him these stories. He listened with what looked like such concentration at first but could only absorb so much. Then he would revert to his new world of childish antics and amusements like gathering up the duvet and hiding under it.

"You can't see me!" he would say with a childish laugh.

It always made me laugh.

Accepting these changes and laughing with him worked so well for us. I could have easily said, "Stop that," to make him act his age, but flowing along with him in his reverie was a positive thing for us.

He was now a sweet child who was as strong as a bull. He was a different Jeff. Most of the old Jeff was somewhere else, but every once in a while he would say stuff from the past. We used to enjoy folding blankets together, and he continued it so often in the home that staff often asked, "Why do you think he is folding the blankets all the time?"

Unlike many residents with dementia, Jeff continued to have a happy, friendly personality. He could easily have progressed to a stage of kicking, lashing out, shouting and cursing like so many residents did. I encountered some aggressive women there, and it really was difficult to believe a ninety-four year old would grab me as I went by and hurt my arm. She could not have weighed more than sixty pounds! We avoided the obvious fighters, but I had seen Jeff holding hands on occasion with this little lightweight and talking to her! They were communicating, and it would have been interesting to know what passed between their brains.

NO MORE ELEVATOR CLASHES. LATE SUMMER

The four units in Montbretia finally got switched around. The unit Jeff was in would be transferred to downstairs—oh, happy day—so we wouldn't have to take the elevator anymore! I did not mention this move to Jeff until the day it happened. But he did ask me, "Why are all the beds in the hallways?" Suddenly he was making sentences out of the blue. I told him we were moving to another floor and room and that was why we had packed all his clothes and possessions.

He had just been sitting there watching all the activity like the rest of the residents. It surely did take lots of organizing to get this move completed, but it finally happened! What an effort by everyone! I noticed some of the residents were confused and they got agitated as they couldn't find their rooms but those in wheelchairs seem more settled.

The move for Jeff seemed like a positive one. I had a preview of the area and certainly liked it better than where he was before. It was double the size when taking into account the outside patio with two entrances, the common room and the kitchen. I organized his room and was glad that it was fairly central, although he didn't get one of the large corner rooms. After we moved him, he told me, "I'm happy." He said, "Stay put," when I was sitting on his bed while he covered me with his duvet and tucking me in. It was quite amazing and surprising to hear him speaking a lot—albeit in disjointed and incomplete sentences.

I wheeled him by a group watching TV, and he said in a loud voice, "Hello everybody!" So many answered. All the staff were laughing with him as he kept saying "Hello, how are you?" We headed to the patio, so he waved and said, "See you later." He was repeating what I often said as I left him for the day.

I took him outside to a superb patio twice on the day of the move for short visits to get him used to it. He listened to Leonard Cohen through his earphones for a good hour.

LATE SUMMER 2016

I've been here for a whole year now and have made some friends. I see Helen four or five days a week and we get outside and share lots of treats.

There was a big move recently from upstairs to downstairs so no more elevators to take. I see a beautiful patio here. We can do standing exercises out there in the sunshine.

No one comes out there except Helen and me. They hang out in front of the TV watching movies and cartoons. They have no idea how lovely and fresh it is out on the patio. There aren't many visitors so that could be the reason they don't go outside.

A few fighters here—three men who want to argue or push and shove. I keep away from them as I think I still could give as good as I would get! So many girls and women look familiar and I know I've seen most of them.

Rosie always comes to see me and touches my arm but she's nervous and angry when Helen comes to be with me. She watches us with a scowl.

My favourite is the tiny girl with the biggest smile who does balloon toss. I like playing just with her though and I get impatient that I can't have her to myself, just her and me playing with the big balloon. So I try to hold on to the balloon and often I've pinched the balloon too hard which really makes me unpopular as it just disappears—no balloon anymore!

Helen has nailed up lots of underwater photos she took during our dives—some cheeky ones of sea lions. We nicknamed one "Frenchie" as he reminded us of a good friend who is a cyclist and rugby player from France. The sea lion had that haughty look like Frenchie had. I really like this new room!

I can picture our diving all over the world when I see the underwater photos. I often say, "Look at that one," and Helen tells me the story of the photo and we chat about our time underwater and what kind of fish we saw. I don't say much but I hear her. Hard to beat skiing, rugby and scuba. Life was busy then. It's different now.

Helen talked about the years we spent in Switzerland. I remember working on the ski lifts there when I was a teenager. She told me many times about our trip to work in Europe.

LIVING IN THE SWISS MOUNTAINS

It was so marvellous to live high up in the mountains. When we didn't have contracts, we spent the days hiking and always went by this farmer's yard that had chickens and roosters running around. She always had freshly laid eggs. There were few stores in the valley, so we would walk to these large buildings where they made cheese. They'd give us a sample from a few huge wheels and then we'd decide which to buy. We could purchase fresh yogurt from these cheese shops as well.

Jeff was a member of a Club Med in Leysin in 1957. Jeff looked up one of the members and we met up for a tremendous reunion. He made us an amazing raclette dinner with the local cheese. We were eating raclette way before it had become a popular dish in Canada. He also pointed me in the direction of a local library so there was never a lack of material to read.

Jeff saw two other friends from his teen years sitting at an outside bistro as we were walking through the town one day. The three of them couldn't believe they were all together again. A few nights later, we joined them for

Swiss fondue at their home. One never moved from Leysin and was engaged in snowboarding competitions.

MY ROOM

Helen brought an original watercolour of a Steller Jay to hang in my room. We bought it from a rugby pal who is a wildlife artist and displayed his art in Stanley Park! I love looking at it.

One of the movers who is also a maintenance guy gave Helen a great lounge chair for the room.

When I started walking, we tried with my shoes on, but I couldn't move my feet properly, so I now walk in my socks. Some days I can walk really quickly. Oliver and my wife were saying I was trotting or canting, like a little run. First time I'd done that. She told me the residence bought the walker for all the residents to use.

Helen taught me to "turn" so I can get out of my chair and into the walker on the weekends when we have nobody to help. She has to show me many times as sometimes I forget the plan.

For safety reasons no one is allowed to help us with the transfer. I wonder why? Do they expect us to fall? They say it's "not without risk" but so far so good. We wouldn't achieve some goals without risks—scuba, skiing, rugby—and I'm lucky we are both strong and get along so well.

We often go to the main common room in the lobby with the walker but can't go on the patio as it's concrete and there are no proper wheels on this walker.

But we get around, see a lot and stop to have a yogurt drink. We visit the gift shop and talk about all the antique items for sale. We go by the hairdresser shop where I get my haircut.

In the afternoons I go out on the patio and there's some beautiful trees and lots of birds that come to visit. There is an overhang in case it rains so there is nothing to stop us from going out there anytime.

When Helen isn't around, the dynamo—I call her "Baby" as she's so tiny—gets us all organized outside for tea and cakes in the afternoon. We often have our headphones on and listen to music.

FALL INTO WINTER 2016

Jeff continued to be enthusiastic about walking, and he never turned down the opportunity, but Oliver and I knew he could no longer walk on his own. He was always unsteady and needed the rails on either side of him to balance his weight. Because this walker didn't have big wheels, it actually was only balanced so long as the person walking was not aggressive or contrary. Jeff tended to be agreeable and treated walking like a special occasion every time.

We continued to be very close and shared comfort and laughter. I missed him so much all the time we were apart, and that was why I continued to travel on the buses to see him sometimes six days a week if there was a provincial holiday on the Monday.

My personal routine was taking two days to myself at my apartment—Wednesday and Friday—and sometimes on Monday. I called them "Helen Days" and devoted my time to chores, groceries, relaxing and re-energizing. I seldom stayed with Jeff for his evening meal. I usually headed for my return buses by 3:30 or 4:00, but it wasn't written in stone.

The staff all knew my schedule, which I had set out on a calendar in the room, and we tried not to clash.

OUR WEDDING ANNIVERSARY. DECEMBER 4

She tells me it's our wedding anniversary today! She brought a special treat from her bakery—butter tarts and a fizzy drink.

She tried to tell me stuff about our wedding day and I didn't have a memory but then she got out a computer for me to look at the photos of our wedding, and then I knew some people. Only some of them. But she filled me in. I've forgotten who I knew. We were all laughing and happy in the pictures!

We got outside in the garden but it was chilly so we only stayed for a short time. We had a cuddle and I had my nap with her next to me. I seemed to be very tired and needed a lot of sleep today.

When I woke up she was reading by the window. She immediately came over and snuggled in beside me.

Baby came and brought me earphones and I listened to my favourite Leonard Cohen tape. My wife was leaving soon as the weather was turning bad and she said the traffic would be quite backed up if it snowed.

THE DAY AFTER

I spent the following evening going through my photo album at home as our wedding was such a memorable, beautiful day! The Inukshuk Statue just off Beach Avenue was such a fabulous venue for a wedding. Despite the blustery weather, a canopy was set up. It's hard to find a photo of anyone NOT smiling! We walked back to our apartment, and the first song we heard was "Mrs. Robinson" by Simon and Garfunkel. Jeff and I started the dancing on this day of such happiness and love!

Jeff had coached rugby students at one of the schools, and both teachers from that school were in attendance as were old friends who used to live in the building on Beach Avenue. One of them wore a kilt! There was only about twenty people, but the apartment filled up quickly; it looked like fifty people! My niece, Debra Ann (who helped me move into my condo in Vancouver), was my best lady, and she came from Ottawa. Best friends of Jeff's from England arrived as a surprise as well! My father had given my mother a beautiful rhinestone necklace and earrings for their wedding in the 1930s, and that's what I wore in their memory. It was a day I'll never forget.

Fragile was the word to describe me the day following our anniversary. Special celebratory days clearly showed how life had changed and how we weren't on the same wavelength. I frequently burst into tears.

It was also a terrible place to be for these residents. They were so helpless, like a child, fighting against unknowns, not knowing where you are, who you are or what you are anymore. As bad as it might seem, they were well cared for by efficient staff and medical personnel.

Thankfully, I continued to meet my psychiatrist once a month. She helped me talk aloud about my fear, insecurities and heartache that never seemed to let up. I tried to stop beating myself up about the guilt of his involuntary admission. That seemed to be the commonality among my friends whose husbands were in care residence: trying to shift some unwarranted blame off of ourselves.

This was the worst thing that had happened in my life, and being exposed to death up close was difficult. I spent a lot of time in Jeff's residences. I met some wonderful residents, we became friendly and then they passed away. It was so difficult and heartbreaking to be in that atmosphere for long periods of time; it would take its toll on anyone.

Would it have been different if we were rich and could keep him at home to be cared for by a bevy of nurses and carers? It remained a question with so many pros and cons that I never could come up with a satisfactory answer. I would have liked to take him home and away from all those residents and staff. The finish line was up ahead, but I didn't know which of us would cross it first. I was concerned that the strength, courage and bravery might run out for me. I figured my brain was functioning as normally as it ever did, but it couldn't have been. Jeff had gone to his other world, and progression in that world was obvious and we had no solution which would alter it.

We all had our burdens to bear and we needed to seek help and support where we could get it. I continued to try my best, never give up and to make the best of what was left of our life together. The top priority was comforting him in any way I possibly could.

The old cliche, "No one ever said life would be easy," often came to mind. It was not. In fact, it was super stressful. We always had choices. We learned as the days went by to be more compassionate, forgiving and as helpful as we could be to others having witnessed what dementia does to someone's brain.

Happiness never just happened, I had come to realize, you had to fight for it and work hard at keeping it once you got it. My love for Jeff sustained me through these tough years, but it was hard to imagine and cope with him leaving. I didn't know how I would face that, but maybe I wouldn't; maybe I would be gone before him. Ah, to be able to look in a crystal ball and see the future.

Who knows anything really in the moment.

MID-DECEMBER

It's snowing. I'm watching at the window. People are slipping and sliding and dressed in parkas and big boots.

The yellow bus comes often to pick up and drop off. Watching all the buses that go by. I'm cozy and warm.

Helen just arrived all bundled up! I am so happy to see her and wave madly in case she misses seeing me. I kept looking and looking.

We get all set for a walk in the big walker and we are both overjoyed to be able to do this together. Afterwards, the treat is fruit cake and coffee.

Then my shoes, hat and mitts appear and I know we're going out! The sun is shining. People help me get into my warm coat! We head for this sunny patio with no wind and I feel so happy and tell her she is beautiful.

I must have nodded off in the sun. She was sitting on my wheelchair armrest with her arm around me, my head on her shoulder and chest. I know she loves me. She always tells me so.

She opened up a whole new career for me by teaching me how to read her stenographic notes. It took about a year to get in the groove of transcribing but it worked for us so well. I learned so much in grammar school in England and was able to answer so many questions she would have relating to the cases we contracted. For instance, if we had a case with a plumbing expert, tiler or carpenter, I could help her understand the terminology. And so it went with all types of cases.

I'm awake now and we're heading back inside. We sit by the fireplace and drink tea. Music is playing, the lovely blonde girl playing the piano.

Hot soup is next. She shares little bowls she brought with pears and even a chicken sandwich with mustard.

I'm getting so sleepy. She knows. We head for my room. I'm in bed so fast with heavy eyelids.

I startle awake. I'm alone. No, she is sitting and reading. She slides in beside me and she whispers nice stuff. It's warm and she is close. I know I will nod off again.

CHRISTMAS 2016

Time was really flying by. It seemed just a little while ago it was Christmas 2015. The routine was set and the plan was followed with Jeff getting lots of fresh air and being wheeled outside if the streets were clear.

We had a beautiful December with lots of sunshine and fresh snow. We did our walks twice a week with Oliver, and Jeff continued being enthusiastic and determined to walk. He participated with gusto in the exercises directed by Y, and I could tell he enjoyed having his earphones on as often as they were presented to him. Mostly, he was always happy to walk. Others were sporadically using the walker as well.

I brought him Christmas presents and told him I bought gifts for me with his money. I think he understood. I planned to decorate a table for Christmas Day lunch and dinner. Y decorated the common areas with Jeff watching closely. I decorated Jeff's door and his room with cheery Christmas items. I spent lots of time with him over the holiday season as the casual staff are less familiar to him. We went outside as much as we could.

I always was a believer in fresh air, and the more we got outside, the better we all would feel. It was sad, though, as many residents didn't get out at all. Some were too fragile and got cold too easily even if they were bundled up. I could perceive their feelings of envy that we were going out and they weren't.

The travelling at this time of year was never easy with buses and trains. I sometimes had to wait half an hour for a bus, so it was tiring. I could do without some of those days, but with any snow in Vancouver traffic got snarled and schedules were off.

I always brought lots of treats, lots to read and photo albums that Jeff looked through with me. I mentioned the background stories and quizzed him about who was who. He couldn't really speak, so he didn't say too much. I was not sure if he really recognized the people he saw in the photos with him.

We often got some old rugby games on my iPad. He loved watching those and definitely enjoyed this new experience with moving his finger on the iPad. We always got live soccer games on the big screen TV on Saturdays, and we would sit together watching them. He was attentive and always cheered out loud when a goal was scored.

The staff were mostly kind to me and gave me a soup now and then if they had extra. Generally, I brought my food or picked up something on the way. I never came empty-handed, and Jeff knew my satchel had goodies. Upon arrival, following big hugs and kisses, he always reached out for my scarf and looked in my bag, spreading things out on the table or bed. I always encouraged him to do so. He seemed to know there were surprises for him. Once he got a hold of my satchel, there was no getting it away from him!

I tried to make arrangements to stay overnight during the Christmas season but that was not approved as it could cause a disruption if he was not used to me in the room at night and woke up suddenly. I understood that perfectly. He had become used to the routine and this would have confused him. I just had to enjoy the chilly walks, the exercise and hopefully some nice snowfalls without traffic backlog. Jeff liked to rub my cold, rosy cheeks, and he often said, "Oh, you are so cold. Let me warm you." We always smiled, hugged and comforted each other.

Chapter 9

NEW YEAR'S DAY 2017

Everyone is wishing me Happy New Year!

She came early and we walked together using the big walker. I was struggling a bit as I've got my own idea where I want to walk, but she's saying, "Don't be stubborn. Where do you want to go?" I point to the locked doors and we head for them. There's a huge, beautifully decorated Christmas tree in the lobby! All kinds of things on the tree and I feel so happy to see all the sparkle! I wanted to open the presents under the tree but she steered me away from there kind of quickly.

It's very busy. Lots of visitors, new faces. We chatted to people and everyone was so friendly to us!

We head back, grabbed our seat by the window watching buses slipping and sliding. She brought me freshly-baked butter tarts from her bakery. A whole one just for me!

I've got visitors—Mike my dive buddy and the Chocolate Lady (I call her that in private as I can't remember her name). Mike gave me a big hug and his wife held my hands. I feel so happy to see familiar faces. We've known each other for such a long time, way before I ever met my wife.

We chat and have tea and cakes! Fruit cake, Eccles cake and of course chocolate!

After an hour I'm tired and start nodding off, so they are ready to go. She's going with them which is good as she won't have to walk on the slippery streets.

"I will see you tomorrow," she says.

Staff tell me we will have roast beef, mashed potatoes and gravy for dinner. Can hardly wait, all my favourites!

MID-JANUARY 2017

Jeff had been alert and chatting more than usual. We were looking out the window drinking a chai latte and he said, clear as a bell, "It's dangerous out there. One wrong move ..." and then he snapped his fingers! For someone who hadn't said much for over two years, that was quite remarkable. His level of comprehension kept fluctuating.

Many people who get Alzheimer's slowly decline and don't come back to where they were a year before—they go in the opposite direction. Staff were quite surprised how much Jeff tried to talk around this time. One day, Jeff said, "You're doing a good job," to one of the staff members who was changing him and getting him into his chair. They had a good chuckle. Jeff was forever thanking them for their care.

Y made all the residents photo books pertaining to past activities in their lives. For Jeff, she made one devoted to rugby. I sent her a few photos of Jeff playing rugby and petting horses and she incorporated them in his book. When he came across a picture of himself, he shouted in a loud, clear voice, "That's me!" He was clapping and smiling. He was able to read some of the words as well. It was really remarkable and definitely not the norm.

He always joined in the activities and liked to excel at whatever game they were playing. I had given Y tapes that he liked—mostly Leonard Cohen and the Bee Gees—and she converted them to the disc players for his earphones.

I brought him treats from my bakery, and when he saw the two mincemeat pies, he did not hesitate. He was on them like a flash, gathering them close and making sure he got to eat them!

Those extra two days of walking on Saturdays and Sundays had kept him limber and enthusiastic to walk. Oliver could only be engaged for two days a week for fifteen minutes. I got permission to do walks with Jeff on the proviso that no assistance would be given to me and that I took full responsibility. It was lots to handle with a big guy like Jeff, but he understood what we were doing and cooperated with the routine.

No one was allowed to lift a finger—all about safety issues—but I differed on that score. It seemed safe to me. Many people, including his doctor and psychiatrist, said Jeff's walking was due to my encouragement. It was why Jeff was not like so many others who never stood or walked. I fought to get Jeff walking with Oliver, and this opportunity could have been available to others by bringing up the subject with their team.

It was obvious that the longer a person stayed in a wheelchair, the less mobile they became. If they didn't exercise their legs and bodies, they would be less able to as the years pass. That applies to whether someone has dementia or not. Oliver had always been impressed with Jeff's ability and determination. To encourage someone to stand holding on to the sides of the walker and then turn and sit down seemed a small risk by comparison to skiing, scuba diving or even driving a car with drunks on the road.

There was no team for walking, just me and Oliver, and everyone just looked on. Staff with trepidation—or could it be admiration?—while I did the transfers myself on the weekend. None of the staff had the time to watch Jeff use the foot peddler, so that only happened when I visited. The same for standing. It was easy to imagine his frustration being in a wheelchair all day. When I was there, I got him to stand by his bed after lunch, turn and lie down for a stretch and a nap if he wanted one.

Much as I liked this residence, it was short-staffed. Half of the residents required assistance with their meals one-on-one, but the food sat in front of them just out of reach while it slowly got cold. Another resident's wife and I tried to feed some of the residents, but it was frowned upon and not allowed. We were told it was not a safe practice to feed someone other than the person we were responsible for. We both appreciated that. This lady was eighty and came every day without fail to feed her husband, who was in his mid-nineties, lunch. Unfortunately, this resident never could stand or get out of his wheelchair. I had made friends with some of the residents over the years, but it was so tough when I would hear they had passed away in the night. Even though it was ongoing, it still remained difficult for the staff and they emphasized many times not to get too attached to the other residents.

It was a busy unit for the staff as almost all residents were incontinent. We tried to get Jeff on a toilet regime, but it didn't work. He got so constipated and the timing became unpredictable. He wasn't able to sit on a toilet seat without supervision and belts strapped on so he would not fall over or forward. He seemed to have lost his understanding of what to do on the toilet and would just fall asleep or try to break away. After an hour sitting there, often nothing had happened. Despite having dementia, I'm sure he knew to some degree that what was happening was beyond his control. A terribly tragic disease which affects hundreds of thousands of wives or husbands or moms and dads.

I read an article about a family who were convinced their father could walk again despite a number of complications. It was like he had forgotten how to walk, but his family encouraged him with standing exercises and said he should try to walk again. Their father did walk again. Never say never! That inspired me to be positive and have hope. Aren't we all trying to give someone we love some quality of life if we can? Small gestures, a coffee or chai latte brought to Jeff, resulted in clapping to have something different to drink. They don't forget others' kindness to them.

LATE WINTER

I've never had false teeth but I've had crowns and other things done to my teeth. I was losing a lot of my teeth at a rapid rate.

When Helen comes she wheels me over to the sink and I get to look at myself and my teeth.

She is trying to show me what to do—not to drink the water I put in my mouth but to save it for brushing. She bought me a battery-powered toothbrush and she tried it out after my mouth healed from the teeth disappearing.

I was sitting talking later and I handed her a tooth that broke off again. But we do the brushing together.

When they get me up in the morning they try to get me to brush my teeth, but they don't wheel me to the mirror and the sink like Helen does. She brushes her teeth and I follow her instructions and now I get it and spit it all out and it's a nice fresh feeling and taste in my mouth. She does the electric brush and I just let her do my teeth as it feels really good and I get how to rinse really well now.

We go for walks to the market and get a sweet frothy coffee. It's chilly but it's great to get outside. I can always see the mountains in the distance.

It's a walking day with her only today. I'm way bent over to the side in my chair. She encouraged me to walk and we did and I feel so much better now. I seem to be constipated a lot. She's been rubbing a new cream on my knees called Voltaren and it's really good. When she's not here others rub it on my knees.

I'm trying to eat with my spoon again. I hit them with my spoon when they try to feed me. I like to do it myself now.

LATE FEBRUARY

I have a new friend. I keep seeing him walking around and today he came over and talked to me.

He told me his name but I've forgotten it already. He's younger than me, looks like, and he's fitter than me, but then he can walk and I'm in a wheelchair. He's friendly. We sat by the window together and talked. But I can't tell you what about as it escaped me. Just stuff.

Helen arrived and found us together and he acted like he knew her. She has seen him around the place I think but doesn't know him. He was extra friendly to her. I got my chair closer to her.

They talked and then he went off with the very tiny deaf lady.

The deaf lady is another new friend who comes and holds my hand and gestures to me as she can't speak except to laugh and yell at people in her space, but she likes me, I can tell. She likes Helen and they get on really well.

Deaf lady walks with the young new guy every chance she gets. They do the circuit together all around the place. She used to walk with someone else before the young guy came on the scene but that person got very sick and was in hospital for a long time. He did come back but he left again and I haven't seen him since. He could be on another floor or moved to a different place.

I always talk to everyone and hope they will talk back.

Helen takes me on the patio rain or shine as she knows how much I like going out.

LATE FEBRUARY 2017

It was so good to see Jeff talking with a new resident, whom I'm calling "The Young Guy." This new resident was restless, young and seemed fit. He did circles around the residence, most often in the morning with the deaf lady. She communicated with many of us, and Jeff and I were friends with her.

The women residents seemed to get into fights more often than the men. The men sat mostly quietly, read, did puzzles, watched TV, but there had been some real screaming and punching matches with the ladies. I'm not sure how it all started.

The Young Guy's wife visited every day in the afternoon, so the four of us would chat. Well, at least two of us were chatting; the other two watched, listened and wondered.

At the end of every month, live musicians attended at Montbretia and played to celebrate each month's birthdays. There was a good guitarist that spring and we both enjoyed it. We had a special cake made in honour of those whose birthday it was. The carrot cake reminded me of our wedding cake. It could be he remembers the cake, not sure about the wedding! But no matter the cake, he always had two pieces and more if it was offered!

We were looking through photo albums again one day—that's a common occurrence—and it was such a joy to stop and reminisce about our beach wedding. Most of our guests were rugby players from Jeff's past, and many of the gifts were connected to games, clippings from the past that his best friend from Cheltenham brought.

I seemed to have a few fans at the home. A new lady wanted me to take her hand and walk with her. She was quite bent over but chatty. I took her hand and walked with her, and she told me she loved me. She was one of the few who could walk unaided, and she was in her late eighties.

A female resident turned seventy-five this month, and she asked me if she looked beautiful like I did. Just so sweet and warmed my heart so much. Her husband visited a couple of times every week and they seemed very close.

The danger with getting close to someone other than who you came to visit can result in residents counting on you. I had chats with staff about that subject. It can be even difficult for them not to get attached to a charming, engaging resident, but caution prevails as we don't want them to count on us and look forward to our visits when it's not them we are visiting.

Many don't have visitors. Could be their husband or wife had passed on, or it could be that they came in the evenings so I wouldn't know. Many hired companions to be with their family, but I could see that didn't work too well at times. The companions were paid. It was a job. They had no connection with the resident, at least not at the beginning. The resident rarely seemed interested in them. I think they wanted someone they knew. In this age of mobile phones, many companions and visitors were busy with their cell phones when the residents wanted their attention. Some of those relationships looked friendly and happy.

Could it be called "giving up" or "goodbye syndrome"? I had experienced that with Jeff's children and family as they didn't call or visit. His sister and her husband did visit at first but we hadn't seen them for quite a while.

If we could just imagine being a resident for a minute, wouldn't we want to go outside in the fresh air and see different surroundings? Forget the dementia, they knew there was an outside and other residents often watched us wheel out there. Maybe they were content watching TV or it was too chilly for them. Maybe they needed to lie down and let their brains catch up with the energy they were using trying to figure things out.

STARBUCKS VISIT

Today was a day for me and Helen to walk without Oliver. I was really motoring along and trying to wave to everybody! They were cheering! My knees were sore but not so sore that they stopped me from doing several revolutions around the halls. My wife looked so happy. We stopped and had a yogurt drink to give me even more energy.

It is such a beautiful day so we are going down to Starbucks for a coffee and to meet The Young Guy and his wife. He hasn't been walking as much and today he's in a wheelchair too so our wives got us these great frothy drinks as we sit outside talking at the mall. But it's chilly so we don't stay too long.

We get back and it's time for lunch and then for a nap—my favourite time to get warm and cozy. As they change me and she waits outside the door, my eyelids are drooping. I'll be asleep very shortly. She's coming in but I'm too tired to look anymore.

I wake up and she's sitting there reading a book. She crawls in beside me and we have a cuddle and hugs. She talks and she always has a lot to tell me. It's time to get up as Y is here with the earphones and I'm going to move by the window and watch her chatting with all of us. My wife says she will see me tomorrow and I'm already surrounded by my friends. Y is playing the flute and it's so peaceful and quiet. We are all attentive but some of us are lulled to sleep. I see some nodding off in their chairs.

MONTBRETIA SPRING DAYS

I had some truly magical spring days with Jeff! He was really anxious to use the big walker, and he amused us all by "running" and laughing and waving to everybody! He was just so happy. And, wow, when he wanted to motor, watch out! We did three revolutions around the area and he said, "That was fantastic, thank you." My heart was singing! I left him listening to music, eating shortbread cookies and drinking tea!

The rotating doctor told me that Jeff was no longer taking the antipsychotic drug Risperidone. They always knew my views on drugs, but I did acquiesce on this one as his team psychiatrist said it was such a low dose. I think changing the meds a bit was making him chat more and be less sleepy. He looked terrific and ate well. When I wasn't looking, I caught him eating my chicken sandwich!

At the end of my visits, I always left him listening to music with his earphones and watching the traffic go by at his favourite spot by the window.

Jeff had a bath once a week, and staff told me they gave him bubble baths! He seemed to be treated well; he was non-combative and smiled and said hello to everyone, so he was a popular resident. Only his constipation had set him back, but that seemed more controlled with fewer meds, especially the painkillers. We used Voltaren twice a day on his knees to keep the discomfort down.

Another resident passed away. She was a Hungarian woman whose husband was also living in the same residence. She was fine, walking, pushing her walker to her room and she just collapsed and died, just like that, out of the blue; a total shock to everyone as she was healthy and got around. At the time of her death her husband was in hospital as he was having his knee looked at. This news must have been such a shock to him. In one day her room was emptied and her clothes given to others. I was so surprised at her passing as there were at least five people I would have imagined would go before her. This couple had been in care for six years and were in their eighties.

The fact that Jeff didn't stand up or have a real nap when I don't visit played an important role in my frequency of visits. Since he had been on fewer meds, he now wanted to stand and walk more, which was wonderful. It was not like I was there all day—from door to door 9:30 to 4:30, give or take. I treasured the naps with him and he always seemed so happy to see me.

Things change, our needs, their needs and how our energy fluctuated. Diet, sleep and exercise had been key requisites for me. Jeff was my priority and I loved being with him, so I had little time for friends. I knew he was in a good place, being taken care of overnight, and there were countless challenges I could never face on my own. What often drew the line of having your partner stay at home or in care was incontinence, especially bowel for someone who was wheelchair-bound. It was like moving, lifting, turning over and totally taking care of a 170-pound child.

What about activities and fun? He definitely had all that in a residence—it was obvious the pleasure he derived from his activities. The weather had been amazing, warm and sunny, we would go outside for three-quarters of an hour looking at all the buds coming on the trees and birds flying about. I sometimes had five days visiting in a row but was getting exercise and reading. I enjoyed being with him so much and missed him terribly when we were apart!

When I wasn't there, he did not have to "perform" for me or others. It was his time to relax, fold his arms in what I saw as contentment, nod off when it suited him. A bit of space, reunions, missing someone is all a part of marriage, and ours was no exception. Of course, this is all speculation.

Jeff was just so talkative that spring. The staff kept mentioning how he was talking more and engaging them in conversation. He didn't seem to fall into the regular

---

category of Alzheimer's patients as he often fluctuated from day to day.

"Anywhere you want to go, can I come along with you?" he asked me one day.

"Yes, maybe we can think about London," I replied.

He even began walking without any direction with the Ultimate Walker; totally holding the bars and walking in a straight line. Wow, that was just so amazing! I got him to peddle cycle for fifteen minutes to limber him up, then five stands. It often tired me out as much as him, so we would have a nap together. Even I seemed to be sleeping better.

MY BIRTHDAY. APRIL 2017

Helen tells me it's my birthday this month, and that I will be seventy-six years old. I find that hard to believe. I'll be one of the ones they celebrate with music and cake at the end of this month!

I'm chatting with The Young Guy and I see him with the deaf lady often. She comes over and adjusts my pillow and blanket as I sit by the window. She does sign language and always asks if I drive. She can read my lips if I answer. Rosie notices that I'm talking to her a lot but Rosie has this really tall man that comes to visit her. My wife was taking photos of them together with his camera today.

I'm doing lots of exercise with Y, balloon toss which I like as I can reach out of my wheelchair. She does all kinds of arm and leg exercises with each person. First she arranges us so we are all in a circle and then we do a group session together. Some sleep. Some nod off. Others who aren't in wheelchairs walk around, sit down, walk around again, but when ball time comes everyone is ready. We all stay far away from the TV during these times.

Helen and I watch soccer every Saturday and no one minds. A couple of the male residents often join in cheering along with us.

This morning at breakfast all the staff sang me "Happy Birthday"!

The musicians have arrived for the monthly birthday party. At the end of their playing they came over and sang "Happy Birthday" to me; everyone joined in.

Helen picked up a lovely lemon cake to share with my friends.

I had such a surprise—there was Wayne, my rugby mate, walking towards me with his hand outstretched. I shouted, "Wayne!" He was smiling and he gave me a hug and wished me a Happy Birthday. He had a new rugby jersey for me. He asked me questions and I tried to answer. We talked rugby and it feels so good to be with him.

We sat together with The Young Guy and his wife and she took some photos of the three of us. I'm eating lots of cake! The Young Guy looks tired. His wife tells my wife that he's got a cold and is not feeling that great.

I get by the window where Y is playing the piano and my wife leaves.

ACHES & PAINS ON THE JOB

I often returned home with a sore left shoulder from helping Jeff transfer to his chair. I always forgot that I was seventy-four years old and not as sprightly as before. He continued to be strong and leaned and resisted. It could have been a simple process if Jeff was able to communicate but he couldn't.

He once caught me and an aide off guard as we were planning to move him into his bed. Jeff was in his walker in front of the bed to get in when he suddenly propelled his legs into the air and onto the bed—an awkward, unexpected position. We were both standing there stunned and almost missed grabbing him, but we got lucky and were able to grab him before he crashed to the floor. It was tricky as he was squirming and had no comprehension he was in a dangerous position. No harm done that time.

One day I left him just for a moment on the patio to grab my coffee. When I returned, his soup was on the concrete and his watermelon scattered about. This was a perfect example of why he needed assistance and close attention for all his meals and snacks. I could see him planning to dispose of a plate or fling his spoon. He might take a sip of milk and throw the rest at what he thought was an open window or on the floor. Fortunately it wasn't too often, but he could be unpredictable and quick as lightning! No wonder he was such a good rugby player!

When I was not there, I was told he would sit at a long rectangular table. They kept an eye on him as he handled his spoon, but sometimes he just wanted to be fed and would keep his arms folded. It was like he decided that's how it would be that day. His behaviour was often out of whack with the norm for a decline in progress. Generally, though, Jeff handled his spoon and ate his soup well, even blowing on it because he saw me doing that.

Jeff was unpredictable. Life was unpredictable. I went with the flow because I'd learned worrying didn't make any difference. I wouldn't say I was depressed, as I was basically a happy person. I was more grief-stricken with the sadness and pain of Jeff's condition. I hated what he had to go through sitting in a wheelchair—something we never expected. I missed him all the time we were apart, but I did my best to see friends and carry on with my hobbies.

It would have been helpful, loving and charitable, though, if his sister and her children, as well as Jeff's two sons and daughter visited, but it was just not happening. They did not call or send cards for his special days. They ignored him as though he did not exist anymore.

My relationship with the staff was mostly friendly. Even the kitchen staff gave me a spare soup now and then when there was extra. Weather permitting, Jeff and I ate out on the patio. It was rare to see others follow suit, but, of course, there was only so many staff to handle the feeding. Unless a resident had a visitor at lunchtime, they would sit indoors waiting to be fed. I never knew what to expect, who might stumble and fall, who might not wake up one morning. The Young Guy had an incident and left us that spring, much to my sorrow. He was only seventy-two.

STAFF CONFRONTATIONS — THE "TERRIBLE THREES"

A troubling situation arose with one of the staff who was assigned to Jeff's team. This woman, I call her "M," added stress on top of everything Jeff and I had to cope with. It was the same staff who got involved when Jeff first arrived at Montbretia when a resident hit me across the head. After I made my complaint to the resident manager, she outlined her concerns to me and said they would get to the root of the problem.

In my opinion (which may not have been shared by others) M was a bully. She was impatient with some residents and it had to be her way when she decided to assist someone, not when it worked with others. I got along so well with the other staff, and that didn't sit well with her. She did her darnedest to be confrontational. That is my personal perception. It stressed me out terribly so I had to raise the issues as I didn't want to keep having to deal with her.

I met once or twice a month with my grief counsellor/psychiatrist, who continued to counsel me even after she was no longer on Jeff's team. We discussed M at length trying to find a solution to keep the heat down. She suggested that perhaps this worker had issues in her past like having been bullied or abused and took the opportunity to target someone who was obviously happy and in love with her husband. She advised me to ignore her and not let her goad me into fighting or losing my temper as that was what she wanted—for people to see me as the "bad guy."

We did some exercises where my doc was the bully who tried to start a fight. It really helped as I could see how a bully would try to get me to argue. It was an interesting exercise that I learned from and tried to apply with M.

When I got back from my appointment, there was an e-mail from the manager telling me Jeff would not be looked after by M for the time being. Great news! She mentioned that she had a general meeting with all the staff and relayed how grateful they were for how much I did with Jeff. He trusted me more than anyone, and I seemed to understand what he needed. They appreciated me helping with his lunch when I visited as well. Sometimes he would grab hold of something (or someone!) in his room and not let go, but I could talk him out of it. Any time I told him we were going to have tea or ice cream, he forgot what he was doing, let go and settled down.

She mentioned Jeff's difficulties with bowel incontinence and suggested that when Jeff was soiled, he responded better when wearing adaptive clothing. She encouraged me to only use adaptive clothing, like shorts that close with Velcro, when walking, so I redesigned some of his shorts.

Jeff always walked in the Ultimate Walker when I visited and did standing exercises and feet peddling as a warm-up. That often made his bodily functions kick into gear, so it was a catch-22. We wanted him not to be constipated but he was constipated when he didn't walk or stand. Having to change him interfered with lunch feeding, which couldn't be a worse time for staff.

His toilet problems triggered so much of the indignities of this disease, and my stress level escalated. Because his system was more relaxed when he moved, he might soil himself twice in a visit. I got in a state and the minutes passed so slowly waiting for help. I had often asked to put him on the toilet, but that rarely happened. Jeff was always distressed when he soiled himself, and I often had to calm him while he cried. His brain was still working and he was humiliated, that was obvious.

I made a few attempts to engage M in conversation about how difficult it was for me to watch dementia reduce my strong, bright husband to a child before my eyes. I tried to communicate that he was the strong one, a leader in his prime. I said my goal was to help him through this really difficult time and do my best not to interfere with the team plan which she and other nurses followed.

I don't know if what I said helped. It was so terrible to watch someone's brain dying. Physical pain is awful but there was still hope for surgery to have the problem fixed. Dementia was the end of the road for these people. Nothing would improve and they don't even know it. It was just so difficult to witness.

We all just live in the moment. We get old, sick or tired, and we try to find happiness or comfort when things go wrong or we get hurt. My sleep patterns were problematic as my brain often refused to shut down or my feet ached enough to wake me up when I finally dozed off. I didn't drink much. I barely took a pill. I tried sleeping pills but gave them up as I didn't like the drugged state I felt in the morning. I could lie down on the sofa and have a nap, but the minute I hit the bed I was awake and restless with my thoughts. Could that be the way for so many of us?

Oliver didn't show up one day but I helped him with lunch. He had a nap, and I left him with headphones listening to music. He wanted to be close and in hug mode so that was nice and the highlight of my visit. All the little changes I and the staff had been noticing indicated he was at another level of acceptance. He looked so good, healthy and handsome!

A couple of residents were doing really poorly and their time was running out. A particularly favourite resident had been there long before Jeff moved in. He was a really tall Italian man, ninety-three years of age. I squeezed his shoulder one day in greeting and he was so bony—thin as a reed—and wouldn't eat much. His wife, who was ninety-four, was not that well either. Their son brought her in a number of times when I was there, but they only seemed to visit every couple of weeks (we probably had different schedules). Sometimes he would shout his wife's name over and over. It broke my heart, especially as he started to cry. He watched Jeff and me often, and I could see how sad he was. I often asked him to sit with us. When his family arrived, he transformed into a happy, smiling person for as long as their visit lasted. His family always was friendly to me and Jeff. His wife looked so fragile, and perhaps that was why they didn't stay long.

These days I usually arrived at 10:00 and stayed until 3:00 or 4:00. I sometimes left around 2:30 on the days Y was there as Jeff was into his headphones. Most people who visited made it short because it was tiring for the resident and the visitor. But I'd come a long way on two buses and the train—an hour plus sometimes each way—so it would be crazy to stay for only a short time. I came armed with a book in case Jeff slept, and I often crawled in next to him on the bed. So comforting. I sometimes nodded off, but I was still always on the alert.

When I look at photos of Jeff sitting on the patio, he so often looked "blissed out"—what one of my good friends said when she saw it. He looked content, happy and mellow with my scarf around his neck and clutching my satchel! We enjoyed our visits. He was wonderful, and it was quite humbling to watch him eat and realize what we take for granted. I felt such love for him and I missed him.

He still knew me. He became so chatty at times. His sheer strength kept him focussed on walking well despite the obvious pain in his knees. He was overjoyed to walk. He kept himself busy either folding the sheets as he sat in bed or looking at the huge underwater photos I plastered on the walls in his direct view. I often stood there pointing out things in the photos and recalling the story. I had his attention! I made him laugh and told him close calls we had on some of our dives.

Every visit included cuddling on the narrow bed for his afternoon nap—good thing I was small so I could squeeze in. He so often tried to tell me things. He was the best storyteller and had a repertoire at dinner parties that made him ever so popular. Jeff never lost his winning personality, and he was ever so charming with a shy smile and a coy look when certain ladies came by. Just very popular with everyone and non-aggressive. A pity he lost so many teeth—just can't bother with dentistry at this stage—but he could still eat most foods. I couldn't imagine life without him. But I tried not to dwell on that subject.

Jeff's moods fluctuated from being enthusiastic to unusually drowsy and non-communicative. He'd be like that for two or three days, and I started thinking it must be due to being in the wheelchair and being constipated. Also, he was having trouble eating sausages with skin on them and unpeeled cucumber as he couldn't seem to masticate enough. He would just chew and chew, and then he started to choke. That led to a diet of minced food.

My life hinged or unhinged on what was happening with him. We had total lack of verbal communication during so many visits. The arms folded so firmly said a lot! Each day when I arrived, he would take my scarf and have me place it around his neck. He would clutch my satchel and make sure I didn't leave. Reaching for my scarf and the way he enjoyed having it around him was so touching. I noticed that he often clutched it tightly to his body, like he did with my satchel, hoping (I deduced) that it would prevent me from leaving.

I was desperately lonely without him in my life, but I was slowly adjusting somewhat. I had changed as well. I had more patience, and I was more compassionate being among residents with this disease. So many of them never had visitors (when I was there), and their plight was painful. I had my hobbies and chores, so decided that Wednesdays and Fridays were the new Helen Days. The other five would be with Jeff.

Montbretia Residence was so fortunate to have such an amazing activities director Wednesday through Saturday who played the flute and piano and did one-on-one exercise with each of the residents. Everyone seemed to adore her!

MID-JULY

Helen tells me July 1 was two years at this hotel! I seem to be one of the longest-staying guests.

The food is good, the music is terrific. And I do all kinds of exercises with Baby. She has the biggest smile and dances like a trouper!

Once a month we celebrate the residents' birthdays. It's my favourite day with clapping, people trying to dance and me watching! Best part is the cake and tea though especially if it's carrot cake.

My wife always comes, at least I think it's her. It can be confusing as there's lots of short people here but when she comes closer I know it's her and she's the one I want on my lap. I know it's her for sure as she wants to hug and there's always the welcoming kiss!

Today we're sitting on the patio in brilliant sunshine. She reads while I nod off but I keep checking that she's still here. I don't want her to leave just yet. She was so insistent on me walking in the big walker but I just didn't want to today. But I pacified her by doing five stand-ups from my chair. Then I got a yogurt drink and a bite of cookie! I was often told I'm a manipulator to get my way and that must still remain.

I'm meeting lots of new people on this floor and I have a big room.

I can pull myself along the hallways and say hello.

Everyone is friendly and Baby came here too.

There is another one—she looks like my wife but way younger; like what my wife must have looked like when she was in her twenties or thirties. Kay is so friendly and we have really hit it off. She's in charge of my new headphones and my activity boards.

HOT SUMMER DAYS

Getting to Montbretia Residence gave me lots of exercise—standing, waiting, walking, running up and down the SkyTrain stairs all counted! I can often find a positive in a negative, so no complaints as I was staying fit and I'm sure it was good for my joints. As I sat on the bus one day, I remembered our trips to Las Vegas.

We couldn't help but go on a trip to Las Vegas when we lived in Vancouver—the deals could not be ignored! We went on a few trips and always to the same hotel with a huge outdoor pool which was seven or eight feet deep. Those are such great memories. Jeff was only interested in the pool, the shows in the evenings and, of course, all the good food, although on one of our trips we found out about a huge Crafts and Antiques outdoor Fair, and we had the most amazing time coming back loaded with antique wine glasses and other treasures. That particular trip coincided with a trip made by my brother, his wife, her family and ours which turned out to be such a special time of us all together! Gambling wasn't Jeff's thing—but I enjoyed Blackjack and the slots!. We caught so many free outdoor shows, checked out so many innovative buildings with European themes. On our first trip there, I played the slot machines at the airport waiting for our flight and won $300—a tidy sum to put away for a future trip.

This was not the future we planned. It had now been almost ten years since Jeff's diagnosis.

His sister contacted me in January to say she was moving into a condo and wanted to see Jeff again. It had been three years this October since she and her husband last visited. I gladly gave her an update and said I would meet her. July came around, six months later, and she never got back after saying she would. I felt it was her loss, the old cliche. She and his kids probably would have been detrimental to his life. He told me last year when we looked at photos of them that they were dead. For them, he was out of sight and out of mind.

Jeff remained anxious to stand. Being stuck in his chair was the last place he expected to be at this stage of his life. He seemed happy and just kept thanking me. Standing and walking exercises definitely resulted in better bowel control. He also walked with gusto—almost trotting! I often forgot just how tall he was, but when he stood up, he towered over me. His favourite spot was this kitchen opening, and whenever he saw staff coming to the fridge he would shout, "What's for me?" Always hoping for treats!

I'd read and heard that personalities changed and were unrecognizable with Alzheimer's. Patients often reverted to how they were when they were in their thirties or forties. Fortunately, Jeff aways had a great sense of humour and welcomed everybody's attention, so the staff seemed to care a lot about him.

He would reach for someone's name tag and read their name—we were all surprised he still could do that. Research indicated that patients with Alzheimer's slowly declined and didn't regain what they had lost, but it was becoming obvious that Jeff was not in that normal classification or category. At one point he needed to be fed, but two years later he was handling his spoon on his own and refusing to be fed.

The exercise in his walker was limited to along the halls. He took every opportunity to stop and read aloud the names on the doors—residents, "linen closet," etc. When he came to his door he would often say, "Godfrey Robinson—that's me!" He would stare at our picture for a long time, and then smile at Oliver and continue walking! He always smiled at Oliver, looking him over. He was so aware that I was taking photos and would pose and smile for me. We were fortunate to have such a strong bond that kept us on such good terms despite the chaos!

Life was simplistic for him. He never seemed troubled except when I first arrived and he caught sight of me.

He would get emotional and grab me, pulling me onto his chair. He would not let me go, so I stayed quiet, no struggling. I wasn't going anywhere; I'd come to make him happy if I could. They don't forget everything and flashes come back. He would often blurt out just a word or two when some memory was screaming to get out.

I didn't have family in Vancouver, but I had some wonderful friends who supported me. They tried to visit Jeff, but it was painful for them to see him in this state. He also withdrew into a shell as if something came back to him about them. He may have recognized that, unlike them, he could not just get up and walk.

He tried to chat or say something and couldn't, so he often just bowed his head and looked so sad. His reaction and how they now perceived him seemed to discourage them from coming back. His friends discussed it with me, and I knew it would be great to have them visit even just a little bit. But it was their decision to make. I could only encourage them to come. If the visits didn't work out, then they would re-think the situation. They would surely be guided by his reaction.

As the summer wore on, Jeff was not good, hunched over, uncooperative at times. He had a swollen ankle and foot, which didn't help things. We had to use the hoist as he wouldn't transfer and resisted. There was no use fighting it, as he was way too strong and my arms hurt from trying to get him to stand. He smiled when I left as he had Leonard wafting into his headphones. They were all happy with the headphones. It was a great resource for the residence.

The tall Italian man's wife died in July, and it was quite unexpected. He interacted with Jeff and me often.

His son told me about his mother and I just broke down. His wife and I used to hug hello. She was there just a few days before having a special Italian lunch with her granddaughter, her husband and her son by the window. I'm glad that will be a memorable occasion for them. It was for me as when I went over and chatted with her she forgot for a moment who I was and spoke Italian to me. We all laughed. When these emotional upsets occurred, they drained me of energy and filled me with fear of what was coming in my life. I couldn't help but think, *Well, who is next to go? Would it be Jeff?*

Few people who are chronically ill really want to die due to fear of the unknown, and those of us who are in love with sick people learn many things about ourselves like compassion, patience, acceptance of their plight or non-acceptance. I didn't want Jeff to suffer. Up to this time he had a mental problem and wasn't suffering physically other than having bad knees and trouble walking.

It was unbearable to dwell on him physically leaving. He had retained a lot of his personality and was still the man I fell in love with thirty some years before. When it was his time, that would be it. I had no say. I wondered if he would then be at peace. I didn't know. I often thought the wrong people died in a home like Jeff's. Some are so healthy but they go quickly while others are in a haze with little knowledge of their surroundings for years. There was no pick and choose.

Every day you spend with someone you love, no matter their condition, you are giving them some comfort. They may not react in front of you at that moment, but many remember how nice you were. I've read much about

Alzheimer's patients. They don't want to be ignored, just that bit of kindness means a lot. It's about them not you.

What could I give him in these last days? Sharing a coffee together, reading to him, bringing him new warm socks, a book with lots of pictures or a card. He was the sick one, and I needed only to smile, touch him or give him a hug to brighten his day. I had to ignore myself and concentrate on his needs. I had a healthy brain.

A resident whose room was next door to Jeff's would be soon celebrating his sixtieth wedding anniversary, so his wife invited me to join with the family gathering for cake. I kept meeting her family members, Italian, who were a lovely, large, supportive group to her and their father. It was a wonderful time on a narrow patio with cake and drinks. I was truly honoured to be included in this celebration!

BALMY, SUNNY DAYS IN LATE JULY

Jeff could not tell us if he was in pain, but when he stood, he sat back down quickly so I would get the message. One day he hugged the bed not wanting to get up. He wanted to keep eating cheese and crackers (making sure he brushed the crumbs off his sheets). After much coaxing and cajoling I succeeded in getting him out of his bed. I think he wanted to be there for the day, and I knew how that felt.

Some days Jeff was anxious to walk initially but then he was uncooperative with the transfer back to his chair. We had another near mishap, but I helped him in a slow slide to the floor. Then we needed assistance to use the hoist. Some days his comprehension was just not there. He wanted to understand but thought I meant to raise his legs and propel himself and not the opposite. Another close call!

It became obvious as the days slipped by that part of Jeff's brain wasn't engaging at all. Months ago he was aware of his bodily functions, but now he was silent, vague, not tuned in. Changed. He didn't say a word, didn't cry, didn't shout, didn't move. It was like it was the new "normal."

It was terribly sad. It was also difficult for others to know just how terribly sad it was. I was losing him. The disease was chipping away at his brain. We didn't expect him to get better, but the new level of acceptance was also mind-boggling and indicated that he was in the last stages of this disease.

EARLY AUGUST

Today she brought me coconut yogurt—so she says—and fresh blueberries!

Denis is a real fighter, small but tough and always in trouble. He was taking rocks out of the two ponds in the patio and throwing them around so now we can't go outside.

Some good friends sneaked us out to the patio while this fighter was busy eating and then drew the curtains. Thank God he doesn't know we're out here. We've had a few fights, fisticuffs! I usually win!

I have two favourite nurses—two Kathleens. I notice they are my wife's favourite nurses too as she is always laughing and smiling with them.

Today Rosie came over to see me when my wife wasn't around. She was rubbing my arm. Rosie is eighty-five and is also in a wheelchair but she had shorts on and she sure is in very good shape. We talk in French.

Suddenly my wife arrives. Rosie gets wheeled away.

We are having a drink and biscuits. I couldn't finish the water and threw the rest out towards the window. Oh no, the window was closed. I threw glass and all. We both got a shock and some water on us but we did laugh hard. I meant to just throw the water but it all went sailing in the air and hit the window!

SEPTEMBER/OCTOBER

I found entertainment when the opportunity presented itself, like going to the opening of a casino in downtown Vancouver.

The old casino was in a beautiful area on the sea wall where a small ferry docked every fifteen minutes, and it was just a lovely venue. Jeff and I often cycled there as there was an inexpensive seniors' lunch on Tuesdays. We could sit outside and have our lunch, and then take a small amount to play a few slot machines. Jeff, who always was a chatty person, engaged a lot of the male staff (mainly security personnel), so they got to know him and had observed that he was changing. A couple of them introduced us to three people they knew who had Alzheimer's. Those Tuesdays we would have a great lunch in the sun. Then Jeff would chat with his new-found friends while I spent a few dollars playing the slot machines.

I had a lovely evening at the grand opening—the machines were paying— and thought about how Jeff would have enjoyed sitting in the bar and watching rugby on their huge screens.

When I saw Jeff the next day I wished I could tell him about my evening out, but he could not comprehend or carry on a conversation other than saying a few words. We moved to the patio and had lunch in the sun. He was sweet, but I could smell "something." There was no alerting us anymore, so when we got in, I made sure staff checked and changed him. They put him to bed and I snuggled in and we slept for an hour!

The weather was so beautiful I decided to stay for dinner as well. He continued to be strong and somewhat independent, but that day he wanted to be a baby bird with his mouth open for his food! I obliged and played it his way. If I tried to push him, he would only fold his arms tighter. He would often pull at my shirt and rip it if I tried to get away. Once he got a hold of me, he wouldn't let go, and, quite frankly, I loved him for that. If I relaxed into him, he would then relax his guard but would link his hands together and lock me in. I don't know how many times he would say, "Don't go," if I made a move to put on my scarf. I didn't go. I stayed. I was wanted. And I wanted him.

I brought the little Henkell bottles of bubbly for our Thanksgiving dinner together! The chefs made really good stuffing and the best gravy!

THANKSGIVING

Here she comes with a big satchel. Goodies for me I hope!
She says it's Thanksgiving and she has gifts for me! I'm happy.
Chocolate, fresh fruit and warm new socks!
We have paper placemats with turkeys on them.

She also has little bottles of bubbly—I'm allowed a bit and try to sneak more from her glass! We have turkey, mashed potatoes and gravy and everything is so good. We toast each other. It's a beautiful day. We are together but I know it's special as there's the added stuff and the chocolate.

THE GRIEVING COUNSELLOR

Meetings with my grieving counsellor helped me tremendously. She never said to "move on," but we tackled the problems. I hated that expression—"move on." Another one that drove me mad was "Sorry for your loss." It was said so often that it lost sincerity. We could try saying things like, "I'm sorry they died so soon," or something different. I don't know, it just bugged me maybe because death and loss was so close to my doorstep.

So much of the time I spent with Jeff was when he was sleeping. My doctor helped me to accept that his brain was shrinking all the time and he needed lots of sleep to recover what was left. Let him sleep, take off, do some things for myself. We worked on times and schedules, and then she gave me a printout about self-compassion. This exercise was called "Mindfulness," and I found it really helped me, so I want to share it with you.

SELF-COMPASSION BREAK

Think of a situation in your life that is difficult, that is causing you stress. Call the situation to mind and see if you can actually feel the stress and emotional discomfort in your body.

Now, say to yourself:
1. This is a moment of suffering.

That's mindfulness.

Other options include:
This hurts.
Ouch.
We all struggle in our lives.

2. Suffering is a part of life
That's common humanity. Other options include:
Other people feel this way.
I'm not alone.
We all struggle in our lives.

Now, put your hands over your heart, feel the warmth of your hands and the gentle touch of your hands on your chest.

Say to yourself:
May I be kind to myself.
You can also ask yourself, "What do I need to hear right now to express kindness to myself?" Is there a phrase that speaks to you in your particular situation, such as:

May I give myself the compassion that I need?
May I learn to accept myself as I am?
May I forgive myself?
May I be strong?
May I be patient?

This practice can be used any time of day or night. It helped me remember to evoke the three aspects of self-compassion when I needed it most. I often did this exercise twice in one day with good results.

Grief is a lonely emotion, so we all treat it differently.

I asked my doctor if she thought Jeff was content when I wasn't there. She believed he was. We had quite a discussion about it. They would call me if he was shouting or asking for me, but no one called and said, "Please come, Jeff needs you." No, he was relaxing with the group. He did what he wanted.

When I was there it was almost like he had to entertain me. It was pointed out that he could be overtired when my visits were long, so I accepted that. I believed that. He loved it when I arrived, but after a couple of hours he often would become vague. He probably did want his space.

Y told me he was doing an activity with another resident. She said they sat across from each other and messed about with the bits that were glued onto the board for two hours!

"Helen, don't worry about Jeff, he's busy," she said. "If he's tired, he nods off. Staff always change him and give him treats, so relax!"

Very good advice from someone who had seen so much.

Jeff continued walking in the Ultimate Walker, and he had lots of smiles for me. Out of the blue one day he said, "You must be careful." I don't know what he was worried about, but he had a concerned look on his face when he said it. I gave him a big hug and said, "I am really careful," and he patted my back. Oliver heard the exchange and said to me afterwards, "You two really love each other." True words.

LATE FALL

I had come to realize we could only be comforted with the good memories as we couldn't change what was presently happening. Aging often comes with unforeseen medical problems, and we can't blame ourselves for the tragedies. They impact us, but we need to find what happiness we can. We just have to face the challenges and do our best rather than worrying about it. People lose limbs, break their spines but still do things. We just have to face it and take what we can from each day with our partner. That was how life was. We did not expect to live apart and struggle with this illness.

I was lonely, tired of life, and aging brought lots more to cope with. But I had a roof over my head, a fridge full of food, and we had to put it all in perspective and be grateful for lots of stuff.

One day I was thinking about Jeff's youngest son and wondering where he was at. I had a flashback of the time he invited us to this decrepit, burnt-out trailer he was living in. He made us steaks on a BBQ. He had no stove, sink or toilet, and he washed in the river. We take so much for granted while some people have nothing. Why it happened was not open to discussion, but it was there. It was reality. To see it right before my eyes was so sad and devastating. This was Jeff's son whom he loved, and it broke his heart that day, I know, as he had no control over his son's whims or habits or anything. To this day, when I ride the SkyTrain and the view opens up to Richmond I always wistfully glance at the spot where we had that BBQ and visit with his son.

Jeff was being well taken care of now, but I had to make sure my affairs were in order as well as I got older as I didn't want to be in a home. Period. Jeff didn't either, but what do you do, give him a bunch of pills? My grief was beyond anyone's understanding. It never went away. I know we all will die, but the downhill with Alzheimer's was excruciating.

NOVEMBER/DECEMBER

Jeff's sister finally came to visit him in November and it went well. I think she was embarrassed to not have been around, but I just ignored all that and tried not to engage with her problems or excuses. I think Jeff was unsure who she was at times, but he might have remembered her. He gave me the big eyeball when she was trying to get close as he was probably confused about where she fit into the scene.

It was disappointing to me that he received no Christmas gifts or birthday cards from his family. I did feel resentful—there was no hiding that. It was great to get an e-mail from her saying she was going to visit again, so it was terribly disappointing that she didn't show up. I waited—Jeff and I waited—for her and her family to visit and she stood us up. I felt so conflicted about our relationship. She sent me an e-mail later saying she slept in.

On December 4, our anniversary, I chatted to Jeff about our wedding day and showed him photos of the wedding celebration at the Inukshuk Statue at English

Bay. He was impassive, not excited; not sad, just a vague, wondering look on his face.

I tried to get the most I could out of my visits with Jeff, and it wasn't easy for any number of reasons, but I always felt excited to arrive and see him after a Helen Day. It was like the butterflies I got when boarding a plane for a fun trip. Our relationship changed so much because we could not have the same conversations we had previously. It must have been difficult for him as he was so blank and vague. Did he wonder why we were not together all the time? It had to cross his mind. Or did it?

When I was having my mind muddled about how to treat his sister's potential visit, my doctor wrote me an e-mail with some excellent advice and thoughts about life and relationships. I've summarized a couple of paragraphs that helped me with forgiveness and compassion, and I think they would benefit any of us on a similar journey.

> Someone once wrote about forgiveness: "One of my greatest lessons in life around forgiveness has been 'Holding on to anger is like drinking poison and expecting the other person to die. The only person who really hurts is the person holding onto the anger. And forgiveness is not about condoning behaviour, rather it is about having compassion for others for being the wounded selves that they are, and at the same time doing whatever is needed to feel safe for you.'"

One of the forgiveness meditations I appreciated the most was:

For the ways you have hurt me, I offer you forgiveness, and if I am not able to forgive you fully now, may I forgive you to the extent that I am able—in this moment.

Jeff's sister visited several times that month, which was promising. She definitely made an effort to reconnect, if I can put it that way. She sent me an e-mail saying they had a good visit and she may turn up at the residents' Christmas party the next day.

This was a difficult part of the year for me, more so than the previous Christmas seasons. The pain never weakened. I was stuck with it. I wanted Jeff back as he was, but he had gone somewhere—a world I was not in. I could only stay on the periphery, which was strange and disconcerting to say the least. I went by our old Beach apartment where we lived together for twenty-two years, then the Inukshuk Statute where we got married, the huge lit-up tree on Beach where we shared glasses of champagne and watched the carol boats go by for years. All of this was within a matter of minutes on a Beach bus.

Jeff and I often made plans for me to fly to Ottawa at Christmas and spend it with my parents and family. He would spend the day with his sister and family in Vancouver.

We went to Mexico to relax in the sun, most often to Zihuatanejo, a number of times as well. Sometimes we would go without accommodation booked. We would simply show up at a favourite restaurant where the owner and his wife were delighted to see us. They would let us sleep on their sofa or mats on the floor for a night while we found a hotel.

It shook me up—really shook my foundation—that he was in his home and I was in mine. No longer together. My wonderful husband had gone but he was still there. I sometimes wondered if it would be easier if he wasn't there. Or would it be harder?

It is amazing and devastating to think there are hundreds of thousands of wives and husbands who felt like I did. Missing someone they loved who was physically in their lives but somewhere they no longer could reach together.

Jeff did not always respond well to seeing people from his past. He looked troubled and concerned and questioning. Much as I would like all his friends and mine to visit, it didn't always work for him. I knew I had the support of our old friends from thirty years ago and others who helped me make the journey manageable. Without all that support, love and friendship I would have been up the creek. My priority was to protect him, make him comfortable and try to balance it so he continued to know and love me and derived some comfort and happiness despite having this terrible debilitating disease.

I had my routine with Jeff. I kept in touch with people who seemed to care about me—it kept me sane. I missed Jeff all the time, and I was trying to always be there for him. I know we both derived a lot of joy and comfort during these visits.

My psychiatrist helped me with self-compassion exercises to shore up my mental strength. Hundreds of thousands of people who face Alzheimer's challenges and loss of loved ones go through this fight for strength and courage. It was frightening for our friends to see the changes up close. I worried, too, about myself and my family and friends as we knew so little about what was happening to our brains.

We must live in the moment, grab our happiness where we can find it, don't let the negatives overwhelm us. Easier said than done, as the saying goes.

Over this Christmas season I planned to enjoy my moments with Jeff. He was still my guardian angel. I bought little bottles of bubbly to share at our Christmas Day meal. He knew the anguish. He was too bright not to, despite what had been taken away.

Chapter 10

JANUARY 2018

Everyone is saying Happy New Year! Smiles and nice music playing!

She's arrived telling me it's New Year's Day and many hugs and kisses. She says it's very chilly out there.

I sit by the window and see all the snow and the buses and I want to be on that bus with her.

She brought me chocolate and butter tarts. I grab them close. We sit together holding hands and she shows me photos of us and lots of people on her small computer. We even watch some rugby!

I get tired easily. I can hardly wait to finish lunch so I can get in bed and snuggle my girl!

It's warm in my room. We are close.

So many new people. It can't be that they are all new but I've just forgotten who they all are.

I look for the new girl with the long brown hair. Her name tag says Kay. She is so happy and always smiles and squeezes my shoulder. She asks me all kinds of questions but I can't seem to say much. But she has big new earphones for me and my favourite music.

I watch her. I look out the window. It's busy out there.

I get snacks. She holds my hands some days.

JANUARY/FEBRUARY

Had another year really gone by? And a new one starting? Here we were in 2018! I had not envisaged these years continuing at the same rate of decline in his stages of dementia. I had been witnessing the ups and downs, more the downs, and such contradictions in some of the other residents' cognitive abilities. I had mostly noticed a decline as the months passed and their lives were ending. There were few like Jeff who seemed to remain at a stall—not getting worse! Jeff was pushing back and starting to do things he could not do six months before—a reversal! That was confusing to staff and to me. The number of residents at Montbretia remained at twenty—ten males and ten females—and when someone passed, their room was swept clean and assigned to someone on a waiting list.

Never did I expect to be going through so many deaths of such a mix of personalities—it takes its toll, no doubt about that, to be exposed to death so often. My feelings were torn with losing someone but at the same time knowing their awful struggle with dementia was over. The death of someone in their eighties or nineties did not seem as shocking as those who were diagnosed with early onset dementia in their fifties or sixties. To see a rapid decline in a youthful, walking, active man or woman who had arrived looking fit and healthy was shocking. I soon realized they were unable to communicate or have a conversation. It was truly frightening to watch that deterioration and their frustration.

Jeff was like an ocean—crashing waves and dead calm. His moods were certainly influenced by constipation, so the more I got him to stand and walk, the more his system worked. It takes a "two people assist" to handle a resident who is incontinent. Residents had to be fed their meals, and staff needed their breaks. Toilet habits with dementia patients were mostly unpredictable, and it was the norm for some to scream, shout, knock furniture over and get in arguments. The exercise sessions played an important part in changing their dispositions, tiring them out so they settled down and nodded off in their chairs.

Jeff was still walking, and it was ups and downs with him. His knees may have been getting worse. He was cozy sitting by the window in the common room or sometimes at the window in his room with me, but he was not as keen to go outside. The weather had changed, and he would say, "It's cold" when we went out. He even pretended he was shivering so he could come back in quickly.

It was difficult to be tough and courageous when watching a wonderful, talented man's brain slowly dying. This journey Jeff and I were on together was hard for others to understand fully unless they experienced it. The salvation for some of us dealing with a husband or wife with dementia was and is gauged by our bond and love together before all this happened.

So you go one way or the other—visit because you want to or just abandon them with token visits now and then. I don't think I was judgmental about others' feelings about this subject. I so often wished I could have him with me all the time and see him every day, but I probably would have become a total basket case. It was so easy to get terribly depressed around all these people with the disease, so I had to back off. I had to find a balance and allow my friends and the staff to support me.

Patients with advanced-stage Alzheimer's needed twenty-four-hour supervision and help with personal hygiene, dressing and eating. Changes in brain function made it increasingly difficult for them to move about, sit up and even swallow. This led to complications such as bedsores, skin infections, blood clots and sepsis. Injuries from falls were common. Difficulty in swallowing made eating and drinking an ongoing challenge and could lead to weight loss, malnutrition and dehydration.

The most common cause of death among Alzheimer's patients at that time was aspiration pneumonia. This happened when, due to difficulty in swallowing caused by the disease, an individual inadvertently inhaled food particles, liquid or even gastric fluids. Because our mouths and throats contain numerous bacteria, these were then carried deep into the lungs to multiply and grow, which lead to pneumonia. Due to the impaired immune systems of Alzheimer's patients, pneumonia was more often than not fatal.

One of my friends gave me four pairs of adaptable trousers from her husband who passed away. I was so grateful, and I sewed some Velcro strips in between some of the missing snaps. The commercial washers had to use scalding hot water and agitate the clothing so much that they shredded and ripped the clothes as they whipped around. Socks disappeared all the time too.

When Jeff walked, he wore shorts so his pants stayed up properly. I gave him knee-high socks with sharks on them too. He just looked so good! I washed those socks by hand as otherwise they would be lost or ruined in the laundry machines. He often had his toes curled around his favourite ones not wanting to give them up for washing when I was leaving for the day, but if I hadn't removed them staff would throw them in the general laundry and we wouldn't see them again.

It was difficult for Jeff to process more than one person at a time, so it was preferable for his sister to have a solid one-on-one with him over lunch. He got confused easily with visitors and would have a deep frown on his face as he searched for a past image of who they were.

I had some amazing days with Jeff that first few months. He was all giggly when I arrived, clapping with such vigour when he saw me. We were all laughing! I felt just so close, comforted and loved. I had a smile on my face all day! He was truly adorable. I walked by and he said "Boo!" and threw me kisses. I was so thankful he showed his love; talk about precious moments.

My doctor sent me this beautiful saying that is attributed to the Buddha:

> You can search throughout the entire universe for someone who is more deserving of your love and affection than you are yourself, and that person is not to be found anywhere. You, yourself, as much as anybody in the entire universe deserves your love and affection.

VALENTINE'S DAY

Here she comes!

Is that huge red heart for me? I gave my Poppet a really big hug today. She knows I love chocolates! Everybody knows I love chocolates!

I have so many choices. Which chocolate will I choose? Helen said I could have as many as I want.

She got a little plate for me and I placed the ones I wanted on the plate.

Then closed the box for another day.

I offered her one. We ate chocolates today and she told me it was Valentine's Day.

CHILLY WEATHER

I spent Valentine's as well as our province's Family Day with Jeff, so it was six days in a row of busing to Montbretia. He was delighted to get a box of chocolates, concentrating so hard on which to choose. Some of the buses didn't behave as we were having a chill spell with low temperatures. Lots of snow in Jeff's area. Less here, but it was not melting as quickly as usual for Vancouver.

Jeff had been walking so tall these weekends with me. We never missed our walks on Tuesdays and Thursdays with Oliver, so he was getting lots of exercise. He was really keen to walk and we had great weekends together! Jeff had no organized activities due to cancellations with activity staff, so I'd been there entertaining him. It was so sad to see all the residents who had no visitors. So many people said, "Jeff is so lucky to have you." It really made a difference, but the reverse is also true: I am lucky to still have him. Despite this confounding disease, we are still together and adjusting to the changes. I couldn't imagine not going to see him and him not being in his world any longer.

But I was glad a Helen Day was just around the corner so I didn't have to face the blowing snow and chill. I had discussed Yaletown repeatedly with the manager at Montbretia and was awaiting an appointment date with them so we could assess together the pros and cons of Jeff moving. I wanted to confirm I was allowed to take him out on the sea wall and ensure the hallways and area space wouldn't be a problem for him. I wanted to know if they had an Ultimate Walker as well.

It had been pointed out that any change would likely result in confusion as he was settled at Montbretia. I had also been encouraged to cut my days down to not more than four per week, but I just wanted to be with him. All our days are numbered, but he was having issues swallowing and coughing over the previous two months. He continued to be strong, but pneumonia or eating problems could have been his downfall, not his fragility. There was a mounting, pressing concern as he was having little coughing bouts when he would drink. We thickened his apple juice and milk, but he just swirled the milk around in his mouth and then vomited it up.

In this latter stage he was in, his throat started closing up or he forgot how to swallow, which becomes the situation contributing to many deaths. Once they cannot swallow, they stop eating and die. Was he reaching that stage? Could be. Signs were starting to manifest themselves. It was not only when he drank; he seemed to cough more in general. He mostly ate minced food due to his few teeth, so he also had trouble chewing and it took a long time masticating before he would swallow. I had witnessed five residents die who had stopped eating due to choking. They were all really close to the last stage. It was difficult to compare them to Jeff because he was physically strong.

We had a couple of episodes during the transfer from the walker to the wheelchair where Jeff misjudged the chair distance as he turned, which put me in an awkward position of holding him up as he was falling. I was too far from the help cord but still managed to get him to stand. I really felt the strain in my muscles and back. I dragged myself to the buses. It was my fault as I shouldn't have been doing it myself. Staff always said I should be careful as Jeff was not a child. Next time I promised to engage someone to stand by as we transferred.

Jeff's coughing had escalated. I received a call at home at 9:00 p.m.. He was having difficulty with aspiration, which resulted in the head nurse removing some of the fluid to help ease his condition. I was anxious to see him. He was sitting quietly in his wheelchair when I got there the next day. He ate his lunch—puréed soup, minced meat and veggies with apple juice that had a wee bit of thickening—quite happily. The rotating doctor checked in with me about whether he could tolerate some cough medicine. He coughed when he was in bed and we were not sure whether it was leading to aspiration pneumonia. He was tired at 2:00 and needed more rest. The head nurse met with me and said his blood pressure was fine and he had no fever, but he was coughing a lot. They thought it was due to poor swallowing and could lead to pneumonia, like what Don (his pal at Wisteria) got several times, requiring hospitalization.

They were trying to get Jeff to spit up phlegm, but he resisted for lack of comprehension. I tried to talk him into stretching out his arm so they could take his blood pressure, but he quickly pulled back. He was suspicious and folded his arms so tightly I had no chance. We were not sure what his problem could be; perhaps he was even allergic to something—it was difficult to know. He ate and slept well, though. He kept coughing, so I got him to do standing exercises; that always helped get rid of constipation.

Jeff was examined later and the doctor told me it was not a cold or cough. She narrowed it down to delayed swallowing and particles possibly going into his lungs. She suggested a type of puffer with a mask respirator with meds, so that was ordered.

My psychiatrist said it was very serious but the respirator might help clear his passageways. She also brought up a decision I might be faced with if he contracted pneumonia: would we let nature take its course or give him antibiotics? I had a non-resuscitation agreement in place if he had a stroke. Giving antibiotics could help if it was a one-time episode or even several if the patient didn't have dementia. But with dementia, aspiration pneumonia can be ongoing. You can give antibiotics and he clears—maybe. But it could come right back.

So that was a decision I would be faced with if this respirator didn't do the job. I didn't want to lose him, but I didn't want him to keep suffering if it was ongoing. He was supposed to get the respirator within a few days, and he could use it four times a day at first. I hoped he would accept it.

One of my sisters had serious medical issues, so I was trying to figure out how to get to Ottawa to visit her. No time was the right time to go with Jeff's stages. It was imperative to see my sister who was so ill, and I would forever regret if something happened to her and I missed the chance to hug her and share some time together. Isn't that just the way we all feel despite the pressing priorities in our lives?

It was like my decision about the cruise to Alaska. I was more or less talked into it by my doctor. I had a couple of friends visit Jeff while I was away, and I was sure they would again if I were out of town for a week visiting my family. His sister was also visiting more frequently, and even if it did confuse him, it was not something we dwelled on. I tried to think in the context that he had another visitor who always brought her sweet dog who licked his face!

I knew I was making Jeff happy as evidenced by his constant laughter and smiles. He always—always—patted my back and hugged me fiercely. I know we continued to share our love. I was grateful for these days with him. He had such a huge loss compared to my grief.

Jeff walked the best he had in three months—he was "motoring" and laughing! Beautiful spring days had been conducive for trips out to the patio and to the local market. Jeff had his nap every day, and I managed to transfer him myself to his wheelchair. I said to him just recently, "Let's go out," and he piped up, "What are we waiting for?" Wow! A whole sentence! And he was ready to turn into his wheelchair from the bed with ease. That was not the norm. That was a surprise and a very welcome one at that. I got him all bundled up, and I think I shocked the staff that I did it without any intervention or assistance from them. I was pleasantly surprised with his cooperation. We went onto the patio, then out the main door, and he was happy. We enjoyed an hour outside—just what we both needed.

So many considerations arose when contemplating moving someone with dementia to another residence. It wasn't just for their adjustment to new surroundings but the level of care that might be different—better or worse. What would I do if he was offered a place in Yaletown? It could be the end of his walking with the Ultimate Walker unless I purchased one. He knew the staff at Montbretia, and although I was only there in the morning and afternoon, I didn't get the impression that he interacted much with the residents.

I decided to continue pushing to get him transferred to Yaletown. At his present stage in this illness I didn't think it would make any difference to his equanimity. Montbretia care (combined with my constant vigilance) had been wonderful, professional and caring. It would be the same in Yaletown. The only issue might be the other patients, but all patients eventually come to the same level, and social standing becomes irrelevant. Dragging myself all the way across the city by bus to be with my loved one was untenable.

My grieving counsellor pointed out that Jeff slept a lot to keep his brain active. If he had fewer issues, perhaps he would be accepted by Yaletown House. He had been getting into things he shouldn't—like emptying his closet or the chest of drawers, playing with the taps until they came undone, removing fascia off the side of the door jambs—a year earlier, but that stage was over now.

Jeff's sister went to see him and left me a belated birthday gift, a bag of goodies which had lots of thoughtful items in it. Three kinds of honey, home-made jam, pure jasmine soap, warm woollen socks, fig and walnut spread, plus a bunch of other neat things. It was an unexpected surprise that I sure appreciated!

It was such a pleasure to arrive there and see him just light up when he saw me. He would wave almost like he was watching for me. Hey, maybe he was. When he spotted me, he started clapping and said loudly and clearly, "You are beautiful," for all to hear. Wow! He made me feel so loved!

He was different in so many ways and so childlike. Jeff had lost some abilities but had definitely not lost his graciousness and manners. He always thanked staff if they gave him a blanket or juice. He also had been sitting on the toilet so we were handling his toilet issues a bit better.

Jeff's residence manager and I met, and she agreed I had a strong case for his move to Yaletown House. Perhaps more of his friends would visit if he were closer, as Montbretia was off the beaten track. His sister would have come more often if he were closer as well.

It was always difficult to get Jeff's attention around noon hour as he was exhausted from tossing the balloon around and the exercises Y gave them. He never missed his meals, though, as he had such a good appetite. He was so anxious to get into bed and was not happy to be so close to it and then moved back in the common room. He would get his bed time only after he walked.

March crept up on us so quickly! Jeff's sister decided to see him and insisted on picking me up as I, too, wanted to see him. He saw me and said, "Hi, baby," with a big smile. We had hugs. It seemed like he didn't recognize his sister. He stood an impressive eight times for us. She took her dog out for a walk as I fed Jeff his lunch. She convinced me to leave as Jeff was sleeping in his chair, and, wow, I agreed to go. I needed to be pushed sometimes.

We went for a fabulous lunch by the Fraser River and watched ducks in the mudflats. It was a brilliant, beautiful day. It was such a lovely, unexpected visit from his sister that flowed so smoothly. She said she would visit Jeff if I went to Ottawa. My confidence was high as Jeff's rugby buddy said he would also visit him while I was away.

A few days later it seemed he had a sudden decline. He was slumped to one side at an awkward angle in his chair and would not straighten. If he had vascular dementia, which was what the neurologist diagnosed, the slumping could mean he was having mini strokes, like steppes. Each day could bring new developments, positive or negative. It was such a far cry from the steady, dependable, strong person he once was.

When Jeff and I first met, besides running a delicatessen, he also got called for work as a stuntman for a couple of TV series: *MacGyver* and *Wiseguy*. He was a stand-in for Jeff Bridges on one occasion because of his height and build. He also did stunts on *Experts* and *Murphy's Law*. He played some interesting characters, and this collage of his roles represents some of them.

He often would work long hours on set for days. They once dropped him off by helicopter on top of a mountain and he slept in a tent there overnight to guard the set equipment. Another time, he had to have extensive make-up to turn him into an Amish man with a black beard and dark hair. He didn't have speaking roles but lots of action, and he really enjoyed this work. He was obviously good at it as he was regularly called. Some days he would leave at five in the morning and return at two the next morning.

A little bonus for me was they often needed a court reporter for trial scenes, so I would get work as an extra. I would bring my stenographic machine and act like a court reporter, which was quite hilarious. I would bring demure clothing to have that professional look. Sometimes I saw myself in the background of the episode or a close-up of my hands on my machine! It was a lot of fun for Jeff and me, and we earned fairly good money doing it!

As I approached Montbretia, it so often crossed my mind what Jeff used be like. I had to remind myself not to be surprised or disappointed as it was the nature of the disease. It would be a huge bonus if he was smiling, hugging and chatting.

As the weather improved, so did Jeff! I took the opportunity to wheel him out to the patio for an hour in the sun before lunch one day. After lunch, staff helped transfer him to his other lightweight wheelchair, so we wheeled down to the market. We looked at flowers. I gave him a bag and he enthusiastically picked out mangos, bananas and mandarin oranges. We went inside and got more yogurt. He behaved so well, and the cashier gave him the purchases, putting it on his lap, and he said, "Thank you." On our return, we could see the mountains in the distance and I stopped and talked about them. The uphill return was always a bit of a struggle for me pushing his heavy wheelchair!

DAILY MUSINGS

Where has Poppet been? I kept looking for her all morning and couldn't concentrate on the balloon toss in case she came and didn't see me. I hope she comes soon.

I sure don't like getting all mashed-up food but it seems I start coughing with bigger pieces so they are mashing everything. But it does go down easily and it always is so good.

We went to a market and I found parking spots for us but she said it was okay, we would just use the wheelchair. All the fruit to look at and she handed me a bag to fill.

I was so excited as I got to choose exactly what I felt like eating. We had a big bag full, went inside and paid and everyone was so friendly to us. I was among a lot of people I hadn't seen before but lots of smiles and hellos to us!

Then we went to a coffee place and she bought a big foamy coffee drink for me—seemed to have ice cream in it. I told her I want to do this again and again!

We have such good times together. We hug and kiss and cuddle and it makes it easy to fall asleep!

YALETOWN

I finally had my meeting at Yaletown House, and I left feeling positive that Jeff was high on the list if—and it was a big "if"—a ceiling-hoist room became available.

Jeff's cognitive abilities were now such that he was unaware of his functional limitations, which gave me some solace. There were glimmers of assertiveness, but he got respite in sleep. My doctor never failed to remind me that my dedication to his well-being had prolonged his life well beyond normal expectancy and there was not one thing to beat myself up over. The best will in the world could not stop his inexorable decline. All I could do was continue to grab the moments of joy that presented themselves.

Jeff and I certainly benefitted from with the respirator gizmo. At first he thought it was food and wanted to eat it. He coughed less, and they were mincing all his food so he could swallow more easily.

There were days when I got to Montbretia quickly with the buses and trains on time. He would walk, eat everything and it was perfect for us both. But his disease continued to be unpredictable. One day he was not doing well, but the next day he'd be alert, chatting. His sister had been dropping in which was great to see.

I looked forward to a Helen Day to catch up with my chores after spending Saturday and Sunday with Jeff. All weekend it was cuddle, snuggle and huddle mode with sleep mode 80% of the time. Sometimes he was vague, but he always knew me and always seemed overjoyed to see me, grabbing me with his strong arms and pulling me close without letting go.

I exchanged e-mails with Jeff's brother and sister-in-law in England, providing updates and photos of Jeff over these past few years. I was not at all familiar with the relationship he had with his brother, but I knew they worked together for many years. Jeff rarely spoke about his brother, and I couldn't remember him suggesting visiting him while we were in London. Both busy with their lives! It was brothers and their dynamics. I only met them and the rest of his family a couple of times when Jeff and I went on a six-week bicycle trip to England and France.

Later in our relationship, we lived off and on in the heart of London around Chancery Lane and six blocks from St. Paul's Cathedral. How fortunate to find this apartment and be right in the hub of busy London! We were contracted for work at the Royal Courts of Justice, which was walking distance from the apartment. We were really busy with a new contract job in London and it was an exciting, fantastic city to explore. I absolutely loved living in London.

Opportunities to travel to the Red Sea for scuba diving were so tempting and were a real steal from London! We had dived there on three occasions, and the variety of fish and coral—not to mention the desert and atmosphere— were exquisite! Such a diverse culture and many rare and unique fish and coral. Jacques Cousteau said it was probably the best diving in the world.

In looking back on our third dive to the Red Sea, at El Gouna, I can't help but wonder if Jeff's dementia was beginning to surface. He always used a compass underwater, and on our last dive we didn't use the line to descend and he plotted our course. It was an amazing dive with the highlight being an encounter with a huge humphead wrasse, a fish I'd never seen before, who hung around and let me take a few photos. When we had used up most of our air, Jeff was looking for the area to ascend but he hadn't made the right compass calculations. When we hit the surface, we were far from the boat. It was choppy, and we were spotted floating on the surface so the dive charter had to come and pick us up. Jeff was so surprised and couldn't understand how he had miscalculated.

The dementia journey was slow at times with intermittent changes and confusion for both Jeff and for me. I was always surprised how the changes got accepted and that we found new ways to communicate and enjoy our visits. Jeff was strong, stubborn and determined, and I guess that was an echo of me as well. We were both alone. Apart. Separated.

Jeff's sister always let me know how her time was spent with Jeff. Her e-mails were supportive and praised me about Jeff's walking accomplishments! She also said she spoke by phone with Jeff's brother and explained "...the magnificent part you are playing in supporting Jeff and we agree he is a very lucky man to have you." She gave Jeff's brother a rough outline of where his health stood and updated him frequently. She said it made him sad, but he understood the prognosis. She said they discussed whether there was any point in having him come from England to visit with Jeff and wondered what my thoughts on that were. I couldn't say. Only his brother could decide whether to make the trip or not.

Another visit to Yaletown House cemented my feelings that it would offer him more outdoor space. The welcoming sea wall with paddlers and boats, all the activity to watch and ponder—dogs running around, cyclists on their bike paths. I got so overwhelmed with grief at times, and I felt guilty that he was not living with me despite all the arguments against it. I was so frustrated that I couldn't do more for Jeff. There he was locked in his chair, nodding off, with time passing by. His music was playing, and he must be feeling so alone and stuck.

Travelling back and forth was draining and, let's face it, I, too, was aging and running out of steam. I hated to acknowledge it, but I was in the category of "old" now. How desperate I was to have any of his friends stop in even for fifteen minutes to say hello to their old friend. He would know. I was so grateful his sister started visiting again. We discussed our loss of Jeff while watching him when we visited together. I tried not to cry, but it was really so difficult to stay in a good frame of mind. I had lost interest in so many things and was solely focused on Jeff's struggle and happiness. I couldn't believe how quickly the years were passing and how old I was.

My flight to Ottawa was on a Tuesday at 9:30, and I'd be back on Sunday morning. Five nights to spend with family I hadn't seen for several years! One of the residents at Montbretia was ninety-six and did physio in the Ultimate Walker before Jeff's turn. Her son, who came to visit often, said he would happily assist Oliver on the two physio days I would be away in Ontario. He often shook Jeff's hand and always smiled at him.

I received an e-mail with bad news from Wisteria about the death of my friend's husband, Don, who passed away from aspiration pneumonia. Don suffered a lot with pneumonia and had several hospital bouts due to that added problem.

Jeff had his bath in the morning on Easter Sunday. When I arrived, his pants were not done up and he had no socks on. Unfortunately, I think nursing staff were giving him suppositories without letting nature take its course. Two days shouldn't warrant laxatives when someone doesn't get to stand up. If he was allowed to stand more, at least once when I was not there, he might be less constipated.

Jeff would turn seventy-eight this year. His sister and I treated him to fish and chips for lunch with fruit and a birthday cake we shared with everyone. The birthday month musicians also showed up, so there was also another cake that day—never too many cakes for Jeff!

There was a flu-related outbreak which affected the residence. Visitors were encouraged to stay away, but no one could stop diehards like me! No sickness was evident in Jeff's unit, but I was still washing my hands constantly and keeping him in his unit, not out in the halls. Despite the outbreak, Jeff was good—the activity director did all sorts with them.

I had this awful feeling sitting at Jeff's bedside wishing him out of this world of his slowly dying brain. I just cried beside him. I felt so utterly helpless and loved him so much. What a life for him. God, it was so terrible sometimes. Forty-five hours of busing a month helped me keep my sanity and keep him hopeful, but we all knew what the outcome would be. I was confused about how long this terrible decline and the loss of quality of life would go on.

MY BIRTHDAY. APRIL 26, 2018

I am being treated so nice today with everyone in my room singing "Happy Birthday." They gave me cards too!

Exercise with Baby and all my friends sang again! They tell me my wife and sister will be arriving to visit me at lunchtime!

A huge cake and lots of fruit!

We gathered around the long table and it was so nice to hear the birthday song. I was in the middle with my sister on one side and my wife on the other!

Music arrived. We celebrated with great cake. I was allowed many pieces! I'm tired now. Need to nap.

LATE APRIL 2018

I became good friends with a lady whose husband was at the same residence, and we used to meet once every couple of months at a café to update each other. On Jeff's birthday a year ago, she and her husband were sitting with us and she took a couple of photos of Jeff. Her husband was not well. Unfortunately, he died a week later.

Jeff's sister was true to her promise and arrived with fish and chips for his birthday. We got the cake and a mixed tray of fruit at Costco. Jeff's sister and I made a happy, cheerful connection on his birthday!

I was not crazy about the live music as their choice of songs got to me. Jeff would have rather been in his room stretched out, but his was the only April birthday so he was sort of obligated to sit there. He enjoyed the wishes and song and, of course, two pieces of cake. After the musician closed up, we put Jeff in bed for a nap. We snuggled a bit. It was a good day. He was pensive and quiet but ate his lunch. We didn't attempt the walker, but he was keen to stand, and so he did.

Days passed with highs and lows from Jeff. I was used to it and trying not to read anything into his vague mode, the tightly folded arms and moody, faraway gaze.

I was off to Ottawa soon, and my plan was to see Jeff before I boarded my flight as the airport was en route. I would be back on Sunday early and drop in on Jeff on my way from the airport. Jeff's sister said she would visit him at lunchtime as he needed assistance at this stage.

Lots of emotions about this trip. My siblings would be together for the first time in three and a half years. One of my nieces sent me a photo of a table full of bottles of champagne they had ready for my arrival! They were setting the atmosphere!

I had just the nicest, sweetest cuddle with Jeff this weekend. He whispered love stuff and rubbed my back and we giggled together. It was exactly what I needed!

In the evenings I often watching taped shows to relax from the bus and train travelling. I was excited for the season premiere of *Dancing with the Stars*. I'd always loved dancing, and my first husband (he had a massive heart attack and died at fifty-four) was a terrific Latin dancer. He taught me cha cha, meringue and a few other steps! What a coincidence that Jeff and my first husband both had the same birth date—April 26th.

Jeff's youngest son moved near us in the West End and invited us over to meet some of his friends. It turned out to be a night of salsa dancing! His son grabbed me and said, "I will teach you!" Salsa was the new popular dance, and before long we all were salsa-ing, Jeff being a natural dancer like his son. Nice memories!

QUIET DAYS

I have asked a few people where my wife is. Where is Helen? When will she be here? Is she coming today? Is she coming tomorrow? Is she sick? They say she will be here soon.

I watch for her all the time but don't see her.

I see lots of Baby and we do earphones often and lots of different exercises. My favourite is when she is just with me and gives me lots of attention and talks non-stop. She sits on a small stool in front of me and rubs and massages my arms and shoulders. Then she attacks my legs and feet. I am not too happy when she stops. I want her to stay with me. I ask her if she has seen Helen and she said she went to see her sister for a few days. But she said she would be back soon and not to worry as she's coming soon.

But my wife doesn't come for lunch or dinner or at all. They tell me when I ask where she is that she will come soon but I just keep waiting and watching. There's others to be with but I just don't know where she's gone. I ask Rosie if she saw my wife but she didn't answer.

Every morning I ask, "Is my wife coming today?"

OTTAWA

I had a wonderful six-day visit with my family. We caught up on news, gossip and got into the champagne most days, but the time went by all too quickly. My sister Pat took the train to Ottawa from Toronto and my brother lived in Ottawa so we all were gathered at my sister Betty and her husband's home.

Betty's husband, Bud, had been diagnosed with dementia recently although his family mentioned his confusion at times in e-mails. Pat and I were shocked to see how much he had changed. He had taken each of us aside privately and told us about his suspicions and what was "really" going on. He wondered if his wife was interested in another man down the street and other stories that worried us.

I could see the changes in him as he was getting confused (although trying to hide it), but he was certainly changing. Bud was sad, too, because he knew he had changed and was forgetting important things. We look from the outside and don't experience what they must feel—the loss of something and not remembering what it was they had lost.

I had read many books on dementia by this time, and the big thing was feeling anxious and not sure if they were still loved—worried that we don't love them. The person with dementia wonders why they can't remember and it plays on their brain. I often saw the furrows in Jeff's brow; they were the same ones my brother-in-law had.

I went through so many "insignificant" changes with Jeff that were clearly happening with my brother-in-law. He had uncles who died from dementia-related disease, so that gene was in their family. It was difficult to fathom that he couldn't carry on with his routines any longer.

Jeff had no ability to write or read early after his diagnosis. I had trouble with it, thinking he could do things. I'd send him off with a list for the store and he didn't buy one thing on the list because he couldn't read. It wasn't his fault. He wanted to help but the confusion was there. Because Jeff could walk anywhere he was easy to lose. He would promise to wait on a bench and forget why he was sitting there. So many times he wandered away when my back was turned. He couldn't sit on the beach anymore—just had to keep moving and wandering.

People with dementia need all the help we can give them. Jeff cried almost every morning as he knew something was not right with him anymore. I took the courses on all the stages and went to the support meetings, so I had heard lots. Everyone was different. I found the books helped.

MAY 6

Where is she? I keep asking them, "Where is she?"
I haven't seen her for many days and asked if she was sick.
They keep telling me she will be here soon. I keep watching for her.
She always comes with treats and takes me outside.
I haven't been outside for a while and hope she comes back.
I wish she would come see me soon.

RETURN TO VANCOUVER

It was a beautiful day for flying, and I went straight from the airport to Jeff.

From a distance, I could see he had a questioning look on his face but he seemed to figure me out. He let out a yell and said, "Poppet, you're here!" He grabbed me in a big hug, almost toppling his chair. Everyone was laughing, and we had a memorable day together. Outside, great lunch, standing exercises, a cuddly nap, eating treats. He was smiling and happy with me, holding tightly. If I moved in the bed, he would say, "No! Stay here," and squeezed tighter. I loved it all; it was just what I needed on my return from Ottawa.

When I went to get a coffee, he swung his chair around and was watching me. Then he held his hands out as I came back. He seemed vulnerable and insecure, and I really felt like his lifeline. I wondered if he had missed me—he was acting as if he had, needing lots of attention. I told him all about Ottawa, about my sisters and brother all the nieces and showed him photos of the family. I think some of it brought a memory from the past as he would smile at some of the photos.

I asked staff if anyone visited Jeff. They checked but didn't see any entries for visits to him. Don't think his sister visited him, and I hadn't heard from her. I checked with his rugby buddy who said he would visit, but he got tied up.

I had these disappointments, but my return brought magical days! I hadn't heard Jeff make so many sentences in years.

One day— Jeff had just started walking in the walker with Oliver— Jeff yelled, "Hi!" and then he turned to Oliver and said—I kid you not—"This is my wife," and broke into a huge smile. We could not believe it! He kept saying all kinds of stuff like, "We have to keep walking." Happy me, happy Oliver! He was lucid all day, so I wondered what cocktail mix he got that morning. It was so unlike someone with Alzheimer's to get "better." Most continued on the downhill slope, so it was a startling change—moments like those were just so precious and memorable.

They had hired another activities director, Kay, who had just graduated from care courses. She divided her time with Y and with a lockdown unit across the hall, so all dementia residents would get more activities.

How terribly sad when someone loses their independence. I looked at Jeff and my heart just broke to see him in the chair. His knees were so lumpy and bad; it was quite amazing he could walk. But we always got out in the fresh air and he seemed happy and smiley. He loved his new earphones and music seemed to relax him.

I was somewhat down despite the uplifting episodes when I returned. It was the trip, in part, the euphoria at seeing everyone but the sadness at the state Betty and Bud were in. It was always on my mind. I felt connected with everyone but at the same time quite disconnected as Jeff was not with me and life had changed so much for the both of us now living apart. Perhaps I was being oversensitive and no one wanted to remind me that Jeff was without me now so we avoided the subject. I was viewing it from the one who had the husband with dementia and now we were presented with Betty's illness and Bud having dementia. It may have been difficult for them to understand my life with Jeff now compared to the years before and so much had also changed in their lives..

But days with Jeff were happy ones. He was mellow after a bath one day, and he reached out to me and said, "You're my wife." Wow, what was going on? I said, "Yes," and he said, "That's right," and gave me a tight hug. It was a whole conversation! I figured staff must have been saying stuff about me like, "Your wife is coming soon." I know it doesn't seem like much, but it was huge for him to be speaking and making sentences.

We went outside for lunch. We had a good nap. We chatted a lot. As I was leaving, all the residents were wheeled to the patio in the shade, including Jeff. Apparently, they had discovered that residents love being out, and it makes me happy. It was one of those days that fell nicely into place in my unpredictable life.

When I arrived for my next visit, Jeff was sitting there happily with his earphones in. We got him walking, and he did amazingly well—three whole rounds of the halls. He was asleep before his head hit the pillow. We had lunch and we had our moments. When he woke up, he said, "Hi, baby, I love you." I was so close to tears. What could I say? I was lucky beyond words.

I left him on the patio in a location he could be seen by nurses. I wanted him to stay outside!

MAY 2018

I like going outside! I hope she doesn't leave me again.

My girl brings me treats. We eat outside.

She showed me lots of pictures of people but little came to me but there were some good-looking people!

She told me she was away. I didn't notice or did I?

I asked one time, "Where is my wife?" They said, "She'll be here soon."

She talked so much this time and I was trying not to fall asleep so I wouldn't hurt her feelings.

All I wanted was to hug her and rest and not walk and just listen to music.

EARLY JUNE

One day when Jeff was sleeping like an angel, I was thinking about my friend whose husband passed recently. I was in a similar waiting game, which shook me up with fear and trepidation. The mindfulness teachings suggested engaging the thoughts but then letting them go and living in the moment of him sleeping like an angel. Not go past that. It is a nebulous state, though, and some thoughts just caught me off guard.

I had two close friends whose husbands had passed away, and we used to meet often for dinners and talk about our experiences. It was obvious each of us had different journeys. We initially met before our husbands were in care. The three of us attended a monthly programme of round table discussions to help us share our current problems and share solutions and tips on how to cope.

Grief hangs in there and we learn to accept it, don't we? Or do we? It was like grief had become part of my life for ten years, and I didn't expect it to go away anytime soon. My friends continued to grieve and try to find hobbies to help them cope. We often discussed how much our husbands suffered and how courageous they were to battle through this disease.

A friend who lived down the hall from me who lost her partner said, "I'm so grateful for having had three years with my wonderful man." It put the many wonderful years Jeff and I had together into perspective. It also reminded me I must be thankful for what I still had with Jeff and to help others stay positive.

Some days ran so smoothly at Montbretia. Jeff was happy listening to music—always Leonard Cohen or the Bee Gees. He managed his spoon on his own at lunchtime. We did our nap. Then he walked and was chatting to staff.

"Where are we going?" he asked.

"Switzerland!" I said.

"Good," he said, "to the mountains."

That thought was clear and there and connected!

I had my two widow friends over for a nice pot luck dinner, and I saw a definite pattern in our chatting about Alzheimer's. You are incapable of handling your spouse at home and, much as you don't want to, you have to give in. I don't know if having tonnes of money would change the equation either; it's a difficult row to hoe regardless.

At these dementia-related meetings I attended in the West End, there was a lady who would not give up her husband and had care assistants coming all the time. One day she broke down crying and said, "I can't stand the smell of shit in everything in my house, my clothes, the furniture, his clothes." So she would go on short trips to get away from the home atmosphere and hired staff to take care of him during her absences.

We all thought we could handle it, but we couldn't. Care was so beyond our capabilities, especially when dealing with a strong, stubborn, independent childlike man or woman. It tore us apart because we felt like we were failing them. But when I saw Jeff sitting there content listening to music, not being aggressive, going from moment to moment, I recognized it was the only way we could survive.

I entered his world. We touched. We looked at each other. We communicated. But he could only take so much activity. He was always trying to speak, eat, please me, and his brain was just not absorbing what it should—things were bouncing off him. He needed lots of rest and quiet time. We were both doing the best we could to survive, and I found it difficult to express the reality to those who hadn't experienced it.

Constant worry.

Sleepless nights.

Endless standing and waiting for buses.

Hoping he would remember me when I arrived.

Hoping he still loved me.

Life was precious.

I always said goodbye to Jeff each visit in case it was my last time. One day I said, "I love you," and he said, "Me too," and patted my face.

The physiotherapist occasionally got delayed or cancelled, but Jeff still had his music and board playing until noon. One day he was listening to Leonard Cohen while I was sitting with him, and he just suddenly started to cry. Then I started to cry. It was so heart-wrenching to see him in that state. Kay thought he was listening to a sad song, so we changed the artist and he seemed better. He was squeezing my hands so tightly. He seemed different, more sensitive than before.

Jeff continued to walk but with knee pain. He was slowly declining, though, and we could see the changes—couldn't understand instructions, afraid to stand, not knowing what it was all about. And then one day he became chatty again, which surprised us all. But that didn't last—it was just short intervals of lucidity.

Jeff was like the last man standing as all his mates from the original group had passed on. There just seemed to be several new—but whining—women. They all wanted to befriend me, and I did my best to ignore them. I had enough on my plate. When new people moved in, staff helped them walk. Two weeks later they were stuck in their chairs. That was what happened. It was a tragedy—like a hospice. But I ignored it the best I could and did my thing with Jeff.

I really was troubled not wanting to let Jeff go, but his quality of life became so humiliating to both of us. Like so many of us in this situation, I had such a myriad of emotions that pulled every which way. I really don't know if one gets a weight lifted when there is no more suffering for them. The despair, sadness and hurt during the last stages of their decline was real. People run from it and often don't visit as they just can't take it.

A new lady visited her husband four days a week, fed him lunch, stayed less than an hour but never stopped pretending life was smiley and beautiful. We were all so different. I just cried many days while Jeff was napping. I felt physical pains of heartbreak in my chest. It was the most difficult time of my life. I had never been this sad ever.

MID-JUNE

Jeff's sister and Newt (her dog) came back to visit—a bit of respite for me!

The rotating doctor and I noticed Jeff was having swallowing problems—something she described as "pooling and pocketing." Essentially, he had been storing the thickened liquid in his cheeks like a chipmunk. It could make him look grumpy (which he may or may not be). When he nodded off, his mouth opened and all the liquid slowly poured out. He was often a mess and did it often these days.

An article I read said his brain was likely losing its ability to remember how to eat—swallow, swish it around or spit it out. It suggested feeding him small amounts of food at a time, watching the Adam's apple bob and giving frequent drinks to encourage swallowing.

He was fine with yogurt drinks, but he couldn't swallow water, milk or juice, whether thickened or not. I tried a half glass of water and he sipped, but it immediately dribbled out of his mouth. His brain had shut off eating, so if pooling and pocketing occurred some could dribble into his lungs and choke him. He continued to be strong and walk well. He was always fit, but aspiration pneumonia could well be his downfall. Another resident had died that way. He was choking, but they saved him and sent him to hospital. He returned to the home but passed a few weeks later.

We monitored this closely. We stopped feeding him lunch in bed as it would be easier to choke. Had to keep napkins away from him as he seemed to think they were food. He'd also started mouthing the bed sheet. How sad it all was. But here was a tiny positive—I could spoon feed him the thickened juice like a dessert, which he would swallow. We could solve some of the problems.

At one point Jeff tried to wear the bedding as he couldn't distinguish a bed sheet from clothing. Dementia was subtle at first or not as obvious when you lived with someone on a daily basis. It was more obvious to visitors.

In the summer of 2018, I had such low moments living with the ongoing grief. We all will die, but Jeff's days were numbered and his quality of life locked in a residence just above the level of hospice was low.

I had to focus on now. That day. Friendly people surfaced in unexpected places. I could write a book about my travels on the buses, the conversations, sharing umbrellas. If we stay indoors, we only dwell on things, and we truly miss the opportunity to make new friends. I needed to make the most of my abilities and talents. We all have something to offer. Tomorrow was gone. It was today. I drilled this into my head—live in this moment, not yesterday or tomorrow but right now. I couldn't say it enough times. If I sat in my apartment and did not go out, I would be depressed. Going out was a matter of survival.

Must have had a foreboding of trouble for this month as I awoke with a heavy heart. This turned out to be a strange, emotional, upsetting week. When I arrived at Jeff's one morning in mid-July, I was told he wouldn't eat breakfast, not a drop, and he was sitting in his chair slumped over sleeping. Nothing could shake him awake. I was told he had a fever during the night but it broke that morning. I wheeled him to his room by the window and he did not stir, would not grasp my hand, would not engage at all. He was catatonic.

Just before lunch I took him outside for fresh air. I spoke with the resident manager about my options for his care if he got worse—no resuscitation and no meds like antibiotics. We gave him painkillers as usual, and he sat outside for an hour. He would not eat a thing. I gave him some liquid, he dribbled it out.

We went to bed and he was just out of it. No reaction. I tried to chat, but he would not open his eyes, hands and legs so still, shallow breathing. I really thought he might die that day.

By 3:30, we got him up. He opened his eyes for a second and had no temperature. He was so frighteningly unresponsive. I shed a bucket of tears, hugged him and pulled him close to me and whispered and he seemed to pull me tighter. I actually didn't think he was going to pull through. I stayed with him for hours, then we got him up and he sat in front of the TV.

I decided to leave eventually as I was so exhausted. When I called around 9:00 p.m., they said he had eaten a small amount and they put him to bed at 8:00.

I went to see him the next day, and he didn't eat breakfast but had three glasses of juice. I shook him and he opened his eyes and smiled at me but went back to sleep. We sat on the patio and I fed him half his lunch.

Not sure if he had had a regression or what. That happened sometimes and then they bounce back. There was nothing I could do when he was sleeping and just out of it. No one called, so I just tried not to worry because I couldn't control what was happening. I felt like he was just waiting to leave this world. It was hard to watch him so still just lying there barely breathing. If he refused to eat, he only would get weaker. He was coughing when he ate at times, so that was a big issue.

All through the week I visited. On the Thursday I held him in my arms and he didn't move and I whispered to him that I was there. He moved his body closer to me so I think he understood. The manager said he might be looking for permission to say goodbye, so that got me really teary.

I rushed to get there Friday morning, and everything had changed! Oh, my god, he was waiting for me with open arms, a big smile on his face. He hugged me like crazy, chatted up a storm and ate his breakfast.

"We have to keep an eye on things," he said.

Hallelujah! I can't express the relief I felt.

I was told to expect this might happen again, but at least I would be a bit more prepared. There was no doubt the quality of his life would get worse, and it was obvious he did not like puréed food; he knew it was not a burger and fries or fish and chips.

I was talked into a day off, but I spent most of my time wondering how Jeff was. I certainly didn't feel like rushing to grab buses and trains—I got exhausted just thinking about it. All I could think about was Jeff clinging to me if he thought I was leaving. He sometimes said out of the blue, "Don't go," and would take a vise-like hold on my wrist.

"I'm here to stay," I'd say, and hug him.

He would then relax. No one could tell me he didn't know the score. When he said, "Go away," I got that too; he wanted time to himself.

Jeff's Monday usually involved music in his headphones in the morning, but Kay didn't show so I decided to be with him. It was important for his well-being to know I was there. I was so dismayed to see him when I arrived as he was sitting all alone in the middle of the room, no one around, chair locked. The relief in his body language when he spotted me was obvious. I was just so disappointed. The staff knew he liked being at the window and he was not supposed to be kept locked in the middle of the room.

I didn't trust the casual staff to know the "plan," as there seemed to be a revolving door of people who didn't know anything about him. They had twenty people to take care of, and when five people had a poop at the same time it was chaotic. Four staff was far too few.

I got him standing and outside right away. His happiness was palpable.

Went to a nicely-presented memorial tribute in the garden at Wisteria where Jeff was for his transitional stay. The place brought back all kinds of flashes of memory, but I tried to concentrate on the good ones and on who the memorial was for. Don had befriended Jeff when he first moved to Wisteria—reading newspapers and eating together. Don had many bouts of pneumonia and his wife told me he died from aspiration pneumonia.

When discussing the big scare with my psychiatrist, she thought Jeff might have had a slight congestive heart failure when he was so immobile and catatonic. She thought his strength might be one of the reasons he pulled through.

At Jeff's annual assessment meeting at the end of July, it was noted that he continued to decline. They mentioned how involved I had been in keeping him focussed and taking him out and always feeding him his lunch when I was there. I received a lot of appreciation from the staff.

I got the feeling that Jeff would not be alive at assessment time the following year. I knew it was unpredictable, but that scare was an indication of where things were going. I thought my grief couldn't get any worse, but the shock of watching him get worse took it to a new level. I tried to kid myself that it was not the end of the road, but these assessment meetings once a year brought the changes into perspective; they shook me up each year. You would think I was immune by then, but it just dragged me down.

One of my friends who lost her husband two years before was not doing well. She was trying to declutter their apartment where they lived together for forty-three years, and it was such a difficult task to decide what to keep and what to let go. By this time, I had moved twice since living with Jeff at the Beach apartment. He hadn't been to either of them so I couldn't imagine him sitting on the sofa or his presence there. After he left the Beach apartment, I would see him and get startled thinking he was in the room with me. Him sprawled on the sofa napping would flash in my vision.

I felt like I was hanging in the air. I worried I would become like my friend—high blood pressure and just so wrapped up in grieving the loss of my husband. I could only hope I would be okay with Jeff saying goodbye. We didn't expect him to continue suffering. His knee pain was a constant. The fluctuation was not the norm for people with Alzheimer's; ups and downs were more common in a vascular dementia.

The weather was unbearably hot that summer, and there was no air conditioning at Montbretia. He walked well, although struggled with his knees. His eyes were vague at times. One day he was studying my face in bed, touching my cheeks and looking at me like he wanted to say, "I wish I could tell you stuff." We hugged and I chatted away and whispered stuff and he smiled. It was tougher than I ever would have imagined.

As he got worse, I felt more helpless. He had this flash of panic on his face which often meant he had soiled himself. I still saw the indignity written on his face. What a tragedy. I cried so often at his sadness and obvious despair.

Jeff's sister found ways to help me with trips to fruit and vegetable markets and paying for my groceries. She would phone and say, "Let's go for some groceries—I'm paying." She did that several times that summer, encouraging me to not hold back and fill my basket to the brim. I certainly appreciated those trips and her generosity!

Jeff and I poured over an album I put together, and I told him who was who. He listened but had a vague look and lost interest quickly. I could tell he didn't want to be reminded that he no longer recognized a lot of people from the past.

Oliver said if we stopped forcing Jeff to walk he would go downhill quickly. There was no doubt that the family of the residents made the difference. Oliver said if family members didn't press to have their loved one walking, they would just sit in wheelchairs. He could only try his best as the physiotherapist to point out the advantages and continued well-being of someone walking a few times a week instead of abandoning that idea. So many new residents arrived on their own two feet but stopped walking within a month.

Jeff seemed happy when he walked. I think we have to be guided by how keen they are to stand. The physiotherapist was covered under the care plan so it was not an extra cost to at least have that in place. Otherwise, it is up to the loved ones to make it happen. Life could end soon enough for other reasons.

In the last scene of a favourite TV series I often watched, the son went to visit his mom, who had Alzheimer's. She would never look at him or acknowledge him, just stare into space, but this time she looked at him. He burst into tears.

"Mom, you're there!" he said, and they held each other.

I burst into tears too. It reminded me so much of how Jeff often stared off into a world we knew little about. I had observed him smile when looking out the window, reaching for something. He got so much pleasure out of straightening the sheets. When he got transferred to his wheelchair and the staff left, I often moved him close to the bed and we would "make" the bed together. We tucked in all the overhangs, and he would say, "Yes," and, "No, wait," as he liked to have some control. Afterwards he would smile.

We spent most of a wonderful August on the patio watching the bird life, eating lunch, hanging out. I busied myself watering the plants and flowers. Our Tuesdays and Thursdays weren't always successful with Oliver, but we utilized the time the best we could. Jeff's body language sometimes said, "I want to sleep. I don't want to walk." I was persistent, though, and used treats to tempt him to stand.

Keeping Jeff's door open helped the circulation as the big fans were in the common areas. We had a number of new women residents who invaded everybody's room whenever they saw an opportunity; they would make off with our personal items and other things. Everything had to be locked up as shavers, photos, whatever they could get away with had gone missing. It meant we couldn't leave the doors wide open for air anymore. There were some exceedingly annoying residents who had joined the group, and the patio became an escape route from them.

Some staff kept locking Jeff in place, and I was getting really annoyed. Often when I arrived, he was shaking his chair wanting to move but couldn't. All this upset me to no end as I had so little control over him when I was not there. I stopped in to see the manager asking her to remind staff about this problem and she said she would take care of it.

DISPLACED ELEPHANT SEAL AT LOS ISLOTES

One day once I got him into bed, I sat down by the window to read. I looked up from my book at a photo I took of an elephant seal. My mind drifted to those days when we were living and diving at Los Islotes in La Paz, Mexico.

The news had spread that a juvenile elephant seal was trying to get close to sea lions at this dive site. He must have been displaced from a colony and tried to join the sea lions, but he couldn't make the grade. That's when he started to pursue the divers. We had heard he was gentle and curious, though always trying to embrace the divers. He'd go from one diver to the next in a state of arousal hoping to have a physical connection. Somewhat unnerving due to his girth and excitement. He weighed at least eight hundred pounds!

Jeff and I had met a German diver on the boat, and she asked if I would take photos of her with the elephant seal if he showed up. I spotted the juvenile seal coming towards us, and he quickly came to me for a hug. He needed to be coaxed to release my thigh. This German diver was quite experienced and was caressing his body so he let me go. Then she posed with him for the photos.

Their interaction was truly remarkable and I took what I hoped were some amazing photos. One of the best showed him like he was laughing. His two big front teeth were showing as she had her hands on either side of his face. I called it *Have you flossed lately?* It was probably the best shot as it was only five feet away. In another photo she caressed his neck and he looked to be howling like a wolf.

The elephant seal took off, but about five minutes later we saw he and Jeff heading into a shallow cave. I used the last of the film on close-ups of their faces. The elephant seal looked like a giant mouse! It was unexpected to be so close to an elephant seal and capture those shots. A once in a lifetime experience!

Jeff used the pictures when he did a lecture at a school in West Vancouver. Hundreds of students were in an auditorium where we had mounted about twenty huge blown-up photos for the classes to examine. Jeff had started to give talks on saving the seas at schools, and how better than to capture the beauty and diversity with these photos to embellish his presentations.

He also did a few presentations for students in his own grammar school in England. The students used the presentation and photos to produce poems about the sea, all of which were given to us. Jeff went there as a teenager and was welcomed back in 1996 for a presentation. He was an outstanding speaker and enjoyed interacting with students about saving the seas.

MEMORIAL DIGNITY QUILT PROJECT

Some family and staff at Jeff's residence made something called a memorial dignity quilt. Those interested in participating were given a block of fabric twelve inches square. They were stitched together, and from then on it was draped over the coffin or gurney of any resident who was exiting Montbretia for the final time. It would be removed at the exit and reused. It was so sad when we knew someone had passed, but perhaps the quilt was a comforting farewell especially for those who participated in making the panels.

EXCEPTIONALLY WARM SUMMER DAYS

I changed the routine so I could see Jeff two days in a row; I could not resist. Besides needing comfort and hugs myself, I needed him to keep standing. One time, Jeff was trotting during our walking exercises, which was quite amazing! I was showing him how fast I could walk and he started this little run. Unpredictable or what? Surprises or what? I don't think it was my imagination when I saw an expression that said, "So there!" on his face. He was grinning from ear to ear.

Jeff's dive buddy, Mike, and his wife (the Chocolate Lady) visited Jeff. It was a difficult visit given our history together. Jeff was shy and didn't communicate, smiled a bit, but I'm not sure he recognized them. He did enjoy getting the Swiss chocolate gift, and the Chocolate Lady fed him a pudding at 2:30. We took him out to the patio and he promptly fell asleep. Probably wanted us gone and some peace and quiet.

It had been an exceedingly hard time as Jeff continued to decline. I felt terribly lonely without the "old, bright Jeff" and had no family living close by—all back east in Ontario. Support from family and friends helped to get me through the more difficult times, but it was a solitary road with conflicting emotions and lots of grief.

My friends tried visiting, and Jeff fleetingly recognized them. The last time they visited it was New Year's, almost a year ago. I appreciated them coming but often thought how much Jeff would have enjoyed their company more often. Perhaps it was worrisome to see Jeff like this as it could happen to any of us and we didn't want to be reminded. This remained a conflict in my mind throughout our journey—why so few friends came to visit him.

When I would get home, no one was there—just me. No one to chat about the day or about anything as it was an empty apartment. It was so easy to break down at the sadness of it all despite how grateful I was being out and having been with people who cared about me and Jeff. It was another stage, a further stage into the disease—the last stage according to the information I'd read. I knew I would be facing even harder days. I tried to stay focussed and to be strong but, of course, it was easier said and hoping for than the reality.

VISITORS

When I see my wife coming I know I will be able to someday chuck this wheelchair, stand up, and walk with the good-looking guy who gives us a hand!

She moves along in front of me at such a pace that I am encouraged to do that too so I start moving a lot faster. I say hello to so many people and they all smile and answer. It is a happy place.

Food is so good and soon I will have a nap.

Out of the corner of my eye I see a couple walking towards me and there is something familiar about both of them—a tall slim man with a redhead—I think it's Chocolate Lady. I hope it is as that means chocolate! They greet me and I try to talk to them but it's not easy—the words won't come out. But we smile a lot and then go out on the patio. Poppet mentions his name, Mike, and I know we dived in our past together—something niggling at my brain about him.

I'm feeling sleepy and we head for the room. They kiss me goodbye. Helen tucks me in.

MUSINGS AT THE END OF AUGUST

It was hazy this morning from the ongoing fires up the coast but had lessened somewhat. They didn't want the residents going on the patio due to the smoke in the air so we stayed in, and I had a really good day with Jeff. When he spotted me walking in, his arms were outstretched for everyone to see (not that anyone was looking but me!).

"You're here, you're here!" he kept saying loudly.

It was difficult to figure out whether he remembered me coming, but he couldn't stop hugging me and had big tears—it was such an up and down scenario.

Kay arrived and she commented how alert Jeff was these days. He even used his spoon on his own from time to time, a significant departure from the normal behaviour of Alzheimer's patients.

The roaming doctor chatted with Jeff, and after examining him she said she was amazed at how happy and smiling he was. It had been difficult to get him to smile when the doctor checked him, so I regarded this moment as a truly special time with him.

"HELEN DAYS"

It was a Helen Day, but I was tempted to go and feed Jeff lunch. If he lived closer, I would, but the transit changes took a toll so many days in a row. I needed the break. Not from Jeff—never from Jeff—but from buses and trains and the despair I saw in his residence.

I could never predict what his mood or pain level would be. He might walk well for fifteen minutes but would get tired. Sometimes when I took him outside, he'd say, "It's cold," and pretended to shake.

"Do you want to go in?"

"Yes."

So his comprehension was not a problem.

It was extremely difficult to make some serious, consequential decisions. In hindsight, they may be the only options because of the unpredictability that dementia brings. The last thing we wanted was to be apart. That always loomed as part of the big picture. But what really worked for the ones immediately facing the choices?

Jeff and I adapted to his situation, but I needed to be with him as much as I possibly could. Staff told me that he asked where I was, when was I going to arrive. They knew my schedule, so they did their best to calm him and let him know I was on my way. As I faced the loneliness and the depth of despair not living under the same roof, there was no doubt that he felt the same way. Even when I was there—especially in the first couple of years—he would wander off and try to open all the doors over and over so he could leave. He often would say, "Don't leave," if he saw me putting on my coat. I didn't hesitate. I stayed. I needed him as much as he needed me.

When he was engrossed in the activities that Y and Kay encouraged, I knew he was happy with their attention. I had to remind myself that I was there for five or six hours but staff were on different shifts for the whole day. I understood the resentment of my presence at times as it undoubtedly interfered or conflicted with their shift routines. Some handled it better than others and welcomed any help, but four people per shift were in charge of twenty residents. Emergencies happened. Deaths happened. BMs happened at inopportune times. There was a constant give and take. Each resident had a different issue than their neighbour's.

It came down to how much time I needed or wanted to be there watching him sleep. It was different if he was in bed and wanted hugs and cuddles, which I was only too happy to give. So I tried to cut my time back.

We could not even speculate about his life expectancy as everyone had different issues. When the time was right for him to say goodbye to this world, that would be his time. His mum had a stroke when she was eighty and incurred brain damage in the process. She was kept alive for weeks, but then the family decided to pull the tubes. Amazingly, she hung on for another two weeks. We certainly couldn't predict someone else's timetable.

One day, he was so impatient to stand when I got there, so I got him to the kitchen opening and he stood the most he ever had—about fifteen ups and downs. He smiled and talked to everyone who came into the kitchen hoping they would offer him a treat (which they often did!) I had no idea why he seemed to be improving.

I got the Ultimate Walker into our unit and hoped to get him walking when he noticed it after his nap. My patience paid off sometimes, and we did some walking. We had an Oliver day coming up soon, and I expected Jeff would walk well. He had been standing with gusto all the previous weekend even though his knees obviously hurt.

He certainly surprised the carers as he bounced back with a vengeance; we could be looking at many more years at this rate. I knew I made a big difference to his well-being and that kept me positive.

On a Saturday in the last weekend of August, I moved the big chair in his room over to the bed, raised the bed and he stood six or seven times while holding onto the back of the chair. This was something new I tried as he was between the big chair and his bed. I'm sure staff would have frowned on it because of safety, but I thought it was OK. It became an exercise we did away from everyone. I know it pained him, but he nevertheless clapped and said, "Thank you." I was often responsible for keeping him in good spirits and vice versa. I so often came home happy knowing we were doing our best together. Sometimes I even bought a bottle of white wine, but I rationed it so that so I wouldn't get maudlin.

I had the distinct impression that fall that Jeff was lonely. I took him outside for his lunch one day, and then I was wheeling him around, but he wanted me to sit on his chair on his knee with him. It was cozy—no one else was around. I gathered up my satchel, scarf and coffee and said, "I'll be right back."

"No, come back," he said with tears in his eyes.

So I gave him my satchel to prove I wasn't leaving and he secured it close to his hip with his hands wound around the straps. I put my scarf back on him, and he seemed happy. He knew I wouldn't leave without my satchel and scarf.

When we went indoors and close to his room, he indicated his bed. He was insecure so I stayed with him longer that day and was close while he fell asleep. It was hard to know what he was thinking at times—fear of being alone, I guess; it was difficult for me to even think about that. Every time it popped into my head, I had to squash it.

After a long discussion with the rotating doctor about his medication, I more clearly understood the pros and cons of drugs like Risperidone. I'd spoken with other wives who had husbands in residences who also thought they were too liberally prescribing antipsychotic drugs which were mainly given to schizophrenia patients. They were trying to find the right mix of drugs to calm aggressiveness. I had many discussions on this subject with his psychiatrist and was told he was to be given the smallest dose if doctors felt it was necessary.

Jeffs sister called to say she would visit Jeff soon and mentioned taking me for a late afternoon lunch. She hadn't seen her brother for a while, two months or more, so her confidence needed to be built up by having me visit at the same time. She arrived during lunchtime and he seemed happy to see her. He was smiling and delighted to hold Newt—there was lot of face licking!

A DATE ALWAYS REMEMBERED. SEPTEMBER 11

One day I was sitting with my coffee by Jeff's window reflecting on that date seventeen years before. Jeff and I were about to land in Germany when the first tower was struck. Many of us remember where we were and what we were doing that day.

We had been hired for an American deposition to be held in Germany. All was cancelled for two weeks, but we made arrangements to go to Heidelberg for a few days. We watched the chaos with horror and sadness in our hotel room. We couldn't tear ourselves from watching and trying to make sense of the situation. We also needed to discuss what we were going to do as we couldn't get flights. Our contact in England suggested we don't return to Canada and see what we could sort out in the coming few weeks.

Jeff suggested we visit Leysin, Switzerland, a remote village in the Alps where Jeff had worked as a teenager operating ski lifts. It was easy to understand why Jeff was so enthusiastic about showing me Leysin! What a beautiful, peaceful, calm mountain village with unique accessibility by a funicular train.

As each day passed, we found another reason to stay. We thought it could be a wonderful place to make our home base for deposition work for six months if the work materialized. We could take the cable-operated train down the mountain and all modes of transport were available to get to London or any European city.

What a turnaround for us. After e-mailing our London contact for work, we took the opportunity that was presented to us to work out of Switzerland if we could find accommodation for six months. A bit of negotiating with a rental agency in Leysin and we were shown a few furnished apartments. Within several hours we had a key to a lovely, fully furnished apartment on the eighth floor of a fairly new building in the mountains. We stood in the living room just mesmerized at the amazing view of the Swiss mountains and cloud formations. Leysin brought such wonderful memories back to Jeff after all the years that passed. Our contacts came through for deposition work in Germany, Belgium and France. The amazing bonus was to ski on these mountain trails where Jeff once operated the ski lift.

Because I was Canadian and didn't have a permanent visa, I had to fly back to Canada every six months, so we had our plans before us. We skied in the mountains, scuba-dived in the Red Sea and walked and hiked a lot. We settled in so easily and acquired many contracts for deposition work in nearby European countries.

Talk about life unfolding in mysterious ways!

Here I was with Jeff now on this journey in care so many years later.

Jeff continued to walk well and did more lengths of the hallways than we thought possible; he never ceased to surprise us! My presence seemed to relax him. Sitting in a wheelchair causes constipation so we were fortunate he still could walk and therefore cut down on the number of suppositories he had to take. I often volunteered to sit in a chair nearby if they hoisted him onto the toilet. At least I could help as staff couldn't sit with him for twenty minutes but I could. That happened often after his walks, and so his mood was uplifted. He really was a wonderful man with his charm still intact most of the time.

My sister Betty was doing poorly and in hospital with serious issues, and I felt so sad and helpless. It was difficult not just jumping on a plane to be there, but I was not sure whether that would be the right move. She had been through so many physical problems. She suffered terribly, and my brother-in-law was in the early stages of dementia, so nothing was the same for them anymore. It was amazing that they were still in their home with stairs and so many issues. Just getting meals together and cleaning up when they were both so tired and irritable must have been difficult. My sister Pat went to Ottawa from Toronto despite my brother telling her to stay put. It was her own decision really. I checked last-minute flights and had to make a decision soon.

I had such a big cry on Sunday when I heard Betty was close to the end. The call came later in the evening. Pat and my brother had just said goodnight to Betty and were in the parking lot leaving the hospital when they got the call. Betty and I shared the same birthdate in January, but five years apart, so we had always had a close connection.

I spoke to my brother-in-law by phone and he was having a difficult time, missing my sister, his wife, and crying. They were inseparable and so involved with their family. Also spoke to Pat, and she was being haunted by how wasted, thin and fragile Betty looked. She, too, was overwhelmed with grief and sadness. My brother always had had a particularly close relationship with Betty so these were difficult days for all of us.

I had beautiful memories of me and Betty from my May trip. We were always the first to get up, and we'd hug good morning in our housecoats and sit with our coffees. A rabbit who thought he was part of the family would appear on their deck, look in and hope for a carrot, which was always ready for him. I'd shed a lot of tears but I hadn't wailed and sobbed. I didn't know if that would still come. It was difficult to imagine her gone.

Jeff's care plan had changed unexpectedly and was now causing lots of problems for us. The manager and I exchanged many e-mails trying to sort out where this new plan came from. A note was posted in his room that said we needed to cut back on the naps Jeff and I had in the afternoons. I finally decided not to get involved and just do what I could by taking Jeff out and being there for him. It was exhausting trying to deal with the bullies who created these problems.

When I got home, I would often jump in a hot bath and turn everything off. It really was the backlash of my journeys; I was often neither here nor there and I didn't really care. I just carried on. It was a kind of numb state before something—a phone call, someone caring, love coming my way—would jolt me out of it. This "nowhere state" came and went, and the only thing I knew was that I never felt this way before dementia descended upon us. I had to be strong. Was I being tested for something? What was the big plan? Was there one? Why Jeff and me? Our reactions were more acute as meaningful days came into the forefront.

We often went to Mexico or the Caribbean for holidays. One experience Jeff and I talked about often was meeting a couple who had a forty-five-foot cutter rigged sailboat on La Ropa Beach in Zihuantanejo. This was in January 1991. They were a friendly couple, and they joined us for New Year's Eve dinner. We didn't know it, but they were looking for a crew for their boat as they would soon be heading to Bermuda and many other ports of call. They invited us, and we said we would think about it.

After returning to Canada, we decided to take them up on it. We planned to meet them in Turks and Caicos to start the journey. A few friends seemed hesitant because we didn't know the couple very well, but we saw it as an adventure. We had each other, so what could go wrong?

We brought two of our tanks with us from Canada as they had access to tank fills at various ports. It started off as a great time, but the warnings of our friends came to mind as we discovered they were not a happy couple. They fought constantly and often pitched plates of food overboard at dinnertime. The arguing escalated and there was a lot of tension about things like how many bananas we were allowed to eat a day. They then curtailed the food we had already paid them for in advance.

Jeff was a capable seaman and took the wheel many times, which he thoroughly enjoyed. My first husband and I owned a similar sized sailboat, so I was comfortable as well. But the drinking and shouting by this couple was not in the contract.

We decided that when we got close to land or an island, we would leave the boat and not go to Bermuda with them. That opportunity arose at a place called Rum Key. We all got off the boat to explore, and we found a hotel which was more or less vacant due to an accident some years before. The owner was still there and he offered us shelter once we told him our story. We went back, got our gear and gave them our good news (of course, it was bad news for them).

We spent the next month on this island, in a hotel that had no locks but that had a compressor for filling our tanks. We took every opportunity to dive. The owner was extremely gracious and understanding about our plight and helped us arrange a flight out of Fort Lauderdale back to Canada.

What a different life.

I was unhappy if I didn't see Jeff every day. It would be okay if I could just see him and come home, but I wanted to feed him, be with him, as he would be gone before I knew it. But it was wearing me down. I didn't have to think about buses the night before Helen Days, but when I woke up the next morning I always felt this need—this pull—to be there. It was like all the rest did not matter anymore.

Just the other day they had three extra soups and threw them out without offering me one. My favourite head nurse wasn't oblivious to the bullies' antics. She snuck me a banana and two quarter sandwich pieces as Jeff and I went outside one day.

"Hide this," she whispered.

Apparently, some residences offer free meals if the carer feeds their loved one. Makes sense to me. At Wisteria I could pay on the spot for lunch, but not here. It had to be twenty-four hours in advance, so I brought my lunch most days. To me it felt like "revenge" holding back the soup; so sad. Jeff was my priority, not them, but it showed how the system could fail at times and hurt people.

Now and again the residence got to me. I just couldn't handle the suffering residents. There was no solution in sight except decline and sadness. I had to mindfully set aside my grief and us out of there—even if it was only to our room by the window. Anything was better than a woman lying in a chair and constantly screaming, "I want to go home! I WANT TO GO HOME!". Another said, "Help me, help me," over and over. It was so raw.

My cup was at the brim and it wouldn't take much for it to overflow. I kept trying to think of ways to make our visits good for both of us, as he noticed what was going on too. I seemed to be in a state. I noticed that the lady who fed her husband lunch and dinner always sat in front of the TV and away from everyone. Another one went to the main lobby. I had to change things as well. It wasn't just me. The atmosphere was changing.

Transferring Jeff to the Ultimate Walker from his chair using the ceiling hoist worked well. He didn't want to turn out of his wheelchair unless we spent lots of time coaxing him. Staff thought we were not safe as he remained very strong. Once he got a hold of my arm or hand, only food offerings would make him let go. A few staff told me he wrestled with them but gets tired and doesn't want to be changed or disturbed. What a sad life for him—actually for all of us who love him.

We were well into fall and following our routines. Jeff had his good days and bad ones—often being tired, moody and distant. I was always grateful for even a tiny smile, but I occasionally got a big hug and back rubbing. I rubbed his knees with Voltaren and he reciprocated (without the cream) thinking, I guess, this is what we needed to do. Fortunately, we had a great manager and she made sure to write on the board in Jeff's room that we were to have naps in the afternoon. That was now the rule.

I was fighting not to break down about Betty's passing most of the time. When Jeff started to cry, then I really lost it. He held me, rubbing my back and crying with me. That was worse than anything as the poor guy had dementia—a broken brain!—and here I was upsetting him. Oh God, it was just so heartbreaking.

Somewhere in all of that I had to find the uplifting thoughts and positive attitude that had been escaping me. I had to remember I was human and flawed. I did some reading about fear and anxiety to try to learn more. I had several friends who had lost their husbands, so I knew what was coming for me next. Even my doctor could not help my attitude. I ended up in a huff and just said at one point, "I've got to leave right now." I walked out of our appointment, which was so unlike me.

All this with Betty, not being there with her at the end, always out of money, scrambling for food, resenting my friends who almost never visited Jeff when they lived right there and all of us did so much together, Jeff's niece and nephew, his sister's kids who never came even once to see Jeff. His useless sons who lived in Vancouver.

Everything was just a bitch sometimes.

I was thankful I had Jeff to comfort me even though he was not able to be the Jeff he was. I only got little snatches of what he was as his brain was terribly shrunken by then. I had to stretch harder all the time to reach him. I rejoiced to hear a whole sentence. I watched him sleep and just shed tears.

He was in such good shape compared to others there, so I felt guilty at times that I ignored them, but they were not easy to be around and the whole place reeked of shit. I couldn't face it. Is that why I got a seat on the bus so easily? The smell that no doubt attached itself to me?

BEAUTIFUL AUTUMN DAYS

We were fortunate to have some beautiful days so we could make use of the patio and watch the bird life. Jeff had on and off days: some days walking, other days slumped over due to cramps. On the weekends, he was often alert, desperate to stand, and was quite verbal about it all.

"That's fantastic!" he would say, clapping.

Jeff had been doing well with his toilet regime, but something knocked it off kilter and the rotating doctor changed the plan. It was not working for Jeff and something needed to be done.

In later November, I kept trying to cheer him up as he was definitely aware of all this bodily handling and did not like it one bit. He would say, "No" to them and not want me to leave the room. He started making many half sentences, but then came, "Are we leaving shortly?" I gave him such a hug, and he laughed.

"As soon as it stops raining," I said.

His vocabulary reflected, I had noticed, what he heard around him in the present. One time when I went to get him a snack, he gave me the diving sign of "all okay." We had been discussing the photos, and I told him how safe he always made me feel underwater. I told him about the dive we had at El Bajo in the Sea of Cortez.

We were side by side about sixty feet deep. I was engrossed in getting a unique photo of some moray eels who kept poking their heads out of the rocks, so I was turning this way and that trying to get the best angle. Jeff signalled he was ready to move on, and I gave the okay sign. He was ahead of me by about two feet with his back to me, but when I tried to follow him something prevented me from kicking my legs. To my horror, fishing line was wrapped around my legs and fins. Jeff was then at least ten feet away. I tried not to panic as I couldn't just shout out, "Help me!" What to do? The more I struggled, the tighter the twine got.

Then our lesson from long ago flashed through my mind. I saw myself on the living room floor fully kitted while Jeff taught me how to use my diving knife. It was always strapped to my lower leg if problems suddenly came about. Here I was in that situation!

I reached down, released my knife from its casing and started to cut the fishing line away. I tried to stay calm and remember that Jeff would turn around and see I was having a problem at any moment. But when I looked up, he was out of sight. I hacked away harder at the line and finally got myself free. I put my knife away and kicked off to follow him. He must have wondered why I wasn't behind him as he was swimming towards me quickly, but he was none the wiser until I described it after the dive.

I gave him the "okay" sign back as I left the room to get snacks from the kitchen.

His eyes started playing tricks on him again. He ripped up a white paper napkin, chewed it up, coughed and spit it out. He also mistook a crumpled serviette for a muffin, and I caught him putting that in his mouth. He was quite reluctant to give it up. He needed closer supervision especially when he was hungry, which seemed to be always. He just never refused food.

His eating habits fluctuated, which was quite amazing to watch from one day to the next. He started eating his lunch with the spoon by himself again, which he hadn't done for over six months. He ate without problems and walked better than he had in a while. He was quite amazing and there were little rewards of joy to see him happy and chatting, waving and smiling!

Little achievements were noticeable to me and Oliver when we walked together, but anyone else would only see his decline. Visitors would undoubtedly be dismayed at how life was unfolding for him, but he and I often clapped at his accomplishing a task like standing and walking. We laughed and joked all the time as we continued to have a close connection.

Some days he just wanted to sit with his head on my shoulder. When I stirred, he immediately squeezed tighter—like, no way you're getting away now that I've got you. That was tender and precious to me.

As our wedding anniversary approached, I planned on doing physio with Jeff and having lunch together to celebrate. Our marriage date was December 4, 2009, but we'd been together since 1987. What a rainy gloomy day it was when I awoke. I wanted to stay snuggled under my bed covers, but that lovely rainbow waiting at the end of my bus trips lured me out the door.

I did give myself permission to enjoy Helen Days without guilt. Jeff would never want me to be chained to his bed. In the past, he always encouraged me to visit my family in Ottawa, which I did at least four times a year. I missed family a lot. I grieved for sister Betty, but at the same time she was really in a bad way so I hoped wherever she went became a paradise of birds and flowers for her.

At this time of year with the wedding anniversary, Christmas, New Year's and people rushing around to buy stuff, stores crowded, taking buses rain or shine, my emotional well-being was out of whack. I just wanted to be nice and quiet, see Jeff and remind myself how thankful I was for his sweetness and love.

I knew at times I was exhausted from worry and sadness, so I didn't want to do much with friends. But there was an underlying falseness of getting together with them as they barely mentioned Jeff's name unless I brought him up. Maybe I was being self-absorbed and trapped in how uncomfortable I often felt—possibly mistakenly—that it was a "duty" to invite me to gatherings. I'm sure I was over-sensitive about the lack of visits.

My perspective changed as the years passed by. Did people even care about us anymore? It was difficult and troubling not to shed tears at gatherings, and I really didn't want that. I had become more vulnerable, and it was so easy for me to damper any party by mentioning Jeff. I was not sure if they protected themselves by not visiting Jeff or not mentioning him, but who was there left to protect me?

My psychiatrist tried to help me with my disappointments about friends and family visiting by pointing out how others had their own priorities and problems. She wondered if, because I didn't complain, they thought I was doing just fine. I was awash and overwhelmed with the whole scene at the residence. What was a day out of their lives here and there to visit someone they once cared about?

One day, Jeff pooled and pocketed his lemon custard dessert and his thickened apple juice. I thought he was swallowing everything, but then I noticed his chipmunk cheeks. He had hung his head and all this gooey mess of lemon dessert just leaked out of his mouth. I tried to mop it up and stop it from going all over his clothes. It was the worst I'd seen, and it reminded me I needed to be more watchful of him swallowing. I needed to see his Adam's apple bob so he did not aspirate the food.

SANTA ARRIVED AT MONTBRETIA

What a lot of activity with Baby and Kay today!

They led a parade with a Santa Claus and he had a huge trailer he was pulling filled with gifts that his elves were handing out!

Everyone got stuff and I got mine!

I kept mine close to me and they said it was Christmas gifts so I want to wait for my Poppet! She should be here soon and we will look at stuff together!

I am not feeling the best these days as the food doesn't seem to want to go down my throat. They tempt me with my favourite desserts and I am enjoying the custard but I then feel really tired and next thing I know my wife is standing there and giving me big hugs. Just as I look at her, some custard starts dripping out of my mouth.

I don't know why that is happening. I know I was eating custard.

She got me cleaned up really quickly and we went to my room where my presents were. I tried to tell her where they came from but I couldn't but I did point to them. We opened them—mostly her tugging at them—and there were all sorts of goodies for me.

I am very tired and need to sleep now.

CHRISTMAS AT MONTBRETIA

Santa came to Montbretia—I don't know when—but our activities director coordinated with London Drugs to give gifts to all the residents. Each received a bag of wrapped gifts, products which Y helped to match with those most in need. Jeff had three parcels to open and he did try but lost interest. He got some Nivea pump action lotion, a huge bottle for his dry skin, a winter toque, underarm deodorant, shampoo, Ferrero Rocher chocolates (but could be a problem with the nuts), three pairs of ankle summer socks, some shaving soap. It was such a nice surprise! I was hoping for a coverlet/blanket as I noted a couple got that, but it will be something I will mention to his sister. His reversible black and red one disappeared in the wash, and I have it on his Christmas list. He always liked having a fuzzy warm blanket wrapped around him when he sat by the window.

Beautiful bright sunny days in mid-December meant I got Jeff out more. We often relaxed with lunch and watched the birds.

A resident who had not been well for a long time died. She was in her nineties, but she was talkative and always said, "I want to go home," over and over. Her quality of life was poor, and I suppose it was a blessing that she got her wish. But it was still a sad atmosphere.

There were four others who didn't have much chance to survive much longer as their decline sped up over the weeks. A sixty-two-year-old resident's progression was alarmingly fast. It was not an easy place to be. I'm sure it's difficult to imagine the stress one is under in an atmosphere of dementia, close to death. I encountered it every day when I walked into the residence. It was overwhelming. I tried to shield Jeff, get him outside and in his room as it could be so demoralizing. I can't imagine what it would have been like without Y and Kay doing activities with him.

Jeff had been walking in a semi-staggering fashion due to his sore knees which looked so obvious as he struggled to put one step in front of the other. But he had been eating well apart from some coughing, and always having good naps!

I was tired, though, and running out of energy while pushing his wheelchair. I was anxious to leave for home at times. I was often hungry and needed to be alone, just sit down, eat and relax.

The holiday season was soon upon us, and I was reminiscing about so many trips we took to the Caribbean and Mexico. Zihuatanejo offered the atmosphere, character and feel of traditional Mexico, and we would often get a flight on Christmas Day and stay until early January.

One trip in particular was most memorable as I would celebrate my fiftieth birthday. One evening we were walking along the beach and were surprised to run into a close rugby friend and his wife who had also chosen this fishing village for a holiday! We talked about my birthday and made plans to have dinner together with them and their daughter at a special restaurant. Drinks were planned beforehand on the beach. They purchased a bottle of Dom Pérignon at a shop on the way and surprised us with it to share for my milestone birthday! We had a fantastic evening! I was looking at photos of me walking back from the restaurant somewhat inebriated being supported by their teenage daughter as the bottle of Dom was only the beginning of the imbibing that night! A bit later my shoes were off, Jeff was carrying them, we were walking on the beach and almost at our hotel in a state of disarray (at least I looked that way!)

After my Jeff visit, I had a date to join long-time friends for appetizers and drinks. We got together around this time every December. Wayne and his wife assembled bags of goodies every year for us. In addition to some bubbly, chocolates and shortbread (for Jeff), they gave me a one-year membership to Costco. I was so excited that I stopped in the next day on the chance it wouldn't be jammed packed with people. It wasn't, so I got my card up and running plus a $20 coupon for purchases and another coupon for a dozen butter croissants and a huge bag of chocolate covered almonds! Wow, I was so excited. I could only carry a little, so after I got home I raced back to get avocados, kiwi fruit and bananas!

As I sipped a glass of bubbly on Christmas Eve, I thought about all my family in Ottawa. I'd had a marvellous dinner thanks to the handy bakery downstairs from my apartment. I took the day to relax and went for a walk earlier. I'd seen Jeff for the past two days and planned to see him the next three, so I squeezed in a time out.

As I walked by this favourite bakery, I saw some staff I knew. We wished each other Merry Christmas.

"Have you eaten?"

I hadn't yet.

"Well then, we have a treat for you—on us!"

They assembled an amazing Christmas dinner: turkey, dressing with apricots, mashed potatoes, peas and cranberry sauce.

"Enjoy! And don't forget the gravy!"

They gave me so much (all white, tender turkey) that I could have the rest for lunch the next day with Jeff! I felt terribly spoilt and loved it.

The holidays were a particularly tough time, but fortunately I had my doctor to consult with as my anchor, and we started to meet on FaceTime once a month.

Oliver came Christmas Day as it was a Tuesday. Jeff did three revolutions around the halls! He was hurting but determined! I'd paid for a turkey dinner with Jeff, so I didn't expect to get in before eight o'clock and collapse in a heap on the sofa. He was so happy opening gifts of socks and treats.

I hadn't heard from his sister. She didn't come see Jeff, but what could I say? Not a lot. It was just me, myself and I for family with Jeff. I was grateful for friends but it was always quiet for me at Christmas as they all had their families to celebrate with. One family always invited me for Christmas dinners, but I always spent those holiday days with Jeff and couldn't go knowing he was on his own.

Boxing Day was uneventful with Jeff, who seemed quite moody. I thought it best to leave early while he was sleeping. I had planned to take a Helen Day on the twenty-seventh, but I was restless and hoped I could uplift him with mincemeat pies and other special treats. I tried to be perky so he didn't catch my down mood.

The forecast was sunny, so I got him outside. He needed the change of atmosphere—as did I. It poured rain, but we stayed under the awning on the balcony. Got Jeff walking on my own, and he did quite well—two hall revolutions. He was constipated for three days and that reflected his grumpiness. He just wanted to sleep, so I opted to leave after lunch. Fewer visitors came during the holidays, but I did notice family and/or friends arrived to pick up some of the residents for their special celebrations at their homes.

I missed Betty so much, and she had always kept me up to date on her children and the grandchildren. I didn't get much gossip and news from her children as they all had their own priorities and Christmas season plans. Betty used to send Jeff $20 every Christmas for a treat.

Holidays were especially difficult times when I was alone and lonely.

I had a chat with a woman whose husband was going downhill quickly. He was in a wheelchair and barely speaking. She said she had cut her visiting time to just two hours as he was eager to acknowledge her when she arrived but then totally ignored her. I think that was a mirror of the previous days for me—eager initially, then distant. We agreed that the key was to leave, don't hang around and get depressed about it, just enjoy that initial greeting and be on our way. I planned to follow suit and not sit in a chair brooding about what I couldn't change while Jeff slept.

CHRISTMAS & NEW YEAR'S

Helen tells me Christmas is upon us again and that I'll be seeing lots of her! That makes me very happy. I know I sleep a lot but I just seem tired and not doing a lot of activities lately.

The place is all decorated by Y—standing on a ladder with me trying to hand her items.

I'm getting lots of treats from my wife and from all the staff—so many things I like to eat—bread pudding and custards! I've been trying my new knee-high socks with African animals and they stay up so well. I also have a pair of socks with all kinds of sharks.

My door is decorated with holly and Santas. Plus I have a line-up of Santas on my bureau, presents all over and we are doing lots of walking and getting around!

NEW YEAR'S EVE 2018

Jeff was happy to see me, and he was keen to do our standing routines. He ate his butter tart with such pleasure and happiness! When Jeff saw Y approaching him with his earphones in hand, he said with a big smile, "Baby Poppet," loud and clear and with joy. I'm his Poppet, but she is Baby Poppet, I guess because she is so tiny. We had such a good laugh! Her adoring looks, huge smiles and much squeezing of the shoulders were magical moments for them both.

Chapter 11

The beginning of another new year, 2019, wow!

Oliver had to coax Jeff to walk as he was crampy, but he was happy after walking and the reward was a long nap. I hoped that by resting and staying home for a few days, I would recover faster from a slight cough. I knew Jeff had activities all afternoon and actually Y was there until 5:00 on Saturdays. When I returned, I wore a mask the whole time and Jeff was kissing my mask! He seemed happy. All good!

Another birthday for me—January 7! I told Jeff, and he gave me a kiss and a hug. I think he understood what a birthday was. I turned seventy-seven on the seventh, but no dollars to spare for a trip to the casino even if it could have been my lucky day on the 7's machines. Thinking like a true gambler!

On Saturday night after three cups of a honey tea I slept all through the night and didn't cough at all! By Monday I was better and Jeff's sister picked me up to treat me with a birthday lunch. I walked home from the restaurant as it was a glorious day. I got lots of contact from my family back east as Betty's birthday was the same day as mine, so it was hard not to remember me too! I had an easy evening trying to wear off half a bottle of wine.

EARLY FEBRUARY

I had fantastic days with Jeff, and my heart was warm and happy! He was so alert some days that we actually had a dialogue going. It was not just me that noticed either. Staff were giggling when they finished changing him and related what he said that amused them so much.

"That's the way to keep it tight," he said, apparently directing them on how to change his pad.

They were laughing so hard as he was so cooperative and friendly.

When I started walking back in, he yelled out, "Come here right now!" His behaviour was so unusual, but we made the most of it. Everyone talked to him and he smiled from ear to ear! He yelled out, "Good morning!" to them when they came in to dress him, and to the residents when they wheeled him out for breakfast. Kay even said he was so excited to do activities and never slept like he usually did—he was just all energy. He was wide awake, humming tunes, smiling at me, eating his treats.

He seemed to be going through a stage in the "late stage" that was not mentioned anywhere. It was a glimpse of his great character from our life together. I needed that boost, and it was a special pleasure as it came in waves out of the blue. I felt fortunate to still have him, much as I didn't want him to suffer.

Jeff obviously missed his sister's dog as one day when I arrived, he was holding a "fake" dog while lying in bed. This dog was soft and opened and closed its mouth, even did a few mechanical tricks trying to fool us into thinking it was real. Y told me he played with it for an hour at a table and gave it kisses. He was snuggling it in his arms when he fell asleep. He was really reverting back to his childhood.

Things turned around for the good when Daniel, a head nurse who was always super efficient, was in charge. He was watching Jeff stand, and I said, "Look at him, how he wants to move his feet."

"I'll get the walker!" he said.

We got him in the walker against the petty rules, and Jeff walked, him and me, and I even got him in bed. Daniel was a gem and would even change Jeff. Just because he was the head nurse did not mean he was above certain tasks.

I was visiting Friday through Sunday, so there was no doubt why I was totally exhausted. I could barely move. I was emotionally and physically spent. I wondered often just how long I would be able to keep up with this pace.

Of course, the "Terrible Twos" came back, plus an unpopular female head nurse who makes them the "Terrible Threes." It was almost like a conspiracy with them when they were on the same shift to gang up on me. Perhaps I was overreacting and just too sensitive about our past issues.

We waited for half an hour just to get his pad changed, and then they couldn't handle him. Their energy was not good around him. I'm sure he noticed their attitude and, frankly, they underestimated him as he understood lots even though he didn't talk.

I must be the least popular visitor at Montbretia. My nerves were on edge, and I was losing my cool. I asked one of them if they would help me with Jeff's coat, and they said, "It's not in the plan." Then they accused me of hurting Jeff's toe with the wheelchair when we were going outside the previous day. I can't tell you how exasperating all of this negativity affected our visits.

Jeff's sister was there, and we took him outside to the patio. All was good with him. I got a ride home with his sister and she commented how rude the nurses were. I'd had no lunch. Nothing was offered to us to drink. The nurses often played favourites, as when certain visitors arrived, trays with treats and tea appeared for them. Not for us. So I was disturbed, tired, felt hated by the Montbretia staff, and I couldn't think of the next day.

MID-FEBRUARY/EARLY MARCH

We were having such beautiful weather, so Jeff was eating outside most days. He continued to show an interest in standing and loved listening to music in his earphones, swaying in his chair, content and having a yogurt bar when one was offered.

My strategy with the three "nasties" was to ignore them where possible, put them on the back burner. Nurses and carers all have different personalities, but these were bullies who lacked people skills. They were not worth bothering about unless they were not treating Jeff well.

There were some wonderful shift nurses and head nurses at Montbretia, and I knew they appreciated my efforts because they said so. Many doctors had told me there was always staff that didn't measure up in residences due to personality clashes. Their advice was to just keep my eyes open but not let them get to me. I also started keeping track of dates when there was bad care.

As the year rolled along, Jeff had been diligent about walking in the Ultimate Walker. He often smiled and said hello to everyone he passed. The staff and many of the residents liked him a lot. He was eating with his spoon again, and that made him more independent. I could see his satisfaction and determination getting the spoon to his mouth without spillage.

Jeff's sister visited him and said he was in good spirits as well.

One day, Jeff was sleeping in his chair but had his arms tightly folded and didn't want to know me or anyone. We tried to walk, but his arm and shoulder were jerking so we gave up and let him have his way. He got into bed with barely any reaction, but I did get one smile.

What puzzled me was why the staff didn't encourage residents to get fresh air. The air was so stale inside while it was warm and beautiful out on the patio.

JEFF'S BIRTHDAY MONTH. APRIL

Jeff was mostly in vague mode and it was becoming harder to coax him to walk. When we succeeded in getting him in the walker, he would only do one revolution or two, nothing like three anymore—but we knew that could change! He was in need of hugs, and once he got a hold of me, he clung and would give me a smile. He said, "Don't go," so his needs were obvious.

We were in our same routine of lunch outside, a nap together and then he would join the others to listen to Y play the flute. What would they do without her? At the end of the day, he would take up his position at the big window pointing out the buses.

Some days we watched rugby on my iPad, in his narrow bed with his arm firmly around me. We chatted. How could I be unhappy? I was truly lucky that he was non-aggressive!

One day, he pointed to a picture of two stingrays and said, "Look at them. Tell me a story about the rays." Such awareness sometimes. He had these lucid moments, and it was amazing how he could even "think" about a dive from the past.

On this dive we were at a depth of eighty feet at a popular site called "El Bajo" in the Sea of Cortez. We must have had at least thirty dives to this site. Stingrays are often seen singly—you rarely see two engaging together—but on this particular dive we saw these two and noticed one was missing his long sting tail. Jeff was making gestures to take a photo as he must have noticed the missing tail. Fortunately, I did catch a photo of them as they settled on the ledge of this rocky promontory. It was almost like they knew one stinger was missing and were staying close for protection being a food attraction to sharks (probably why his tail was missing). This photo caught the eye of many students during Jeff's lectures on saving the seas. I would classify this as one of my ten best photos in that area for its rarity—two stingrays together and one with a missing stinger!

I was still riding my bike, and we had such a cold spell that winter. It was great to see everything blooming and birds visiting the patio.

The apartment I moved into was a godsend—everything I could ask for and more with large rooms, a spacious balcony and a view of the gardens; very cozy and quiet. My hearing had continued to deteriorate, even with my hearing aids. I eventually lost comprehension in my right ear, but it still balanced the tones. I tended to avoid loud restaurants and preferred one-on-one conversation.

My priority had been my sweetie, and that he was—charming and non-aggressive. I tried to remain a happy, positive person who was devoted to Jeff. We comforted each other, laughed together, and I couldn't help but think of how much I would miss him if he died before me. I often had visions of pushing a walker onto buses when I was ninety to see him.

I had no success moving him closer, but perhaps the distance was meant to be as I got some space from the stale air and grumpy, ill people. Despair hung in the air. The activities directors changed the atmosphere the minute they arrived, and the residents all wanted their attention because they were cheerful and positive.

I organized a gathering on Jeff's patio to celebrate his seventy-ninth birthday—mostly the same friends who came for his seventy-fifth at Wisteria. A Costco cake, the casual, open venue with two large tables with a few snacks and drinks—bubbly for sure! The venue for the birthday gathering changed to a quiet spacious area on the main floor which was closed off from the public. Jeff had his scheduled dinner at 5:15 and we wasn't good for long visits.

Fifteen people gathered for the party. Jeff was alert, he tried to talk, smiled a lot. Jeff wore these neat shark socks a good friend gave him with shorts and his favourite pink shirt he'd worn on our wedding day. It was a great turnout, people loving Jeff and me, it seemed. I enjoyed it very much. He was watching everybody, not sure what to make of it all, but he loved the cake.

Most everyone came with treats and cards for Jeff— even one from a cousin in England. As usual, his sister's children didn't acknowledge the day. I invited them through her, but there wasn't even a card for their uncle who they'd known all their lives. So much for his family. A few nieces from Ottawa and Newmarket sent him happy birthday greetings as did my brother and sister.

I rejoiced to know Jeff connected us, and I was grateful to have these constant friends after all these years—thirty years together. Jeff barely said anything but he did engage with Chocolate Lady and started blinking his eyes quickly at her and she reciprocated so it was a sweet moment.- He was definitely affected by the noise and the number of people. At one point he had Newt sitting on his lap and his were eyes closed so we knew it was time to say adieu!

At the end of the day, I felt like a truck had run over me as I was up since five in the morning, so I soaked away some of my aches in the tub. The peace and quiet was just what I needed after all the emotional activity of the day.

MY SEVENTY-NINTH BIRTHDAY. APRIL 26

Everyone is wishing me a happy birthday! It's come around again! Rosie came over and took my hand. I have lots of friends here and they sing "Happy Birthday" to me!

I am being treated so nicely with extras for breakfast. Baby Poppet gave me a hug today and said I looked so nice.

My wife has arrived, all cheerful with lots of hugs and kisses and presents for me—socks and chocolates and butter tarts.

I have balloons attached to my wheelchair. I see Wayne and we shake hands. I see Mike and the Chocolate Lady, my French rugby mate and others, and we shake hands. I have visions of meeting them but can't keep the images in my head—they just pop in and pop out but don't stay long enough. I see a dog that comes to see me sometimes.

Helen looks happy and she has a beautiful cake for me—people take turns talking to me and serving me cake and drinks.

I'm tired though. I would like to get in my bed.

A couple of days after Jeff's birthday, he walked so well. We snuggled and he looked at all his cards and I read them to him. He was quite adorable. He wanted to get out of the bed and walk, but he couldn't just stand and walk away. He tried to push me away so he could stand on his own; he was being so stubborn.

MID-MAY

Lots of birds on the patio! Two families of purple finches. I've counted five babies being fed. It was such a pleasure to have this patio with all the gorgeous flowers on display! Flowers and birds made the atmosphere out there.

May had brought such beautiful weather and Jeff was surprising us with his cognitive abilities—in fact he improved marginally. He was talking more and eating on his own, which he hadn't done for a while. It is a misnomer to use the word "improved" with dementia-related diseases, but he had been chatting like he hadn't done for years.

One day, Jeff fell out of bed just as I was about to leave. The bed was at its lowest and he kept leaning way over. I went for a pee and heard a noise but no sound. When I got back, there he was on the floor. I think he fell on his head, but he was close to the floor, so no injuries or even bruises. The nurse checked his vital signs, and he said nothing. We kept asking if he hurt and he said only once, "I'm okay." We got him into his wheelchair and he went to sleep immediately. I left after a million hugs and kisses.

Another day, Jeff started to cry when I arrived; those big tears just broke me up. It was like he was so happy to see me he cried, but he also looked so sad and worried. How he must have been struggling. I jumped into bed with him and made him giggle. He liked all the attention and was very clingy. I sat him by the window and didn't want to leave him ever.

As I've often said to family and friends, you have to live with someone with dementia on a daily basis to fully understand the whole situation and to see the journey of changes, including the tremendous work staff do.

We had noticed a bad rash on the top of one foot so I asked him about it, but he basically ignored me. It was the first time he'd acted as though he didn't know me; he did the same with Kay. Was it mini strokes? Worrisome thoughts. He ate everything I fed him but was just staring out the window all slumped over. We got outside but he spit out everything he collected in his cheeks, so he wasn't swallowing earlier.

On my Helen Day, I got a call while I was grocery shopping that he wouldn't eat; always a bad sign. I had to rush home, grab a bus and get in there to confirm he was "okay." He came around after some fresh air on the patio for two hours. I fed him and he ate, but he was still slumped over and continued to be quite tired. I left about 8:00 p.m. and waited to see how it would all unfold.

No calls from his night nurse so that was a good sign.

I was there the next morning, and he was not doing well. They tried to feed him but he wouldn't swallow and he was pooling, pocketing and spitting everything out. He had some mucus, so I got them to use his medication with the puffer. He eventually fell asleep in his chair. He was quite still, and was acting like he had in January. He came back with a vengeance after that episode, so we just had to wait and see what would happen.

He had perked up overnight. He ate his lunch and smiled at me. I was not sure whether I should stay or go. He only "pooled" with the thickened juices, so I skipped them. I think the puffer helped. He was congested, but they didn't seem to have a clue except for Daniel and Kathleen. Daniel said, "Get him out in the fresh air," but the nurse in charge on the shift said, "Keep him in his room."

In any event they changed him and put him in bed to stretch out as he couldn't stand; that was better than being in the chair all day. I could give him a massage. I knew, without a doubt, that my presence helped him. The staff made attempts to wake him but moved on quickly—they had many residents to care for. I didn't fault them, but I persisted and got him to respond. He was in another world, and it was a challenge to break through. I felt I was losing him. It was the dementia game. He wanted me close; I was there and that was what counted. I gave him what he wanted, and he hung on to me, pressing hard on my arms to keep me from fleeing. Then he relaxed and fell asleep. Every time he woke up, he knew I was right there, squeezing tightly. What can I say?

The next day, he was awake and recognized me immediately.

"Don't go," he said.

He had bounced back! We thought he was on his way out the door, but he was not ready for that final exit. He moved slowly but still wanted to walk. I asked him if he wanted to go outside, and he said, clear as a bell, "I'm not properly dressed." He was grabbing my iPad and phone every chance he got. He had made a remarkable, unpredictable recovery!

The pain in my hip and knee reminded me to stop carrying so much in my back pack. I was not heeding the signs of too much strain on my joints and was barely able to get home overloaded with groceries. I had been lifting heavy pots and earth for my balcony plants, and I paid the price. Sometimes I carried too much in my satchel for Jeff, so I decided to pay more attention to my well-being. I needed my energy to keep visiting! I used the Voltaren rub, which helped relieve the pain in my knee, so I'd been let off lightly.

EARLY DAYS OF JUNE

The "Terrible Twos" were back on the scene creating the usual problems. As a result of their lack of interest in changing Jeff, we waited and waited. I had to have the nurse intervene.

It was so beautiful sitting outside on the patio in a nice breeze; it also cheered up the residents to get outside. They often had earphones on while being supervised. One time, a table was filled with tea, coffee and biscuits. I could feel the atmosphere change. Who doesn't like being in fresh air and treated kindly?

Jeff had to be coaxed to walk during some of his physio appointments. We actually had a dialogue, which was so rare at this stage of Alzheimer's.

"Let's get going over there," I said, pointing to the far window.

"Do you mean the far corner?" he asked.

Oliver and I both said yes.

"Okay, let's go!"

His mind was in high alert, but what was going on in there? Staff chimed in and said, "Keep it going, Jeff, we all love you!"

Jeff's neighbour of four years died one day. It was quite moving to see her wheeled by with the beautiful handmade quilt covering her coffin. All the staff lined up, and I just stood by Jeff's door and watched it go by me. Just a few weeks ago, I'd given her a hug.

Gloria Vanderbilt died on June 17. Her son, Anderson Cooper, of course, was an anchor on CNN. He gave a loving interview/memorial about her death. I think she was in her late fifties when she had him. I mention this as it brought to mind a gift from my sister-in-law before I left for Vancouver in 1986. It was a beautiful umbrella signed by Mrs. Vanderbilt. I still had it, but it had some spokes in need of repair. It was probably meant to be used once in a while or carried as a fashion statement, but the Vancouver weather meant it got used an awful lot. The handle was so unique—a swan. It brought back so many memories of my plans for Vancouver and what might lie ahead.

I had many memories of dinner parties with friends. We both used to love one particular meal of prime rib roasted on a BBQ spit—you just couldn't beat that! The host always made sure I got a rib bone. Another close friend's partner, a Frenchman, was a part-time chef and, wow, he was an amazing cook. I learned lots of cooking shortcuts and tips from him. I reminisced aloud with Jeff about those times.

My Mom could bake like nobody else. Being Eastern European, she made noodles by hand every Sunday on this huge wooden board my dad made for her. The dough was rolled until it was paper thin; it was extremely difficult to duplicate this in a store-bought product. Unfortunately, I didn't inherit her talent for baking. I remember throwing the crust dough I made on the floor and stomping on it in a fit of rage at my lack of prowess as a baker. From that time on, I never made pies unless I bought pre-made crust. Jeff and I would pick buckets of wild blackberries and make five or six apple and blackberry pies and freeze them. Jeff was a great sous chef until he wasn't, but he never forgot to bring me flowers as and when the mood struck!

Our connection seemed magical in those days at his residence. We often had an easy, cozy time on the patio with birds and blooms! As the gorgeous montbretia blooms attracted the hummingbirds and Jeff's attention, we often talked about Jeff's life in Rhodesia.

He was seventeen when he moved there to live with his aunt and uncle. He quickly secured a job as a tobacco farmer on a plantation and described to me how poisonous the tobacco plants were because of the chemicals in the leaves, stems and flowers. He wore boots which would get covered with this sticky, dirty residue when he walked along the rows of plants. I was never sure if this cemented his vow never to smoke, but he discouraged anyone who would listen whenever the opportunity arose.

One Christmas in Ottawa with my family, we were all sitting around Betty and Bud's kitchen table and someone asked about his life in Africa as a teenager. Bud always so curious, wanted to know all about his job on this plantation. There were quite a few smokers in the kitchen, and with their permission he started talking about cigarettes and proceeded to take one for the demonstration he was about to give. He meticulously took that cigarette apart bit by bit while describing all the chemicals in it and what each component of a completed cigarette looked like inside. He connected that to his work with the famers in harvesting tobacco for commercial use. To this day, some of my family bring up that utterly fascinating Christmas Day listening to Jeff's stories about South Africa.

My grief seemed to be closer to the edge as Jeff often had that forlorn look in his eyes. He was not oblivious to where he was. Just because he had dementia didn't mean he had forgotten everything. It had become a long grieving process.

Being among friends was difficult because I knew Jeff was a near invalid sitting in a wheelchair with no chance of a cure.

I so missed hearing from Betty, who used to write an e-mail or two most weeks. Now I seldom heard gossip from the Ottawa crowd; a few photos now and then but little news.

Constipation so often results if people sit in wheelchairs all day, so Oliver and I tried to give Jeff as much exercise as he could tolerate with his bad knees. He continued to be healthy compared to the other residents on his floor. Lucid moments came and went. One day during physio, he was walking and he piped up, "What is this place? Who are these people?"

"We're in a five-star hotel that is free, and these are the other guests," I said.

He smiled but looked a bit puzzled.

A lot of people might be faced with difficulties visiting a family member who is in a care home, but they should still, in my opinion, try to visit occasionally. I always thought that if they knew about the regularity of my visits it would spur them on to give me a day of respite now and then. But that didn't happen. Why was it so difficult to visit someone you cared about or interacted with most of your life as this family did? What about sending an e-mail to me asking how Jeff was or mailing him a card? There was nothing from them, nada.

I had a lovely surprise encounter with one of the carers on Jeff's shift. After we ended our walk (which took some coaxing), this carer beamed when she told me how Jeff had given her the "all okay" scuba diving sign and a huge smile when they got him up. He was engaging and charming despite the odds! We had to treasure those moments and not be disappointed if it didn't go as planned or expected.

To add to our happiness, a hummingbird came to the montbretia blooms only two feet away. It was Jeff who told me about this beautiful plant when we first saw it blooming in the front garden of the Beach Avenue apartment; how lucky we were to have it on this patio! I was confident he recognized the plant as he was always pointing to the flowers.

He was his happiest in that hot July outside in the garden among the plants and birds, his feet up on a chair. Staff would bring him drinks, and Y and Kay often brought the earphones out for him. My main patio chore was filling the bird feeders while Jeff chastised me for climbing on a flimsy chair to reach them.

"Watch out, Poppet!"

A new visitor arrived on the patio one day, someone whose sister had become a resident at Montbretia. She was a keen gardener and brought two hummingbird feeders. She gave me magazines on birds of America, which I read aloud to Jeff as we sat on the patio. R usually came twice a week to see her sister, so our paths were frequently crossing and we had a lot in common being so interested in plants and flowers!

Just when I thought life could do us no wrong, the "Terrible Two" reappeared. They continued unabated, which, given Jeff's advanced condition, seemed petty and uncalled for.

Our manager at Montbretia alerted me to the fact that the Vancouver Coastal Health system had introduced new protocol and criteria for special care unit residents. If the resident no longer displayed disruptive behaviour they could be transferred to the general population unit. This would be the same process that Yaletown House would follow. Jeff would not have been special care because he couldn't get into trouble anymore. He had become complacent and just settled into his lot in life.

I then learned that Yaletown had refused to take Jeff because of the size of his Broda wheelchair. It was difficult to understand why they had indicated earlier that it had to do with the hoist lift in the ceiling. We had been waiting "at the top of the list" (as they told me) for four years to move to our first choice residence. I was upset at this information and there was little chance that he would move.

I followed doctors' advice and put my complaints in writing, but there wasn't much more I could do. Perhaps there were other mitigating circumstances that prevented Jeff from moving to Yaletown House, but I often cried out of sheer frustration with the whole process.

I started questioning whether I wanted this change to Yaletown for me or him, and I kept coming back with the distance I had to travel to see him. Fall and winter were just around the corner again, and constant travelling on buses and trains plus standing in the rain and cold was taking its toll. Jeff was still strong, so he could have lived for many years. I was discouraged but still hopeful.

My grieving counsellor advised me to be careful what I wished for as even though I had problems with a couple of carers, they were the devils I knew. I couldn't be sure who would be at the new residence. Also, my doctor and I discussed whether a move might escalate his decline.

In the meantime, R and I had been taking good care of the patio garden, put up another hummingbird feeder and installed a lovely bird bath. We enjoyed weeding together, and she was easy to be around. She even brought me a hummingbird swing as a gift. She planted new plants and bulbs for spring. Jeff and her sister enjoyed watching us garden.

Many times I got Jeff to stand outside by the fencing. He would have a nap after lunch most days and I encouraged him to get up from his wheelchair and he did quite easily.

I was over-tired from four days in a row at Jeff's with more than two hours in transit. This isn't a complaint so much as a fact about why I was exhausted. Yet I could not scale back seeing Jeff. He was my priority, and I was fuelled by love and devotion. So many times when I arrived, he was just sitting there in his wheelchair with six or seven people, all doing nothing, not speaking or anything. Hot room, curtains drawn. When he spotted me, his whole persona changed, and he waved like crazy. We would embrace and I knew why I felt such a pull to be with him.

I knew I was contributing to his happiness. He would hold my hand with a big smile! Sometimes he would nod off or eat a treat I brought him. We would sit together. Most times I read or talked to him, showed him photos on my iPad, talked about the flowers blooming, the species of birds who kept arriving and departing.

A new female resident arrived with some obvious cognitive confusion. She kept mistaking Jeff for her husband and yelling to staff that I was with her husband. Staff locked Jeff and me in and she almost broke the door down. She was tall and seemed strong. It was sad to see how lonely and frightened she was without her husband.

I was thankful for so many things. I had some great friends. My apartment was a dream because it had the balcony and the birds. I had my husband who still remembered me. I figured I was fairly fit for a seventy-seven-year-old. In addition, I was truly fortunate to have my grieving counsellor who continued to guide me through the dark times of acceptance by giving me her perspective and sound advice. I figured I was better off than most.

Jeff had been short of amazing and was walking a whole revolution without stopping. He smiled a lot, watched R and me watering flowers and messing with the plants in the garden.

Jeff's chair was repaired yesterday, which was $300. The guy who repaired it asked me to make sure staff did not use their feet on the locking hand gears, but I saw them doing it all the time no matter what anyone said. He said it was no wonder they broke as our feet were not meant to work the hand brakes.

I needed to put $85 in the "slush fund" as it was down to $15 and needed to be a minimum of $100 to cover different expenses that might crop up—his haircut every month, body lotions and foot powder. Also his extra meds came out of our account, and apart from the puffer expense the previous year, most months were not over $25. I always did his pedicures and bought his Voltaren cream for his knees at Costco.

Unfortunately, the terrific deaf lady did not wake up one morning. She had been a sociable and likeable person who I hoped was at peace. She always taught me words in sign language, and she interacted with Jeff a lot. I would see her resting a hand on his shoulder. She came and "spoke" with us many times when we were on the patio.

I had been in ongoing communication with the manager about the "Terrible Twos" They had received other complaints, so better rules were put in place.

Jeff had been quite talkative around then. He was looking at a photo of him and his two sons, but he didn't acknowledge or seem to know them. We then looked at photos of a six-week biking trip to England and France in 1990, and he said, "That's Cheltenham," which really shocked me! His long-term memory surfaced in a flash as that was where he grew up.

I told him about that trip and how I met his mum and relatives. We arrived at Gatwick Airport, put our bikes together which were in boxes, cycled to a pub, and our first night of our trip was spent overnight in accommodation at that pub! We then toured the Cotswolds first. Then we took three weeks to cycle south towards Plymouth and the Cornish Coast. We would then take a ferry to France for the next leg of our journey crossing at Roscoff.

Jeff was the leader and guide. He didn't even need a map as he knew where the best places to go were. We went to Bourton-on-the-Water, Polperro and Looe, just to name a few places. Our panniers were full of our gear and clothing, and we stayed at lovely little bed and breakfasts in both countries. Although we were equipped with rain gear, the unbelievable happened: not one drop of rain fell during our six-week trip!

I took many photos, and we spent quite some time looking at the fields full of artichoke hearts and sunflowers in France as it was the height of the season. We spent glorious days cycling through the Loire Valley. Jeff would pick up baguettes and cut meats, olives, pickles and, of course, a bottle of wine. We would spread ourselves in front of a castle and have our picnic.

We discovered amazing beaches in Les Sables-d'Olonne and spent a whole week there. Jeff taught me to play chess on the beach there. Having once played a rugby tournament in the area, he reunited with some mates and their wives and we had a lovely time together.

We referred to these two albums many times so we could reminisce together. It was surprising how much he remembered when looking at the photos.

The days always unfold differently.

Jeff was sitting there staring into space when I arrived one day. He wasn't wearing a shirt, and he was stuck with his chair locked in the middle of the room. I could see his frustration. Once I got him ready, he walked well, was chatty, and it was all good. We snuggled and chatted, but he seemed vulnerable and would not let go of my wrist. I gave him my satchel and scarf, and he finally decided to let me take my coat off.

We had a hummer at the feeder and R brought a suet cake which we put up. The chickadees were flirting with it, but they didn't seem to trust anything new right off. R and I would plant bulbs in two weeks among the perennials she'd brought. She was a true gardener and was so good at planting and designing.

AUTUMN DAYS

The leaves turned during some lovely days in October, and there was a chill in the air despite the sun often being out. Jeff had been in such fine spirits and was still regularly walking; it was slow, but he still walked!

Out on the patio one day, R and I were so happy to see hummers. Loads of chickadees were such a treat. It was not often you would see five or six together. Then they disappeared as a Steller Jay—British Columbia's bird—graced us with its presence. It was the second one I'd seen since moving to Vancouver. Our hard work on the patio had paid off with this rare sighting. The jay had some suet, and I dared not go closer to get my iPad or he might have taken off. But he stayed five minutes making all kinds of calls. He had found a fully stocked menu! He was bigger than a blue jay and had a black head with a tufted crown and a gorgeous blue body. He spent time with us screeching for others. Was Jeff excited? You bet! We all were! The juncos came at lunch that afternoon, so it was a fantastic day on the patio.

The "Terrible Twos" were around but the manager said I was not to engage with them. These two nurses would not be taking care of Jeff at all, so we simply ignored each other. Perfect solution!

Coming home on the bus one day, I dropped my beaded black purse on the street. In that small purse was my passport, wallet with my bank card, and care cards. I still had my backpack, keys and bus pass, so it could have been worse. I spent hours searching and trying not to think about my passport and having to replace these important documents. I stopped in the police station to give my details of the loss and my contact information.

Eventually, I had to replace cards, so I went to the bank and got a new ATM card. I then headed to Costco to notify them and get a replacement card. I got my replacement card from a sympathetic cashier and decided to pop in for some bananas. When I checked my messages, there was one from my apartment building manager saying the police called and someone had turned my purse in. I was over the moon and abandoned any thought of shopping. I grabbed a couple of buses and got my missing purse from the police station. Everything was there! I just couldn't believe it; I was so grateful and amazed.

I then walked to a fruit store nearby only to discover my beaded ladybug change purse was missing. But I knew I had it at Costco. Was I distracted or what? I retraced my steps but had little hope. Back to the police station, then to PC, then to Kim's, and back on a bus to Costco. I never gave up. No kidding! Nothing was turned in at the Costco lost and found, but I had been at the photo area earlier. When I asked there, the cashier broke into a big smile. There it was—OMG! My $12 in change was even intact. Someone up there was looking over my shoulder for sure. I was in tears and just so happy and thankful that someone spotted my purse lying in the road and turned it in. I was exhausted after running around in circles on buses.

But wait—the story does not end there!

A couple of weeks later I went to meet a friend at our new downtown casino. I was walking towards a favourite machine and this woman was staring at me or, as I soon discovered, at my purse!

She stopped me and said, "Helen? Are you Helen?"

I said, "Yes, have we met before?"

She said, "No, but I recognize your beaded purse. I'm the one who found your purse, checked your passport and name and turned it into the police station."

I was just blown away! What were the odds that we would meet?

EARLY TO MID-OCTOBER

One day a Steller Jay landed under the feeder and ate seeds, but I was not quick enough to get a photo—but the highlight of a fabulous day!

Hard to believe we would be together thirty-three years in December. So often I thought how fortunate we were.

Jeff's sister stopped coming to visit and hadn't communicated, but I heard she had been in hospital. I didn't visit her as I didn't want to run into her son and daughter and their children. I didn't trust myself that I could be civil to them.

One day I had dinner with Jeff at Montbretia; it was unusual for me to stay past his afternoon nap, but we'd had such a great day watching the birds. He was more talkative than he had ever been, so it was unpredictable what each day would bring. I felt lucky to have an even-tempered guy, as I knew of some hitters, especially the female residents. I was so glad to stay with him longer than usual, but I was tired now. I poured a glass of wine, heated up some leftovers and tried to ignore my scratchy throat.

The following morning my throat was very sore and I had developed a cough, so I decided not to see Jeff. Didn't want to pass on any germs. I had been quite tired due to all the bus rides, waiting in the rain, inhaling germs and being around some pretty desperate people (through no fault of their own).

Chapter 12

JEFF'S FINAL ONE
OCTOBER 17

I was exhausted but decided to visit. I almost fell asleep on the Canada Line. Filled the feeders and did a bit of gardening.

Jeff broke the footrest on his wheelchair, and I think it will have to be replaced. More expense. He wants out of the wheelchair, I can tell. He was hard to handle today. But he did walk and then he wanted to stand, so we also did standing exercises.

Apparently, he didn't walk on Tuesday when I wasn't there. They don't push him unless I'm there, so he was probably fed up by Wednesday. Today he was roaring to go, but after lunch he was sleepy, so I didn't stick around as I was worn out.

It was also the last day Oliver would be dealing with Jeff, as he goes on holidays for six weeks and then he's joining another team, so it will be a new team for us next week.

During the night, one of the residents passed away in his sleep. He was about eighty, and I spoke to him and his wife just on Monday. All of a sudden, he was gone. There were three or four right on the brink as well.

As I bounced down the stairs and started walking to Canada Line it flashed through my mind that I was not feeling that great. I seemed to be his anchor, and I always convinced him to stand up, so I knew the score and that was why I was there. He would walk as I could cajole him into it. I pushed like crazy as I knew his muscles would atrophy if he didn't stand or walk. He was capable or else I would not push him.

The activities director told me she saw Jeff stomping his foot on the footrest and trying to rip apart the new wheel caster connections. Was he bored or what? One thing we did know was that he was still strong!

Jeff has had a real rattle in his throat on and off these past few months. He was very restless lately, and I had noticed he was sweating a lot. He could have all sorts wrong with him and we wouldn't have a clue. But he did walk Thursday, Oliver's last day with him, and didn't want to stop, so that was quite amazing.

The beautiful, quilted cover was draped over the gurney of the older gentleman who recently passed. It was difficult being around decline and death for these past five years. I often thought that the travelling kept me fit and focussed on my priorities.

I basically crawled home so it was a pleasure to sleep in on Friday.

OCTOBER 18

I had a new mobile which I was just learning to use, and I missed two calls around 2:00 in the afternoon—the manager and doctor at Montbretia were both trying to reach me but did not leave messages. I didn't check my phone as I was not used to having one, so I was not even aware they were trying to reach me.

At six o'clock in the evening another call came, which I did hear. I could not understand the message, so a friend called the nursing station to find out what they were calling for. It seemed Jeff had some serious choking problems earlier in the day, aspirating, and they were trying to reach me. He didn't have a fever, but he definitely had rattling in his throat. Apparently, he ate some dinner, so I need not rush on buses to be there. Jeff was calm and asleep. She emphasized that no one seemed on high alert or overly concerned. Daniel also relayed the message that if I had a cold or cough to try and stay home another day or be sure to wear a mask. I would see how I felt in the morning. They would call if anything changed.

I stayed home recovering and may not go tomorrow as Jeff was always busy with activities on Saturday. I would see how I felt in the morning.

OCTOBER 19

This morning, the manager sent me an e-mail message at 9:30 that said Jeff was congested and may have aspirated some phlegm. They are being careful feeding him. They will call if they need to. She said I should stay home and rest another day. He was being looked after and resting to get past this.

OCTOBER 20

Such a relief to see Jeff today as I had barely slept. He has been in bed for two days with the chest rattle. He barely ate yesterday but had breakfast and part of lunch today. He had been on a mister/inhaler three times a day for ten minutes. I plan to be with him most if not all of this week. Apparently, he was better than he was yesterday. When he coughed his chest was breaking up, so that was probably a good sign. Mostly sleeping. I came home to sleep as I was not getting enough rest lately.

OCTOBER 21

My friend, E, relayed a message to me this morning that if they need to call me, they will call her. Because of my hearing problems, it was best they communicate through her. It seemed that Jeff had a cold in his chest, not his lungs. He was on oxygen because his blood pressure was low, but he was comfortable. The fact that he was on oxygen was troubling and serious, so I was ready to go and be with him.

I got to Montbretia early and it certainly was his chest. He coughed a lot, but he ate three-quarters of his lunch, a really good sign. He was sweating and looked so wasted, but through all that he managed to smile at me, reach for my hand and clutch it tightly.

He had had these setbacks, but this one was more serious than all the others. It was so worrisome, but I had to keep in mind that I had no control over this—what will be will be—and at this stage I just had to roll with the punches. He was not verbally communicating, so I knew he was stressed and maybe even in pain. So hard to know. Four residents had come down with colds. The place was deserted.

I thought it best I leave as he was being well taken care of and mostly sleeping. This rainy weather really makes for a complete slowdown of buses. Looks like only more rain in the forecast.

OCTOBER 22

No change in Jeff. He hadn't eaten today so far and was in and out of sleep. Coughing a bit. Was very restless lying in bed. Tried to feed him pudding but he wouldn't take anything. Still on oxygen. Doing our best.

Buses were fine today. When I arrived there was no sign of any team around him. I think it was due to lots of flu in the unit. No music or entertainment. Probably staff have alerted outsiders not to come in.

Met with the rotating doctor today, and I was quite alarmed to learn the prognosis was not good, 50/50, so she said. Jeff was not responding, barely moving, wouldn't eat anything or even drink water, so it's hard to know which way this will go. Actually, I was quite shocked and, quite understandably, I would have reacted with real panic sooner if I had thought this was heading to his impending death.

I decided to stay overnight but am always open to a change of plans if we see improvement. I would rather be with him either way rather than sitting at home wondering.

A spiritual carer came in—that was telling—and she was going to call Jeff's sister as she thought it would be better that we informed her. Thankfully, she was fine to take on that task. A nurse friend of mine, CA, had been in touch this past month and texted she was driving to Jeff's today and would arrive shortly.

I expected it would be a long night. They just gave him a pain injection. For some reason I thought today was a critical day as it was the first time he skipped all his meals and not even had a taste. It was certainly worrisome and heart-wrenching. I kept getting these physical heartaches like butterflies, but panicky ones. And I kept checking that he was breathing. Everyone was so quiet. No one said anything. I asked the nurses, but they didn't have any information for me.

OCTOBER 23

I think he knew me, but his eyes were vague. Every once in a while, I saw recognition, especially if I stood up when he tried to reach out but his arms seemed unable to function. They were just limp. He caught my wrist a couple of times and held on, but then his strength just dwindled.

The nurse came in at 1:00 a.m., so I woke up from my mat on the floor beside his bed. I had slept for an hour. I was trying to be positive, but it was not easy when I saw how he looked.

CA and I sat outside in the sun for a bit, and I counted eight male juncos. The bird book says the males go around in little flocks. R, my gardening partner, was here today and she said it was the most amount of birds we'd had this summer. It was sunny and lovely. She came to see Jeff and we cried together.

I was glad to be with Jeff but anxious to get home at the same time. My awareness of him right beside me in the state he was in made it difficult for me to rest. I needed to go home and gather up some toiletries and extra clothes. It was a long day of inactivity, so I wouldn't linger much longer. Maybe he would eat something.

I would go home and try to get some sleep. I had been saying little prayers. I hoped HE was listening as mostly I thought I had been a good girl. Maybe I had scored some brownie points for all the transit changes and standing in the rain.

I did sleep off and on at home. CA is picking me up at 1:30 to take me back to Jeff. Staff knew when time was almost up and that seemed to be the look of it—so they said—but I was still hopeful. He had pulled through lots of times, and maybe the fat on his body will carry him through a week of no food. I did not want him to struggle anymore, but I still found it difficult to accept that he might not be here anymore.

I'm lucky to have good friends, especially in the absence of relatives. It was gorgeous out there, but the buses had been so crowded lately so I sure appreciated the ride. It was likely I would be sleeping over beside him.

He had been on oxygen for four whole days now. I had a bad night next to him but he seemed comfortable. He ate nothing yesterday and not this morning. It could go either way, but it was so different this time, and I became more worried than ever.

As the days continued, nothing had changed. He couldn't eat or swallow. It was painful to see him like this, but they wouldn't do intravenous as they said it would just prolong the inevitable. He had mild aspiration pneumonia or it could lead to it. If he took some food and couldn't swallow, there was the huge danger it would go into his lungs. He must be starving.

I was having lots of teary outbursts, but how could it be any other way?

A VERY SPECIAL MOMENT WITH JEFF

Tonight I spent a solid hour talking to him about our life together. Every once in a while, his eyebrows would go up and twiggle, so I knew he was listening. That encouragement got me into unclenching his hands and doing exercise, circles and lifts. He resisted at first and then relaxed and really got into it. Next came the legs. By now his eyes were wide open and I could see half smiles, very alert.

Then he grabbed me and hugged me. I was absolutely floored as he had been so unresponsive.

A nurse chose that moment to come in, and he broke into a big smile. She was bowled over too. Then he took drops of juice. I could see the concentration on his face as he slowly and deliberately crossed his ankles (always a favourite position of his) in a relaxed pose. He had his moment and so did I. We could go out on that note—it was just so concentrated, close and meaningful. A precious hour of his awakening.

OCTOBER 24

I slept over and would again tonight. I tried another recliner which was so uncomfortable. I tried the floor again but ended up crawling in beside him. He was in a sort of catatonic state, but I held him close and I hoped he was as comforted as I was. I had never experienced anyone dying before me, and I tried not to think about that.

He was going to go his own way when it was his time. Not eating would certainly speed things up.

Waiting for Jeff to wake up but he had lots of meds.

The spiritual adviser came to see me again, and she told me she had phoned Jeff's sister again. His sister told her it was too depressing to see Jeff and had decided she was not visiting anymore. She did say she admired me. His sister left a rambling five-minute message on my mobile, but with my hearing I could only make out some of it it. A friend said she would listen to it. No other family came. None of his sister's children nor his three children.

But our friends are very supportive. CA rubbed cream on Jeff's lips and knew what to do with the suction apparatus to help relieve the rattle. A close friend, E—we were like sisters—came today. She lost her husband two years ago to dementia. It looked like my turn was coming.

When she arrived, we talked about whether I should go home and sleep as I was so tired and had barely slept for days. She also listened to the phone message from Jeff's sister. His sister said it would be too depressing to see Jeff, so I wrote her an e-mail telling her I barely understood her due to my hearing. I said having our good memories was important. She left another voicemail that contained some platitudes about how good my care had been. She said if I really wanted her to visit Jeff in his comatose state she would. I didn't answer. I mean it was up to her, not me. I was with Jeff. She had to decide, not me. She could do whatever she thought would work.

E and I were going to take a cab but decided to drag it out and have a bite at Starbucks then take the bus to Expo Line and Beach bus. I knew how difficult it was for her to see Jeff in that state, but she gave me strength and love.

I was home and hoping I didn't get a call tonight. I didn't expect to sleep much, but maybe being home would energize me. I felt good in my bed, and no phone calls.

OCTOBER 25

I was up at 5:00, walked to Canada Line and went to Starbucks for a breakfast sandwich and coffee. Got to Jeff's at 6:00. He was fragile today, shallow breathing. I was staying the night as one nurse said he may not make it. I would rather be here than scrambling to get back in the middle of the night. Staff were generous and giving me lots of meals.

Jeff was almost totally unresponsive. A few flutters of his eyelashes when I was able to tell him stuff and give him kisses and hugs. He had been given pain meds, probably morphine, to be comfortable and couldn't eat or drink a thing. I kept thinking it was close to the end, and I hoped it was quick and did not go on for another week.

I was a mess, numb and heartbroken. I'd had years to prepare but, as so often had been said by others in my position, I don't think you're ever really prepared.

I was talking up a storm and hoping he heard some of the memories and love I was drawing on from our amazing life together. He had suffered for eleven years. Ten days ago he had been walking in his Ultimate Walker, so his decline had been quick and quite pronounced.

Jeff looked comfortable and calm.

R and I filled the feeders and she burst into tears again when she walked in to see Jeff. He was well liked, and everyone was so sad and couldn't believe how quickly he declined.

OCTOBER 26

Nothing too much had changed. Daniel was incredible. I held the flashlight at two in the morning and Daniel brushed Jeff's tongue as it was caked with residue. We spent half an hour slowly cleaning his mouth. He brushed old food that was stuck like glue in his mouth. We could even see there was a green pea from his last meal, could it be? He really worked hard.

I knew nothing of this procedure before, and he explained how this situation happens with a build up of residue. He used a toothbrush to brush his tongue and loosen the residue.

Staff came by in the evening and were comforting, giving me hugs and food.

CA said to tell Jeff he was free to leave.

"Sometimes they won't go because they are worried about you," she said.

So I had that conversation with him.

At around 4:00 a.m., he had a fever, so a new nurse did some misting and pain injections. He had a distinct non-stop rattle in his chest, but he looked comfortable. I slept on my mat for a couple of hours.

When I woke up, I headed to Starbucks, got my egg sandwich combo, and sat outside on the patio. I was rewarded with a pair of gorgeous towhees, lots of juncos and chickadees looking for Jeff and me. The sun was just coming slowly into the patio and it looked like it would be a beautiful today.

I was then in the room, sitting in his big chair with the sun shining on me watching my "rainbow," trying not to break down. We tried water but he couldn't accept anything it seemed. Moistening his mouth helped. I was so thankful Daniel was here last night on this shift. All the staff were so kind.

In the afternoon, Jeff's daughter in San Diego called the nursing station wanting to talk to me.

"No, I can't," I said to the nurse. "Tell her I'm busy."

I just couldn't.

She had not been in touch with Montbretia, me or Jeff for four and a half years, not even a card to him at Christmas, his birthday. Nada. Nothing. I told the nurse to tell her to e-mail me her wishes.

I heard that Jeff's sister was trying to find Jeff's sons. Good grief. What? They are going to come here after six or seven years of pretending their father didn't exist?

If she wanted to find out about Jeff right now, she could call and ask. Stop stirring stuff. Jeff and I were at peace together here. We could do without platitudes from his daughter, his sons, his family. He had a brother-in-law here in Vancouver who had never called or visited (except for one time when they brought Newt to meet Jeff). His nieces and nephews saw him all their lives but never once came to visit their uncle.

OCTOBER 27

The Chocolate Lady came for a visit tonight but not her husband, Jeff's dive buddy. She told me she was glad her husband hadn't seen how thin Jeff was. I was so grateful that she came. I was just so lonely, panicky at times, and sad.

A long, wide-awake night with little sleep. There was a spot in his bed for me, and I hoped he was made more comfortable by my presence. He was going through a range of racing chest and different breathing from yesterday when he was so quiet.

I didn't think I would be bushy-tailed today, but you never know when adrenalin popped up. The nurse on this early morning shift did suction as he had lots of phlegm in his mouth. I'm sure it relieved him. He also got more comfort meds, but his chest was making a terrible rattle this morning.

Maybe I would be able to doze off for an hour, never know. I asked some staff what happens physically when death was so close, and they said his hands and feet turn bluish. His hands were turning blue, so he may not last the night.

It was beyond sad, but I have accepted the inevitable now. He can't come back. I was glad I was next to him. Will I sleep? A huge question mark.

I lay down beside him.

Epilogue

Our struggle and story is finished. We did it.

I am a shell lying in the bed. I'm here in spirit. I have a short time left to tell you a few last things before I depart to my other world. There is a space of time, a very short space of time, between the end of your breathing and your spirit world. This is mine now.

The head nurse came with a doctor to pronounce my demise. The vicar came to console my wife, who stands by taking everything in after having held me in her arms as I took my last breath. There was a little pop of my eyes opening wide. I saw her and then I was gone.

Two staff come to wash and clean me, so she steps out. They put a clean gown on me, say goodbye to my body, cover me and shed tears. They leave the room, talk to my wife, and she comes in and closes the door.

There's the donation of my brain to the Alzheimer's Society at UBC for research which will happen today after the hall procession to the exit and goodbye to the earth world. It is early in the morning, just past 7:00, and the donation centre is not on 24-hour service, so we still have some hours to share, although there is little time.

I hear Helen talking to her sister, to our psychiatrist, a few other people by phone. She makes plans for my rugby buddy who is assisting her in these next few hours.

But, again, it's early. She removes all the blow-up photographs on the walls that I used to look at every day. Everything is being removed quickly. When I watched her hang these photos years ago, she stood on a chair and I know I told her to be careful. I don't say anything this morning about the chair and how reckless she is climbing on it. My body is lying here under a sheet. She leaves me covered, but every fifteen minutes or so she pulls the sheet back and chats a bit. She says how young and peaceful I look. She is calm. She is grateful that I left peacefully, and she does not wail, shout, sob out loud. She is quiet, trance-like.

The vicar comes in, and they plan for my wife to cut locks from my hair. They chat. I listen. I think they love me. She fills a small cellophane bag full of my hair and seals it. The sheet is pulled over me again.

She continues collecting things from cupboards and putting them in boxes. She leaves a few items which could be passed on to others, like adaptable clothing.

She pulls the sheet back. She talks to me. Then covers me up again.

There are knocks on the door, and she talks to nurses who have just come on shift. Lots of sad people comfort my wife with pleasantries and say how they will miss us.

Around 10:15 in the morning, Wayne arrives. My wife is outside my door. He hugs Helen and talks to her. She cries. He cries. He walks in and gives my knee a squeeze.

He carries items to his car and they speak to people about the procedure for my wheelchair. Helen pulls the sheet down many times to check me out. My eyes are closed. I haven't moved. She says goodbye to me many times, and I know that she loves me.

Everything is packed and in the car to take to her apartment.

Then a gurney arrives to transfer my body to a special vehicle, and I will be off to the donation centre.

There is a procession organized to leave the room for the last time. Wayne and my wife walk side by side behind my body, which has the dignity quilt carefully laid over.

We are outside now. I am leaving now. My body is leaving. My spirit is fading into the sky as the gurney is secured into the vehicle and leaves.

My wife and Wayne leave too.

I'll be in an unknown place somewhere, silenced in secrecy, listening over her shoulder. Her day will come, too, possibly many years from today, but it will inevitably come, and we will be together again.

Afterword

November 3, 2019

Jeff and I have now both let go and he is free. He is out of that wheelchair, will never again have to eat puréed food, will no longer be prodded by unwanted hands, and he will never have to suffer the indignities of having dementia again. I am thankful for his easy passing. He was ready to go. He had had enough.

In the past six weeks, four men, including him, died and it was so terribly sad to watch them through their journeys. A resident's sister and I planted about two hundred spring bulbs and perennials in Jeff's patio garden, so I expect we will visit to see the beauty that unfolds in the spring.

Four months after Jeff's death I received a copy of the autopsy report from a neurologist at UBC Research. Jeff and I had appointments with this same doctor before Jeff's involuntary admission to hospital. He was quite surprised that Lewy body dementia (LBD) was the main culprit (it was "diffuse") compared with Alzheimer's being "moderate." He also mentioned that LBD explained a lot of Jeff's fluctuation during his years in care. We couldn't know such answers until there was a brain autopsy.

Parkinson's disease is often present in LBD, but Jeff did not have Parkinson's symptoms that were apparent to his team of care professionals. Jeff definitely had fluctuation in cognition—as evidenced by starting to eat on his own again and handling his spoon after years of being fed, as well as his ability to make sentences after declining to do so for years. It was only speculation to think that reducing his medication as the years went by had a lot to do with the change of his abilities.

I have done some research about the differences between LBD and Alzheimer's, so I wanted to quote it here.

"How do symptoms of LBD differ from those of Alzheimer's disease?

Many patients with Lewy body dementia also have overlapping Alzheimer's disease, which is why some patients are misdiagnosed. While the two forms of dementia have similarities, there are some important distinctions.

Alzheimer's affects the brain's ability to store new information in the form of memories, while Lewy body dementia targets a different set of cognitive functions—specifically problem-solving and reasoning. Hallucinations occur early in Lewy body dementia but only after about four years in Alzheimer's disease.

Lewy body patients are also more likely to experience the presence of REM sleep disorder, disruption of the autonomic nervous system and Parkinson's-like movement disorders.

Understanding which form of dementia you are dealing with is important. Lewy body dementia responds differently than Alzheimer's disease to commonly prescribed dementia medications."

It's been tough writing with all these flashes of positives and negative memories, but I wouldn't be human if I did not say, "If only I had …"

Could we have stayed together for another year at our home? Would he have fallen down the stairs? Would he have flooded the downstairs neighbour's place again? He was unpredictable. There was always that. He was strong and fit, but his brain had changed. No way could I know what mood could be triggered by a situation. You don't remain the same couple. Your friends and family know he's not the same. I found myself shielding him from strangers when we took the buses and trains. They knew.

He was not the Jeff I knew anymore. He became childlike, but, unlike a child, he didn't learn, absorb new things or grasp what conversations were about. He was also unable to answer simple questions. He could not write or read in the first stage of the disease. He became insecure, suspicious, possessive.

He was physically strong and fought right to the end. It was so enlightening to learn from the autopsy of his brain that he had diffuse Lewy body dementia with moderate Alzheimer's. It explained how he didn't JUST decline—he fluctuated and we never were sure how he would be one day to the next.

Life changes so much when death enters a happy world. I am still so glad Jeff died when he did as he and I would have been battling COVID-19 in the residence. I probably would have been arrested for breaking down the doors to get in!

It's like he knew it was time to say adieu, but it was still unexpected. He suffered and struggled, but our love never wavered. We always had a strong bond and a magical love even under those dire circumstances.

I will never forget his face lighting up the minute I walked in to his care home. He'd wave like crazy from his wheelchair as if I didn't see him. As I got near him, he'd pull me on top of him, practically upending the wheelchair. We would laugh and cry and hug like it was our last moment, our best moment, our only moment, to cherish.

I am isolated and alone now. There are no two ways about it. Loss and grief still plays a big part in my life, but it often still feels like he just died. The COVID-19 pandemic didn't help me move along as I might otherwise have done. I was just not in anyone's bubble, and depression and despair showed up more often than I thought possible.

I wrote an essay for a seniors' community centre in early 2020 entitled *A Bubble of One*. I am including it here as it really expressed what I felt about the isolation caused by the pandemic.

A Bubble of One: A Sidebar to Our Dementia Journey

The dictionary says the word "bubble" is used to refer to a good or fortunate situation that is isolated.

What a perfect word to grab a hold of in this COVID-19 pandemic. I never dreamed eight months ago, in October, I would be encapsulated in a bubble of one as my husband died in my arms early one morning.

I have lots of stories to tell later, but this "sidebar" is about the bubble due to the pandemic. From late October to March 15, 2020, I was wailing in grief mode. I wasn't sure what was happening at times. Then the new rules and regulations due to COVID-19 came into effect—distancing, masks, no get togethers, no dinner parties, no popping in to chat with friends and neighbours. No nothing. We were locked away, slowly coming outside but distancing, many unrecognizable even in our apartment buildings due to masks.

But here's the thing: Partners, husbands, wives, children, people who are families stayed together, ate together, drove together, but others weren't allowed in that circle as there seemed to be a theory going around that if you lived together before COVID-19 you were deemed to be safe together or you also could be infected together. What was the choice here? Families should break up and live in separate places? Families should try and live in separate rooms? Nope.

The consensus seemed to be a household stuck together, walked together, ate together, slept together. And that became their special circle—their bubble!

Some called a FaceTime or Zoom get together a bubble, but the "real bubble" was the person to person in your group, from two people (usually partners) to five or more depending on your household. This bubble kept you safe from others psychologically and physically. You could comfort each other, touch, hug; it was your risk.

It's pretty obvious what a "bubble of one" would consist of: you! No one else, just you. Think for a second how sad that is for a person to be a bubble of one. No hugs, no touching, no sharing. If you are a bubble of one, you know exactly the feeling.

You can phone everyone. You can e-mail everyone. You could make some of your own rules, but with the unpredictability and not knowing who tested positive for COVID-19, it was and is a scary unknown.

Back to my personal experience. I lost my husband of thirty-three years to Lewy body disease and Alzheimer's. I am in the vulnerable category: over seventy but without health issues, fortunately. The virus is not abating. It's so lonely and isolating being in a bubble of one. Add the grief of loss, and it's a huge setback. I can't get invited into anyone's bubble. I have no family here. I live alone, and my husband was my life. I know I'm not alone in this isolation as so many others share a similar circumstance.

As April and May moved by, a bit of social distancing with a few friends took place. No touching, no hugs, no meal sharing. We all seemed safe, but we all knew we had to get groceries, get out, and there always seemed to be the underlying fear you weren't all that safe from others. A cough and you felt panicky. So my bubble of one continues.

Your fears threaten to keep you even more isolated as you fear the runners coming up behind you passing too closely with their droplets as they don't wear masks. I'm one of the few who wears a mask as I cycle as I'm old and think I'm more vulnerable than the youngsters zipping by me.

I looked with envy at the big bubbles enjoying their picnics in the park today. I understand

I could be a risk to be invited into someone's bubble. No one wants a lone wolf from a bubble of one. I might feel the same way if the roles were reversed.

Would I? Would you?

Maybe things will change soon, but for now I have to content myself with my bath bubbles!

Jeff died on a Monday. For the first year, Mondays were always a bad day with me breaking down in tears all day. He's everywhere in my apartment—can't be any other way for me still. But I've tried to only keep happy photos at hand and not look at him in his decline.

My book has been difficult to write. I wonder just how much I can say without sounding like I'm ranting and raving about friends and family not coming to visit or help me out through those six years of visiting him every week, four to five days, taking all those bus changes and trains. It was like a nine-to-five job, and it put my life in turmoil. It has not been easy coming out of it.

We have the same wonderful old friends, but Jeff is the only one who died. It's not the same as breaking up with someone as death is so final and permanent. I have to say my heart is not mended yet. Will it ever be? I know I've aged and don't know how to smile much anymore. I'm still meeting my psychiatrist every month on FaceTime, and she helps put things in perspective.

I know deep in my heart that Jeff didn't want to live the way he was, but we made the best we could with the tragedy of him having this illness. I am thankful he is now free, but I can't change how much I miss him and the pain and tears that go with it. We are both free of struggling after all these years of coping with the changes and his continued decline. I know he was always happy to see me, but I often sensed his frustration. In his lucid moments, life was terrible and I found him in tears a number of times.

Not long before he passed, he said, "Who are all these people? Where am I?" So, contrary to what some people think, they are aware as their memory comes and goes. I remember so clearly handing the photo of him with his two sons on a rugby field. He looked at it closely and just dropped it on the floor. It seemed to me that he thought they probably didn't exist anymore or he knew where they were, couldn't put it in words and closed the chapter.

So much passed between us in our visits. I'm especially pleased that he enjoyed the birds and flowers so much during his last summer on the patio. We ate out there every chance we got.

I am at peace with it, but it's just so hard that he's no longer physically there to hold and be comforted. I never wanted him in a residence, but somehow the time we had on our own apart only cemented our love and made us so uplifted every time we met again. Our five or six hours may have been more meaningful than had he lived at home. He enjoyed the activities and earphones so much and was lucky to have two superb activities directors. You could always catch Jeff smiling and joking with Y and Kay. I tried to work around those times so he wouldn't miss the ball tossing and listening to the tapes of Leonard Cohen and the Bee Gees!

I feel like I'm writing another chapter in my book. I've documented our last months and days together, how we lived in the moment. All I can do is hope, as so many of us do, to combat the isolation of the pandemic, to be free to mingle with old friends, to make new friends, and to follow a path that leads to happiness and contentment with the years that remain.

FEBRUARY 2023

As I was sitting on my balcony reading a book, a thought kept interrupting my concentration. It was startling in its naivety but gave me some peace. The words were, *I'm healing.* That is where I am right now. I accept that it's not easy for me to be focused on projects like my book, meeting new people, the laundry, cleaning closets. Instead, I'm just resting and letting the flow of my life with Jeff move along, loving so many special moments— thousands of them—savouring the years together, the tenderness and love we shared during those tough times, how we smiled, laughed and cried together.

I feel like I have reached another hurdle in life but I can leap over it, embrace whatever happens and still have the quiet and peace.

Acknowledgment

This book was six years in the making. Writing a book was certainly more challenging than I ever imagined but also was so therapeutic and rewarding. I especially want to thank Cora and Roger who first encouraged me to write this book and for giving me early advice on a style I sought to adapt as Jeff's "shadow writer." Using that technique allowed me to be blunt, naive and child-like as a "declining Jeff", but it also added some lightness and humour!

Big thanks to Sylvia for a first evaluation of my early attempts at writing and to Kristene (all the ups and downs of writing) and her husband Fred for their long-lasting friendship and encouragement in this endeavour! To June and another Lynda in Scotland!

I especially want to thank all my immediate family and extended family for their love and support in this undertaking, my siblings, Pat, John, and my sister Betty, who passed too early, and whose birth date she and I shared but five years apart — those countless emails in the wee hours of the mornings which effectively and factually became a journal I could refer to as the chronology of years and stages in this book.

Thank you to staff at Tellwell Publishing, in particular Scott, who started me off, to Rhea, my patient project manager, to Darin, my editor who drew out of me little stories from our carefree life in the 35 years we shared making the pronounced comparison to what our life was like now, and what an amazing job he did of smoothing out the rough spots; to Gerardo's patience with my continued changes for the cover design but the result was perfect!

Thank you to Nita, Michael and Chelsea at Paul's Club for their extraordinary programme, care and devotion to those who suffer early onset dementia like my husband — those walks that kept everyone fit!

Thank you to all the medical professionals on Jeff's team, in particular those who inspired and motivated me from Dr. D. Foti and Amy from UBC Alzheimer's Clinic, Dr. Jeff Bowlsby, our GP for 30 years, to Dr. Elisabeth Drance and Paul Edmundson who took me under their wings, and to countless staff in several venues who were so caring and diligent in their jobs. To Oliver, Jeff's Physiotherapist, whose cheerful demeanour always brought smiles to our faces!

To our friends from 30 years ago who were always there for me endeavouring to lighten the pace and sadness and give me the respite I so often needed: Wayne and Helen, Mike and Linda (and their family), Alain and Sandra, David and Caroline, Denise and Geoff, Linda R.

Many new and old friends also includes Heather & Doug, Pam, Jackie and Geoff (and their family) Myrna, Karen and Les, Anita (RIP) and Karen, Carmen, Dawne, Elmon, Steve, Owen and Tim, Laurinda, Kendal, Karen and Rhonda, Rosemary, Jimmy and Mary, Frank and Janet, Trudy, Bobbie and Maxwell.

CPSIA information can be obtained
at www.ICGtesting.com
Printed in the USA
LVHW071938070623
748680LV00002B/4